The Ordinary Genius   *A Life of*
Arnold Platt

The Ordinary Genius

*A Life of
Arnold Platt*

Ken Hoeppner

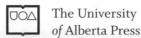 The University
of Alberta Press

Published by

The University of Alberta Press
Ring House 2
Edmonton, Alberta, Canada   T6G 2E1

© 2007 Ken Hoeppner
ISBN-13 978-0-88864-480-0

Library and Archives Canada Cataloguing in Publication

Hoeppner, Kenneth, 1948–
The ordinary genius : a life of Arnold Platt / Ken Hoeppner.

Includes bibliographical references and index.
ISBN 978–0–88864–480–0

1. Platt, Arnold W. 2. Plant breeders—Alberta—Biography. 3. Plant breeders—Canada—
        Biography. 4. Farmers' Union of Alberta—Biography. 5. Agriculturists—
        Alberta—Biography. 6. Alberta—Biography. I. Title.

S417.P55H63 2007   630.92   C2007-903516-7

The University of Alberta Press is committed to protecting our natural environment. As
part of our efforts, this book is printed on Enviro Paper: it contains 100% post-consumer
recycled fibres and is acid- and chlorine-free.

The University of Alberta Press gratefully acknowledges the support received for its
publishing program from The Canada Council for the Arts. The University of Alberta
Press also gratefully acknowledges the financial support of the Government of Canada
through the Book Publishing Industry Development Program (BPIDP) and from the
Alberta Foundation for the Arts for its publishing activities.

Contents

Abbreviations

ORGANIZATIONS

AFA	Alberta Federation of Agriculture
AFU	Alberta Farmers' Union
AIC	Agricultural Institute of Canada
CIL	Cooperative Implements Limited
CIMMYT	International Maize and Wheat Improvement Centre
CSTA	Canadian Society of Technical Agriculturalists
FU&CDA	Farmers' Union and Cooperative Development Association (later REDA)
FUA	Farmers' Union of Alberta
FWUA	Farm Women's Union of Alberta
IFUC	Interprovincial Farm Union Council
LRC	Lethbridge Research Centre
NFU	National Farmers' Union
PFRA	Prairie Farm Rehabilitation Act
REDA	Rural Education and Development Association (formerly FU&CDA)
SPARC	Semiarid Prairie Agricultural Research Centre
UFA	United Farmers of Alberta
UGG	United Grain Growers
USDA	United States Department of Agriculture

ARCHIVES AND HOLDINGS

LLRC	Library, Lethbridge Research Centre
NAC	National Archives of Canada
PAA	Provincial Archives of Alberta
SPARC	Holdings, Semiarid Prairie Agricultural Research Centre
UAA	University of Alberta Archives
UCA	University of Calgary Archives

Preface

Arnold Platt said that nothing he had done merited special remembrance; consequently, he spent two days at the incinerator, burning most of his private papers. Perhaps he did not want to make the work of the biographer entirely impossible, so he left a few things behind. Most significant for the story of his early life, in late 1989, when he was eighty years old, he tape-recorded his recollections of those years. The recollections end in 1931, with the birth of his first child, Wayne. Arnold also wrote an account of his farming experiences in the Westlock district for his family. The family has made the tape recordings and the account available for this project.

Much of the narrative is taken from these tapes, as are direct statements by Arnold in Chapter 1. Arnold also left a 30-page account of the
move from Innisfree to Westlock, and elements of that account also
inform the story in the first chapter.

Because he truly had "been there" in so many events and occasions
of public record, documentary evidence provides considerable insight.
In addition, a considerable number of people—some who knew him as
early as 1940—have willingly shared their recollections to corroborate
and extend the public record. The sources of information are identified
throughout the text. Where I refer to a person's recollection or narrative,
the source is an interview or discussion with that person; those interviews are listed in the References section.

In the Platt family papers, documentation of the years in Swift Current
consists of copies of the scientific papers that Arnold published while at
the experimental farm. Included in the family papers are the letter from
Claire Taylor referred to in the text, a copy of Baden Campbell's history
of the Swift Current Research Station, and an envelope from the Kansas
State College of Agriculture and Applied Science containing Arnold's
transcript from the University of Alberta. Had the materials available
been limited to what Arnold left behind, the story of the development
of Rescue wheat would have lacked the drama that is so significant a
part of it. Except for Arnold's report of work in California, which was
occasioned by Charles Jenkins' accident, and associated memos dealing with the payment of costs, the National Archives contain no records
from Arnold's time at Swift Current. The Experimental Station records
for the years 1936 to 1949 seem to have been lost. Neither the library at
what is now the Semiarid Prairie Agricultural Research Centre (SPARC)
at Swift Current nor the library at the Lethbridge Research Centre has
any records related to the events of those years.

Interviews with three of Arnold's co-researchers from that era, Stewart
(Stew) Wells, Ruby Larson, and Stu McBean, contributed significantly to
the story. Stu McBean's suggestion that papers might still exist prompted
an inquiry to Dr. John Clarke of SPARC, which drew a response from
Dr. Ron DePauw, saying that some boxes of papers in his office might
be relevant. Those boxes contained reports and memos documenting

the achievements and frustrations associated with the development of Rescue wheat. Copies of the documents are now in the files in my office. I do not believe that the originals have been included in the SPARC archive.

At the Lethbridge Research Centre, the librarian, Ms. Ronning-Mains, had kept a small file of archival materials related to Arnold's time there. The file contains memos regarding the move from Swift Current to Lethbridge, Arnold's memos regarding his unmet requests, Alice Wall's two-page note on Arnold that was published in the Centre's newsletter, and Chris Farstad's tribute to Arnold on his resignation from the Centre. It also contains a special section of the *Lethbridge Herald* celebrating the opening of the new research facilities on September 17, 1949. It does not contain Arnold's letter of resignation.

Archival material held in the office of the Agricultural Institute of Canada (AIC) provided a useful context for understanding the development of Arnold's ideas about agricultural research generally, and the importance of marketing and marketing education. The Institute does not maintain a formal archive, but it does have several scrapbooks of historical materials. The files related to Arnold being made a Fellow of the AIC seem to have been lost, although he is mentioned in the lists of members honoured by that designation.

Arnold kept no records related to Sundance Farms or Red Crow Limited. The Department of Indian Affairs located files related to the awarding of the lease and the farming operation on it, and made them available to me in Calgary. Interviews with Shirley (Platt) Deneka, Margaret (Platt) Oikawa, Stewart Wells, Dean Lien, and Gerald Schuler, as well as my recollections of Arnold's account of that farming operation, inform the narrative in Chapter 4.

Harry Patching provided his firsthand account of Arnold's earliest involvement in the Farmers' Union of Alberta (FUA), while Dean Lien, Alex McCalla, Jim Lore, and Gerald Schuler recalled many of the events and incidents associated with Arnold's presidency. Arnold kept a complete bound set of *The Organized Farmer* published while he was president of the FUA and editor of that paper, but that was all he kept from that era. In a collection of the materials Carrol Jaques used in writing her history of Unifarm was a complete set of *The Organized Farmer* as well as a file of materials related to the establishment of the Goldeye Centre. She made these materials available to me.

Arnold's experiences in Geneva in 1959 affected him profoundly, as Jessie Oxford observed. Yet the only material evidence Arnold kept of that time is a collage of photographs taken during the proceedings. Published materials such as Charles Frederick Wilson's *Canadian Grain Marketing* (1979) provide little information about the actual negotiations. Alfred Gleave's book provides more of a personal insight, but suggests that the role of the producers' delegates was quite minor. Archival sources offered little hope at first. The archives of the Canadian Wheat Board are closed and, although Arnold was a member of the Wheat Board's Advisory Committee from 1956 to 1959, the Board made no exception to its policy of keeping its archives closed. J.E. Brownlee, president of United Grain Growers (UGG), was also a delegate to the 1959 meetings in Geneva, but the UGG archives at the University of Manitoba contain no papers related to his involvement in those negotiations. The National Archives contain the Charles Frederick Wilson Fonds, but access to the volumes and files associated with the Fourth International Wheat Agreement is restricted; however, the National Archives arranged for me to have access, and those files provide the context that corroborates Arnold's account to me of these events.

Arnold kept the three volumes of the report of the Royal Commission on Transportation but none of the associated correspondence. Interviews with Helen Platt provided essential elements of the narrative, as did Shirley (Platt) Deneka's recollections. Archival materials, both in the National Archives and in the Diefenbaker Centre, are comprehensive, and I have drawn on these.

The archives of the University of Alberta and of the University of Calgary contain documentary evidence of Arnold's contributions as member of the Board of Governors, chair of the Agricultural Economics Advisory Committee, and chair of the rural campaign for the 3AU fundraising drive. The Platt family papers contain Arnold's speech to Convocation at the University of Alberta, and correspondence related to his being awarded the honorary LLD in 1966 by the same institution. They also contain his account of the change in the composition and powers of the Board of Governor's finance committee, an account corroborated in the interview with Dr. Joseph Richter. Dr. Richter and Dr. Warrack added detail to the account of Arnold's contributions to the Department of Agricultural Economics, as did Gerald Schuler.

The files associated with Arnold's time at the United Farmers of Alberta (UFA) Co-op seem to have disappeared. They were thought to have been deposited with the Glenbow Archives in Calgary, but had not been. Arnold kept very few items of correspondence associated with his work at UFA, but his memo to the manager and his letter of resignation provide some insight, as do his speaking notes on the dedication of Blunden Manor. The Platt Family Papers also include his appointment calendars from the mid-1960s to the early 1980s. Helen Platt provided significant insights, as did Dean Lien. The interview with Arne Olson gave another insider's views. UFA Co-op, through its office in Lethbridge and the coordinator of its history project, Gordon Tolton, made available the complete minutes of the Board of Directors, a file of photographs, and the issues of the *UFA Co-operator* and *The United Farmer* for the years that Arnold worked for UFA.

Documentation in the Platt Family Papers related to Arnold's work on farm organization and farm policy during his time at UFA consists of copies of the reports and papers he presented; Arnold did not keep any working papers or notes. However, Arnold tape-recorded his thoughts about the changing role of farm organizations and deposited that tape with the Provincial Archives of Alberta. (Had Arnold not told me that he had made this tape, it is possible that it would not have been available, as an initial search of the Provincial Archives failed to find it; the tape was located after the archives moved to their current location.) Interviews with Gerald Schuler and Jim Lore filled in the background.

Documentation of Arnold's work on communal property, land use, and on the management of water resources in southern Alberta is quite good. The Platt Family Papers include extensive files of newspaper clippings related to these projects, as well as copies of various reports. Most of the files related to this work are now housed in the Provincial Archives of Alberta although I had access to these archives as they were compiled.

Gerald Schuler, Allan Warrack, Jim Lore, and Dean Lien provided valu-able perspectives on the work Arnold did during these years, while Helen Platt shared her insider's knowledge. I have drawn on conversations I had with Arnold over the years while having the good fortune to work with him.

Acknowledgements

This story of Arnold Platt's life owes much to the encouragement and support of those who knew him. Their contributions are noted in the sections on sources and in the notes. Helen Platt and the Platt family entrusted me with all the materials they had and they shared their recollections without reservation. While Helen Platt read the manuscript as it developed and suggested ways to amplify a point, she never said or implied "you shouldn't say that."

Michael Luski, acquisitions editor at the University of Alberta Press continued to believe in the project through the years that it took to go from an idea to a draft, even though he had never met Arnold Platt. Brenda Belokrinicev edited the manuscript, created the index, and ensured that the notes were accurate and complete. Her improvements to the text took away the usual anxieties about revision as they so obviously respected my intentions as they made the narrative more readable.

David Marshall, president of Mount Royal College, provided me with the year's leave that allowed me to stop talking about the project and actually do it. A research grant from the Alberta Historical Resources Foundation made possible the necessary travel.

Kathleen Hogan, my wife, not only was my first reader whose knowledge of both substance and style prevented innumerable inaccuracies and infelicities of expression, but was also, in her professional capacity as a librarian, an invaluable guide to sources.

In spite of all the support and assistance I've received, readers will undoubtedly find inaccuracies and may note omissions. For these, I alone am responsible.

Dr. Hugh Horner, Minister of Agriculture, inducting Arnold into the Alberta Agriculture Hall of Fame, 1972.

Introduction

Occasionally, if we're very fortunate, we meet someone who inspires us, whose way of being makes us aspire to be more than we had imagined possible. Arnold Platt had such an effect on the many whose lives he touched. I was one of those lucky people. I first met him in April 1973, in a government office in Calgary's Bowlen building, where he interviewed me for the job of research officer. He had just become Chair of the Special Advisory Committee on Communal Property and Land Use, and was hiring his office staff of two.

Newspaper stories had told me that Arnold Platt was a prominent agriculturalist, renowned for developing Rescue wheat; that he had recently been corporate secretary of the United Farmers of Alberta, a farm supply cooperative; and that, the previous year, he had been inducted into Alberta's Agriculture Hall of Fame. In preparing for the job interview, I had discovered that all this was just a very small part of his story. There were more news stories about him, and he was included in the 1971 *Who's Who in Canada*. Clearly he was an important man, a man of influence.

Not having any connections to the agricultural, educational, or political spheres in which he travelled, I was intimidated even before I met him. That first meeting did not make me feel any more confident. During the interview, his keen eyes never left me, and he seemed to listen intently to my answers to the other interviewers' questions. But the only question he asked was, "Do you smoke?" When I replied that I sometimes smoked a pipe, he remarked that, if I hadn't taken it up seriously by then, I never would.

It seemed to be a clear signal that I would never work for him. Evidently, though, I did not know Arnold, for three weeks later I was once again in the human resources office in the Bowlen building, browsing the job postings, and the manager of the office asked me what I was doing there. I already had a job with Arnold—he had simply been too busy to call and tell me.

On May 1, 1973, I showed up for my first day of work. Arnold welcomed me, introduced me to the other staff member, the office administrator, and showed me my office. He pointed out two filing cabinets, which contained the records of the former Communal Property Board and the materials that the Select Committee of the Legislative Assembly had used in preparing its *Report on Communal Property 1972*.

Arnold had a real presence. At five foot five, it wasn't his height that created it. Nonetheless, he was noticed in a room. His shock of sometimes unruly dark hair, which curled up on the left side of his face, created an asymmetry that offset the roundness of his face. The poker face gave itself away in crinkly lines at the corners of his eyes when he smiled in acknowledgement of a friend or in admiration of a well-expressed point. His small, although not delicate, hands constantly worried his pipe, stoking, tamping, cupping, and covering it. When he assumed his position as chair at the head of the board table, he dominated the table because his upper body filled the space; his legs were disproportionately short. His deep voice seemed intimidating at first, and he seemed to be all business. As one listened to what he had to say, one saw his concern for others' well-being and his lack of concern for his own ego. As Dean Lien, who joined the district executive as the Junior Farmers' Union of Alberta (FUA) district president shortly after Arnold became director and chair of the executive meetings, put it, "You knew he was the farmers' friend."

Arnold suggested that I come and see him in about two weeks, after I'd had the chance to acquaint myself with the contents of the filing cabinets. When we met next, he invited me to give my analysis of the way the current controversy over Hutterites' purchases of land had been influenced by what had been done. He heard me out and, apparently satisfied that I had some semblance of an understanding of the issues, he said I should get out and meet some people.

So began a mentorship made remarkable by his generosity, his wisdom, his range of knowledge, and his tolerance for the arrogant ignorance of the young and inexperienced. During one of what would become our weekly seminars, I told Arnold that I did not really think I fit the mold of the specialist, that I regarded myself as more of a generalist. After a few pulls on his pipe, he remarked a bit wistfully, "Being a specialist is easy."

He was the model of a generalist, but it took many years before I had any sense of how he had come to know so much about so many things. Arnold did not talk much about himself; he talked about ideas. Mostly his ideas were concerned with making the world better, and most often those ideas were related to particular events. One did not listen to him for long without realizing that he had been a part of those events. He had the knowledge of an insider, and yet the popular public record seldom recognizes his involvement.

As I came to know Arnold well enough to talk with him about this apparent disparity, I came to understand that he made a distinction between having power and having influence. For the public good to be realized, good people needed to have power. Such power, however, was always constrained by the compromises made necessary by having to satisfy competing interests. Effecting those compromises for the greatest possible good required much background work by knowledgeable but disinterested and self-effacing people. Arnold chose the path of influence rather than the path of power. If that meant his contribution was seldom publicly credited or even acknowledged, then that's how it was.

How Arnold came to have that influence, and how he used it, is a good story. It's also a key to understanding the role that agriculture played in shaping Canada's political, economic, and social life. This story is set in the context of some of the greatest changes to affect North American agriculture, as it was transformed from a way of life to an industry. Arnold played a role in those changes; just as importantly, he played a role in mitigating their most damaging effects. His story invites us to think about today's paths to influence. If a person wanted to make a difference in the nation's affairs, how would she or he go about doing so? Are Arnold Platt's principles of disinterestedness and self-effacement still valid?

This book about his life won't answer those questions directly, but I hope that Arnold's story will provide occasions for considering the ways that his path can be translated to fit contemporary circumstances. Arnold's life, both public and private, was multi-faceted and so diverse as to make him a true generalist. Hardly anyone knew him in all the contexts in which he acted, so it's not surprising that few ever felt they knew him fully.

A few glimpses and impressions demonstrate the varied nature of his life. On election night in 1921, Arnold was with his father William, when William called on John Reid as Reid was milking his cows. They called to tell Reid that he had been elected as the United Farmers representative for the constituency, and that the United Farmers were forming the government. Arnold's father was Reid's campaign manager.

In the summer of 1927, Arnold drove a steel-wheeled tractor, with lugs, from the family farm at Innisfree to the new holding at Westlock and back again—more than 130 miles each way—struggling with his conscience and the sign on the bridge that said "Tractors with lugs prohibited." In the early 1930s, he ran a gaming house in a garage near the University of Alberta in Edmonton, to help finance his education.

Then, in 1938, he was the geneticist, in the greenhouse in Ottawa, who made the cross that resulted in Rescue wheat—the first sawfly-resistant wheat to become commercially available. Then he drove a beat-up truck loaded with Rescue seed stock from Swift Current in Saskatchewan to the Imperial Valley in California, so he could grow two crops a year and get seeds to the farmers, who were losing more than $20 million each year to the sawfly.

In 1953, when he had a leased, eight-section grain farm on the Blood Indian Reserve, he went into Lethbridge wearing greasy overalls for parts for the clutch on a five-ton Dodge he used on the farm. In 1955, he was at the Hotel MacDonald in Edmonton, being elected president of the Farmers' Union of Alberta. In 1959, he was spotted by the Soviet delegate, unlit pipe in his mouth, in an art gallery in Geneva, where negotiations were on for the Fourth International Wheat Agreement. Back in Edmonton, at the Board of Governor's table at the University of Alberta, he persuaded his colleagues to hire North America's lead ing agricultural economist as head of the new department he had just convinced them to approve.

In 1961, he was at Prime Minister Diefenbaker's office at 8:00 am on a dark wintry morning, trying to convince the prime minister that the Royal Commission on Transportation should recommend changes to grain transportation and the Crow Rates even though those changes might not be politically popular in the short term. In 1964, he drove his Chrysler around Hanna, Alberta, assessing the feasibility of expanding the United Farmers of Alberta Cooperative's operations in the area.

On a night in 1973, he drove along a back road near Mossleigh, Alberta, with his lights off, leaving a meeting protesting the establishment of another Hutterite farm in the area. As Chair of the Advisory Committee on Communal Property and Land Use, he'd just taken three hours of abuse for supporting Premier Lougheed's decision to repeal the Communal Property Act.

In 1979, chairing an inquiry at a public hearing on the construction of the Oldman River dam, he listened attentively as a young girl spoke, standing on a milk crate so she could reach the microphone. In April 1996, at a celebration of his life in the Ranchmen's Club in Calgary, Arnold's spirit was there as John Stahl of the Starland Hutterite Colony remembered him.

This book cannot tell the complete story of Arnold Platt's life. His accomplishments suggest his genius, but his genius also resides in his conviction that nothing he did was extraordinary. He considered his life so ordinary that he did not think his papers worth keeping and burned most of them before he died. The following account takes us through the major moments in Arnold Platt's life. The man of genius and the ordinary man, the public man and the private man, were one and the same—deep and reserved, yet sociable and engaging. He was delightful to know.

Arnold's grandparents' house near Innisfree in the mid-1960s. Arnold's half-sister, Ethel (Platt) Larson, in the foregroun•

ONE

Farmhouses, Schoolhouses, and the Quest for Home

1909–1935

I n the late 1960s, when 58-year-old Arnold Platt returned to the district near Innisfree, Alberta, where he had grown up, he sought out three houses. The first was the one that his father William had built on his homestead in 1907, just before he married Gertrude McKinley, Arnold's mother; Arnold was born there, in July 1909. When Arnold's mother died of acute appendicitis in 1910, Arnold's father William left that house and never went into it again. He took Arnold and moved to his parents' home four miles north of Innisfree.

The third house was a small house across the lane from his grandparents' house. William had built it for Arnold and his grandmother Isabella in 1913, shortly before he remarried and soon after Grandfather George Platt died. It was Arnold's and Grandma Platt's home from 1914 until 1927. Although his grandmother provided a home for Arnold there, she also traveled quite extensively; whenever she was away, Arnold stayed with Aunt Nellie (Mrs. Bob Bruce) in Innisfree, or with Aunt Mabel (Mrs. Albert Bruce) in Minburn.

The first house was gone. Although Arnold had not been in it since he'd been ten months old, this was the house that held the most meaning for him: the house of his mother, a mother he knew only vicariously. When, some years after his mother's death, Arnold had asked his father to show him the house, Arnold's father had refused to do so.

The second house was abandoned and in disrepair. This farmhouse also was an abiding presence in Arnold's life. Life on the family farm in Western Canada, with its dynastic dreams and the circumstances of their fulfillment or failure, would always be part of Arnold.

The third house was also gone. Although Arnold had lived in it for most of his childhood and youth, this house had never really been his home. As Arnold was to discover, home was something that repeatedly had to be made anew.

What the loss of his mother, Gertrude McKinley, meant to Arnold, we can only guess. Arnold never knew her, but she was an exceptional person, whose influence extended beyond the short span of her life. He tried to learn as much as he could about the McKinleys in hopes of understanding what kind of a person she'd been. He said he did not think he had found much that was useful, remarking that "it is idle to speculate on these things or on how it might have affected my life had she lived."[1] From what he was able to discover, it seems obvious that she was a powerful presence in his development. It was said she was very intelligent. She was an educated woman, a school teacher, member of a family of some means and accomplishments.

The McKinley family came from the Belfast region of Northern Ireland, emigrating to New York or Boston probably in the 1820s or 1830s. They

Grandma Platt and
Arnold, 1912.
[Platt Family Collection]

were Protestants and landed gentry of considerable means in Ireland. As
Arnold said, "it is reasonable to suppose that they originally came from
England or Scotland and dispossessed the Irish peasants of their land
during one of the many sad periods in the history of that unfortunate
country." In New York, the McKinleys became successful merchants very
much involved in politics; United States President William McKinley was
reputedly of this family. Arnold's grandfather, William McKinley, came to
Ontario in 1867, settling on a large farm on the Grand River near Grand
Valley, a village between Guelph and Orangeville. Arnold remembered
the big house and the great lawn sloping down to the river.

    While Grandfather William McKinley had a large farm, he did not work
the land himself. He worked as a tax collector and had other government
jobs. In later years, he was the librarian of the Carnegie library in Grand

Valley. Arnold recalled meeting him once when Arnold was six years old. He was on a visit to Ontario, accompanied by Grandma Platt:

When I was about six, Grandma Platt scrubbed me good, put on my best clothes and took me to see my grandfather. I was scared to death but impressed with the building and the man behind the desk. We shook hands and while I can't remember anything he said, I sort of liked him.... I never saw Grandfather McKinley again nor did he ever write or try to get in touch with me. I have no recollection of when he died or what became of my grandmother [McKinley].

That image of the man behind the desk in the library, "a large, square granite building with great stone steps and big wooden doors," would stay with Arnold all his life, a symbol of the world that could be accessed through books and education.

Arnold started school in Ontario, in the very school where his mother had taught when she met Arnold's father in 1901 or 1902. Gertrude McKinley had taught at the Luther School, about twenty-five miles from her family home near Grand Valley. While teaching there, she boarded with William Platt's parents, George and Isabella. Later, in 1902, William left Ontario for Western Canada, but Gertrude and William continued their courtship, mostly by letter supplemented with the occasional visit from William. Gertrude agreed to join William in Innisfree, taking a job as teacher in the Innisfree School in 1908.

How Arnold came to start school at Luther School in Ontario even though he lived with Grandma Platt in the small house on the farm near Innisfree is not clear. Grandma Platt had taken Arnold to visit her family and the McKinleys in the summer of 1915. She returned to Alberta and left Arnold with her daughter Emma (Mrs. Winters), who lived in the Luther School District.

It was an inauspicious start to his formal education. As Arnold recalls,

I seemed to be constantly in trouble, with the teacher, with my fellow students. Unquestionably, at that point I was a rather rebellious young

person. I suppose because of my moving around from place to place and that sort of thing, I learned to take advantage of my elders and know that almost anything I did could be forgiven. I don't really know how bad a boy I was but I gather that I wasn't the nicest youngster in the world.

Arnold returned to Alberta from Ontario partway through his first year of school. He stayed with his Aunt Mabel Bruce in Minburn, and went to Bowling Green School there. He got along much better at Bowling Green, and started to enjoy school. After a few months at Bowling Green School, though, he was sent back to his grandmother's house, and in the fall of 1916 he started at a third school: Loree School.[2]

Altogether, Arnold was only in school, off and on, for at most five years. His relocations were not the only reason his schooling was somewhat erratic and irregular. Sometimes the local school district could not afford to pay the teacher or heat the school; sometimes no teacher considered suitable was available; sometimes winter temperatures were too cold for the students to travel safely to school; and, in spring and fall, the children were needed at home to help put in and harvest the crops. Nevertheless, just before he turned twelve, Arnold passed the provincial grade eight examinations, achieving very high marks.

In spite of the sporadic schedule and the frequent change of teachers, Arnold enjoyed his time at Loree School and was an exceptional student, being only the second student from that school to have passed the grade eight departmental exams. Three teachers at that school would influence him greatly: Mr. Howson, who sparked his interest in biology; Mr. Thompson, who taught him baseball; and Miss Agnes Young, who prepared him to write the departmental exams.

Mr. Howson helped Arnold discover the natural environment in which he lived. As Arnold recalled, Howson interested him in insects,

and I started to make an insect collection. Goodness knows, the sloughs, the prairies, the bush that was in that country at that time had a great variety of insects about. I soon accumulated a rather large collection. I don't know how many boxes of butterflies and beetles and whatnot that

I collected—I eventually became quite specialized in butterflies and beetles, which my teacher helped me to identify and label. Unfortunately, neither he nor I were aware that there were other insects that eat dead insects and one spring when I got my collection out to see what I had so that I would know what I should be looking for, I found that they had all been eaten up by little bugs.... Anyway, it was an interesting experience, I suppose one of the things that got me really interested in biology and plant life. I enjoyed it very much.

Howson taught at the Loree school for two or three years, teaching school when he could get enough students to come, and working in the harvest fields when school was not in session. Arnold remembered him as a quiet man who never seemed to worry very much about whether he was going to be paid or not, but who was very interested in all the students. Howson

spent innumerable hours both within the so-called school time and in other time with the young Ukrainian children, teaching them how to speak English and visiting them in their homes on weekends and getting to know their families. He was one of those people who had a tremendous influence on our community, but I have never seen his name mentioned in any of the histories of the area.

From developing his insect collection, Arnold learned that going beyond the rudiments of education cost money. He was not deterred by the cost. Instead, he used the available resources to raise the necessary money. His neighbour, Henry Kvindegard, a fellow student at Loree school who was two years older than Arnold, was Arnold's mentor in such things as how to shoot a gun, how to trap weasels, and how to play cards.

Arnold started to run a trapline as part of his daily walk to and from school, trapping mainly weasels. Each weasel skin sold for between two and three dollars, quite a lot of money for an eight- or nine-year-old in 1918. This was but the first of a series of creative ways of financing his education and advancement that Arnold discovered; gambling and farming would come later. First Arnold had to finish grade eight.

In having been the first student from Loree school to finish grade eight and pass the departmental examinations, Henry Kvindegard was also Arnold's role model. Encouraged by the teacher, Agnes Young, who boarded at the Kvindegards, Henry successfully wrote the departmental exams at Primrose school in June of 1920. Arnold wrote copies of the exams but did not do so well.

The following year, Miss Young came to board with the Platts. She determined that Arnold should write the exams in June of 1921 and proceeded to work very hard to ensure his success. Arnold worked very hard as well. Arnold believed that, without Miss Young's encouragement and commitment, he might never have finished public school. She was a pretty, charming young woman, herself only about sixteen or seventeen years old when she came to Loree school in the fall of 1919—although she had finished normal school—and Arnold was "sort of in love with her." He did not want to let her down, and he did not. He passed with very high marks and felt that he had completed his formal education.

Like many other twelve-year-olds at that time, he was ready to take his place as a young adult in the life of the farm and the community, a community of which the Platts were a significant part. The Platt family, associated with both town and farm in the Innisfree community, had established itself in business, agriculture, and politics. Descended from an indentured Dublin machine-shop apprentice who had escaped his forced servitude by stowing away on a ship whose destination was unknown to Arnold's great-grandfather Platt, but which happened to be Montreal, the Platt family had become established in Ontario.

Grandfather George Platt, who was born in 1856, had started out in the logging business, cutting and hauling trees out of the Dufferin swamp. He was a roving man, however, and soon left the timber business to take up farming, first in Ontario, then near Brandon in what is now Boissevain, Manitoba (1897), back to Ontario, then to Manitoba again near Oak Lake, back to Ontario, and then finally around 1908 following his sons William and Sam to Innisfree. George Platt was known as a man of considerable skills—as an entrepreneur, a stone mason, and a master of the broad axe.

Grandma Isabella Platt (née Isabella East in Ontario, 1862) married George Platt in 1881. Her family, the Easts, originally from England, came to Ontario in the 1860s and established themselves as merchants. Some members of the East family also participated in the Canadian migration westward; Isabella's brother John East established John East Iron Works in Saskatoon, and it was at the Easts' house in Saskatoon that William Platt married Gertrude McKinley. Isabella and George Platt had six children, and five of them established households in the Innisfree/Minburn area. Isabella also had a sister who married King, head of the King ranching family of High River, so Arnold's Platt family community included fairly well-established and prominent people in Alberta and Saskatchewan, along with some Ontario connections.

By the time that Arnold began to think of himself as a part of that community, his father William had become the chairman of the school board for the Loree school as well as being active in farm politics through the United Farmers of Alberta. He raised livestock, sold breeding stock, grew hay and feed crops on about 480 acres, and rented additional pasture as well.

William had come west to work on the construction of the Canadian Northern Railway, operating a pile driver and working with his team of horses as railway construction proceeded between Innisfree and Edmonton. That section of the railway completed, William returned to Innisfree, where he and his future brother-in-law, Bill McKinley, built a livery barn in about 1904. As part of the livery business, William also helped settlers to identify their homesteads, and transported them and their effects across the prairie to their new home sites.

By the time Arnold was born, William had sold the livery business, but it had brought him into contact with most of the settlers in the district. Shortly after the United Farmers of Alberta (UFA) became established in 1909, William joined and he signed up as members some 90% of the farmers in the Loree school district. When in 1919 the United Farmers of Alberta decided to form the UFA Provincial Political Association,

William supported the move to obtain a voice in the provincial legis-lature by putting up candidates in the next election. He became the campaign manager for R.G. Reid of Mannville in the election of 1921. Arnold's recollection of that event captures the surprise that members of the UFA felt at having been elected, not only to be a voice for farmers, but to form the government:

> *I recall the election day and the great excitement there was in 1921, how we got in the old Ford car and drove over to Reid's place that evening. I remember that he was milking the cow at the time. My father was the one who informed him that he had won the seat.*

Arnold attributed his father's involvement in politics to his deep compas-sion for the poor and the unfortunate, a quality that Arnold also exem-plified in his subsequent life, both public and private. But Arnold also became aware while still a student at Loree school that fair-mindedness and compassion were sometimes not enough to counter the forces of narrow-mindedness and prejudice. His father's experience in hiring a teacher who did not quite fit the accepted image of moral rectitude stayed with Arnold:

> *A lady teacher was hired who came with two daughters and seemed to me and I think to all the students to be a wonderful teacher. However, she had not been there more than a month or so until I remember a delegation of the lead cows of the community calling upon my father and putting the proposition up to him that they had heard the story that this woman was a divorcée. My father had to admit that such was the case and that he had known she was a divorcée when she was hired but pointed out that she had excellent recommendations and that they desperately needed a teacher. However, it was not to be. He had to let the lady know that she was not acceptable in the district and of course she had to leave and the school was closed down.*

When Arnold started to take on adult responsibilities, farming, politics, and socializing with family and friends were the main constituents of community life, but they were not the only ones. For Arnold, baseball was important. Of the teachers who influenced Arnold while he was at the Loree school, Thompson was the one who taught him how to pitch, hit, and field.

When Arnold's father had to replace the divorcée teacher, he hired Thompson to teach in July and August. Thompson had just graduated from high school and had no teaching experience, but he was an excellent baseball player and it was baseball tournament season. Thompson and his students spent about half the school day on the baseball diamond. Baseball became one of Arnold's enduring pleasures. It also gave him an opportunity to demonstrate his ability to lead.

Thompson left Loree school to go to school in the United States and play in the minor leagues. Two or three years later, when Arnold was almost twelve and finishing school, he and others in the district who were considerably older than Arnold came up with the idea of establishing the Loree Athletic Association to form a baseball team. As Arnold tells the story:

> We went ahead and called a meeting for the school of all the people we could think of in the neighbourhood to come and discuss this idea. At which point it occurred to me that I should ask father for permission to use the school because he was chairman of the school board. He was rather appalled at my brashness and suggested that I should not take such a lead role at my young age amongst people, many of whom were twice my age. So, using his good advice when we came to the meeting, all I did was suggest they elect a chairman for the evening who later became president and that was done.

In later years, Arnold would draw on this experience in leadership as he perfected the art of leading from behind the scenes.

The Loree Athletic Association formed its baseball team to play in the district tournaments. Arnold made it onto the team and became its youngest player. The team was led by its star pitcher, a thirty-six-year-old semi-professional who had been in the great war. Arnold played right field. He wasn't much of a fielder, but he was very successful as the lead-off hitter. His short stature did not give pitchers much of a strike zone, so he got walks. He also mastered the bunt or the short drive just past second base, but he never could hit the long ball. Instead, he used cunning and speed to steal bases and score runs.

These were great times for Arnold. He was doing a man's work at home, participating in a sport he loved, and assuming his place in the life of the community. For three years, this was enough. He worked with his father at home on the farm, he worked for other farmers occasionally, and he worked for the municipality building roads. His father hired an excellent baseball player, Fred Bohr, to help with the farm work, so Arnold had the company of someone who shared his interests.

But the experience of the insect collection was not entirely forgotten. And the books that came into the house reminded Arnold of the existence of a world of knowledge and experience beyond what his community offered. An incident from his early childhood, from the Christmas of 1917, kept coming back to him.

That year, his grandmother was away at Christmastime and Arnold was staying with his father and Daisy. They had guests for Christmas dinner: the local doctor and his wife, and the local druggist and his wife. All were newcomers to town. Because William had been chair of the local committee responsible for bringing these two medical people to Innisfree, he felt responsible for seeing to it that they were properly fêted.

His wife Daisy was in awe of people who were used to what was, in her opinion, high society, and the preparations for the occasion made it clear to Arnold that this would be a momentous Christmas. Extra coal was brought in, and a special foot-warmer for the sleigh was ordered from Eaton's so the guests could keep their feet from freezing on their trip from Innisfree to the farm. Daisy outdid herself and the dinner was a great success. Eight-year-old Arnold ate at the table with the adults, and he "stuffed himself to the gills."

After dinner, the women moved off into the kitchen, and the men sat back from the table to enjoy their cigars. Feeling tired from the big day and the copious meal, Arnold crawled under the table to take a nap. But the men's conversation kept him awake and alert. They talked about their experiences and their time at university, how one learned to become a doctor and how one learned to handle drugs and chemicals. Arnold remembers that he

> *was completely fascinated by it. I suppose it was at that time that I thought, "you know, this is something I want to do when I get older." It was probably one of the most important Christmas presents that I ever received—this inspiration. I got up enough nerve to get out from under the table so I could listen better and ask some questions on my own and they were most kind in answering them and so the Christmas present I got at this, one of the first Christmases I can remember fairly vividly, was the desire to see more of the world and get an education.*

Books helped satisfy the desire and intensified Arnold's desire to experience for himself the world beyond the district. Arnold loved to read. Before he learned to read, his grandmother had read to him, holding him entranced while he listened to her read works of English poets such as Coleridge and Browning. As soon as he learned to read, he read whatever he could find at home and in the school library. The library extension service provided by the University of Alberta became the mainstay of his continuing education, much as it had supplemented the education he received at the public school. Arnold described the program:

> *The University Extension Department had a marvelous program. They used to send out boxes of books. They would arrive by train of course, and somebody in the district would be responsible for picking them up and making them available to anyone who wanted them. I suppose there would be anywhere between twenty-five and fifty hardcover books of various kinds in each of the boxes, which it seems to me we used to keep for three months and then return them to the university. Then another box would come our way. Usually these boxes were kept at our place.... This was a great thing for the whole community because we had no newspapers except for a few farm journals which were largely propaganda outfits.*

Continuing his education became Arnold's goal. The question was how to do it. Going to high school was out of the question because the school schedule interfered too much with work on the farm.

The farm's hired man, Fred Bohr, had been to the agricultural school in Vermillion and spoke very favourably about it. It was one of three established by the provincial department of agriculture in 1913, the others being at Olds and Claresholm. These schools were intended to provide practical courses to young men and women who wanted to farm, while also serving as feeder schools for the agricultural program at the University of Alberta. The school year was only five and a half months long, which allowed students to work on farms during the spring, summer, and fall.

But students had to be sixteen years old to be admitted. By the time Arnold was fifteen, the Vermillion school had closed for lack of students. The agricultural school in Olds was still operating but, like the Vermillion school, it required students to be sixteen years old in addition to the basic requirements that they be from a farm and be able to read and write.

Without telling his father and grandmother, Arnold wrote a letter to the Olds school of agriculture, saying that he was not only able to read and write but that he had his certificate proving that he had passed grade eight. While he was only fifteen, he was anxious to get on with going to school. Would they make an exception and allow him to attend? The school responded that, under the circumstances, he would be welcome. Now Arnold had to broach the matter with his grandmother and his father. He needed money as well as permission.

Money was a problem. Although Arnold had been working, he hadn't been paid. A series of troubles—the great frost of 1918, the drought of 1919, and the recession of 1919, which had caused cattle prices to drop to almost nothing—had almost ruined William. By the fall of 1923, he was getting back on his feet, but money was still scarce and he needed Arnold's help. The fact that classes did not start at Olds until after the harvest was an advantage, but money for rail fare, tuition, clothes, and board would have to be found. Tuition was modest, but the Olds school had no dormitory and Arnold would have to arrange for room and board in a private home, at a cost of about five dollars a week.

Finally, William agreed that Arnold could go. Going to the unknown, getting up in the middle of the night to catch the train on its way to the city…these have become conventional images of prairie youth in

Arnold's first suit, 1923.
[Platt Family Collection]

the early twentieth century, and they were part of Arnold's experience that day. Arnold had never before been on a train by himself, he had never been to Edmonton—where he would have to go from the Canadian Northern station to the Canadian Pacific station to take the train south to Olds—and by 2:00 A.M. on the sleepless night of his departure, he had almost lost his nerve.

But his father was up too, the night's sleep was ruined anyway, and they might as well go to the station to meet the 4:00 am train. William sketched a map of downtown Edmonton to guide Arnold between stations. Arnold had his letter of acceptance in hand, the name of a land-lady in mind, and a desire for new knowledge greater than his fear of the unknown. And so the adventure began.

New experience was not long in coming. Before he left the station, Arnold met a black person, the first he had ever seen, who worked as the train's porter. Arnold couldn't keep the shock from showing on his face, but the porter treated Arnold with kindness, showing him how to arrange his seat in the day coach so he could get settled in for sleep—even if it did not come.

By breakfast time, the train was at the Edmonton station. Arnold walked along 101st street, amazed at the number of stores of all kinds lining the street. Breakfast over, he went in search of a suit. He had never owned a suit, but the school required its students to have one. Merchants importuned him on the sidewalk, the suitcase in Arnold's hand being their invitation to try to sell him stock they had been unable to move. A clothier persuaded Arnold that a brown suit fitted him perfectly and Arnold agreed, the only problem being the price of fifteen dollars. Arnold showed his developing business sense by negotiating a price of twelve dollars. But that money was the price of a lesson in bargaining and clothes. The suit fit badly and looked worse, and Arnold soon realized he'd been taken.

With time to fill before taking the train to Olds, Arnold stowed his baggage at the CPR station and walked on to the Legislature building. He toured the grounds and the building, awed by the chamber in which the members conducted the affairs of the province when the House was in session, and wondered if he might ever take a seat there.

The boarding house provided Arnold's next lesson. The house looked small from the outside, but it was not until the mean-looking, angular landlady showed him to the room in the attic that he was to share with a fellow student from Lacombe that Arnold realized the house was even smaller than it had seemed.

In a space that might have accommodated one, the landlady housed four. The attic was divided into a front room and a back room. To get to the back room, it was necessary to go through the front room. The two boys in the back room were from Vermillion, and they provided a connection with home, and Bob Cunningham, Arnold's roommate from Lacombe, was a jovial fellow who made Arnold feel welcome.

That faint feeling of welcome aided by wishful thinking lasted until the first meal. The food wasn't bad, but it was like the room—adequate for one, not four. The amount did not change after the landlady had become acquainted with the appetites of four young boys, and Arnold and the others were constantly hungry. After a week of getting by through supplementing the meagre fare with five-cent chocolate bars, Arnold asserted himself. The landlady promised that things would get better by and by, and that Thanksgiving would mark the beginning of the improvements.

Thanksgiving dinner featured a scrawny chicken divided among four half-starved boys and two adults, the landlady's husband—an infrequent visitor—having come in from the farm for the occasion. The boys let the landlady know that this was not their idea of a feast. She agreed that she should have prepared a little more food but promised a great dessert. Dessert was improperly home-canned cherries. The seal had broken and the cherries had begun to ferment. Arnold remembered that they "smelled like hell but we were hungry enough that we ate them." The Dickensian workhouse atmosphere intensified, the boys shivering in their poorly heated rooms as winter temperatures set in. They were so cold that they took the filthy rugs from the floor to use as bedding.

Fortunately, school itself was wonderful. Arnold enjoyed everything about it—the fellow students, the subjects of study, and the teachers. The principal, Frank Grisdale, Arnold remembered as

> a tall, strong man who understood farm boys and understood how discipline should be maintained. When he cussed you out, you were cussed out but good. But you nevertheless learned to respect this man and to obey the rules that he had laid down.

The curriculum emphasized the practical things that a farmer needed to know and do: woodworking, blacksmithing, caring for and feeding animals, and selecting and growing field crops. The fundamentals of the biological sciences and classes in English literature provided somewhat more academic elements.

Athletic and social programs helped to round out the educational experience. Skating and hockey were the main outdoor sports, but Arnold did not own skates and had no great interest in getting any. Boxing and wrestling, especially boxing, did interest him though. He took up boxing, although he did not become greatly skilled at it.

Olds was a co-educational school, and there were girls at the weekly dances. Arnold claimed that he wasn't interested in girls, or more accurately that he was scared to death of them, and that he had no idea of how one did this dancing thing. Members of the teaching staff decided that lessons in ballroom dancing would be a good thing, and Arnold got up the nerve to go to these classes. While he did not become a good dancer that year, these classes and dances introduced him to an activity that would give him a good deal of pleasure in later years.

The Olds School had a serious debating team, with an excellent and demanding instructor. Arnold was fascinated by public speaking and debating, but was desperately shy. His fascination overcame the fear at last, and Arnold joined the team. Just before his first debate, the terror returned. He excused himself, went to the bathroom and threw up his supper, and then returned to take to the stage. Once up on the platform, he managed to hide his nervousness and demonstrated considerable skill in making his prepared points and in the more spontaneous rebuttal. So began his development as a debater and orator.

By early December of that year (1923), Arnold had decided that he needed new lodgings. When he learned of an upcoming vacancy in a house that was some distance from the school but was reputed to serve excellent meals, he jumped at the chance. He arranged to move before classes started again in January. In the meantime, he had the prospect of Christmas by himself at the loathsome boarding house. The other boarders were going home for the holiday, but he had no money for travel. Filled with panic and loneliness, Arnold was close to despair. At the last minute, he was able to scrape together enough cash for the train fare to Innisfree and he went home to his grandmother's house for Christmas.

The second semester of the school year proved to be wholly delightful. His new room, in the home of fairly recent immigrants from Denmark, lived up to its reputation for delicious and sufficient food, the large room shared with only one other boarder provided a good place to study and sleep, and his new roommate gave him free violin lessons.

Arnold and cousin Ralph Barber, c. 1924. [Platt Family Collection]

At school, lessons gave Arnold the opportunity to distinguish himself in ways that the violin lessons did not. Arnold wrote the examinations, and his efforts drew the principal's attention. Grisdale sent Arnold a note saying that he hoped Arnold would continue with his schooling and that, judging from Arnold's marks and from his own knowledge of him, Arnold had a better future in the academic world than in the world of the mechanic, woodworker, or blacksmith. Grisdale predicted his future accurately; most of Arnold's life was in fact lived in the academic world.

That future was not apparent in 1925, when Arnold returned to the farm at Innisfree for spring seeding. William's financial situation seemed to have become worse as he continued to pay off the debts incurred to cover the losses suffered in the early 1920s. Through the rest of 1925 and the summer of 1926, Arnold again worked on the family farm and for other farmers, and worked for the municipality. In the summer of 1926, Arnold worked building roads for the municipality, driving a twelve-horse team pulling a road grader. The work was hard and the hours long, but the pay was decent.

The crops were not so good. Consequently, most of the money Arnold earned that summer went to pay the taxes owed to the municipality and the school board. However, the Vermillion School of Agriculture had reopened, and Arnold wanted to finish the second year of the two-year diploma program he had started at Olds.

Once again, Arnold and his father were able to work out a plan. William would pay the tuition. Arnold had saved a little money, and if Arnold took in a roommate and held a part-time job, they thought Arnold would be able to get through. The farm would provide all the food he could eat. They rented a shack on the outskirts of Vermillion, with a kitchen and two small bedrooms, for ten dollars a month. Arnold's cousin, Ted Barber, agreed to share the house and the rent, and Arnold got a job at the livery barn. The schooling of Arnold Platt could continue.

Arnold was now seventeen and more interested in girls than he had been in Olds. One of his first discoveries was that the job at the livery barn precluded a social life. The job required that he clean up the barn before school each morning, and that did not leave time for him to get himself cleaned up after he finished at the barn—their house had cold water only and heating water would take too long. So the smell of the barn went with him to class.

Arnold had to find another source of income. The instructor of veterinary medicine, who had recently immigrated from Ireland, gave him an idea. As Arnold put it, the instructor, recognizing in Arnold a fellow Irish reprobate, told him that the town needed a place for "the boys" to get together for a game of cards and explained how Arnold could make himself and his house available to people who liked to gamble. The house would take 10% of the pot.

Arnold thought this to be a considerably more interesting way of making a living than cleaning out barns, and he sounded out his cousin Ted. As it turned out, Ted also needed a little extra money. The two of them set up a gaming house, knowing very well that the enterprise was completely illegal. The instructor provided leadership in bringing in card players, and soon the house was making more money than Arnold had been able to earn at the livery barn.

Business became even better when Arnold became acquainted with the "house of ill repute." This house, as innocent in its façade as Arnold's shack, was directly across the street from his, and he became aware of its operation through the disreputable characters who sat in on his game. Arnold and the madam began to refer customers to each other's establishments, and as he said, between the two of them, they had quite a good thing going. If the representatives of the law knew what was going on, they had other things to do and they left these two enterprises alone. Creating a cash flow from a gambling house proved to be a good lesson in farm economics, and complemented Arnold's more theoretical education in the classroom.

With the supplement of provisions from home and monthly visits from Grandma Platt, who brought with her baked goods, Arnold survived quite nicely. Occasionally his budget allowed him to follow his developing desire to become better acquainted with girls, one in particular. For most of the term he and a first-year student from Saskatchewan, Marjorie Carnarvon, enjoyed each other's company at the movies, at the ice cream parlour, or on the river ice-skating.

School in Vermilion proved to be even more satisfying than the first year at Olds, not so much because the program was better but because Arnold had a good deal more self-confidence, which allowed him to ask for help or more information, and a better idea of which things interested him. Two of Arnold's teachers were outstanding, both in their knowledge of their subjects and in their influence: Mannion in organic chemistry and Hopkins in English literature. Mannion had a masters degree in science from the University of Minnesota and pursued his research interests as well as teaching. He was completely devoted to his students, who became his family, probably because he had no family close by. Hopkins, a splendid lecturer who could arouse enthusiasm for the classics of English literature in students who had had little previous exposure to such works, invited his students into his home. On Sunday afternoons, Hopkins invited those he thought might be interested to take tea with him. Here Arnold learned to balance a teacup while sitting on a chair and eating a cookie, engaging in spirited discussions led by Hopkins. This was a kind of social activity Arnold had not experienced before.

Arnold continued to develop his literary and linguistic abilities by working on the school's magazine and by belonging to the debating team. His debating and speaking skills won him a ten-dollar gold piece for being the best public speaker in his class. The *Vermilion School of Agriculture Yearbook* for 1926/1927 describes Arnold as a

> *"good scout"... [who] has made notable success of his work in Botany and Civics, and who has been one of our favourite debaters. As defence lawyer in the mock trial held at the School during the Winter, he proved himself a splendid counsel, and should he enter into the study of law it is felt that he would attain more than an indifferent success.*

Law was not to be his vocation, but this combination of scientific inquiry, verbal skill, and social engagement formed the basis for much of Arnold's subsequent success. Arnold passed his exams with high marks and received his diploma in the spring of 1927.

Further schooling would have to wait, however. Because of changing circumstances, his father needed his help to relocate the farm from Innisfree to new holdings near Westlock, about fifty miles north of Edmonton.[3] The farm at Innisfree was mainly a beef cattle operation, with the home half-section of cultivated land providing grain for feed and sale while leased land provided the pasture. William believed that a looming loss of leased land and the coming mechanization of grain farming made it likely that grain farming would become more profitable than cattle ranching.

Until the mid-1920s, leases had been cheap, running at about twenty-five dollars a year for a quarter-section, the only additional cost being the expenditure for barbed wire fences. After the ruinous losses to drought and blizzard in 1919 and 1920, rising prices for both cattle and crops had made farming and ranching quite profitable in the early 1920s. The general profitability of farming attracted prospective buyers.

The rangeland that William and others in the area leased was owned mainly by the Canadian Pacific Railway, which had acquired land in exchange for building the transcontinental railway in the 1880s, and the Hudson's Bay Company, which retained land as part of its compensation for ceding lands granted to it in the original charter of 1670 to the Dominion of Canada in 1870. The leased rangeland now promised to be worth considerably more as crop land than its leases paid, and the companies were interested in selling rather than leasing the land. In addition, poplars were taking over the pasture lands, and the lands would have to be cultivated to stop the encroachment.

William Platt did not want to buy rangeland that, even if cultivated would be too rocky and hilly to farm with tractors, and his partnership with his younger brother Sam was not thriving. William's close friends, the Lorees, had also decided to look at land elsewhere, and had chosen the Westlock area. When Lawrence Loree called William from Westlock in the late winter of 1927 to tell him about a half section of land for sale at a very good price, William bought it.

This deal resulted in William having a crop to put in on the 320 acres at Innisfree, land to clear and break near Westlock, and no partner to help him. He needed Arnold. To the eighteen-year-old Arnold, this was an adventure. Running a lugged tractor the 125 miles from Innisfree to Westlock at about four miles an hour, blasting out stumps with stumping powder on the 50 acres they cleared that summer, then running the trac-tor back to Innisfree in time to harvest an outstanding crop—"this was the life" said Arnold. "All you needed was modern machinery and you could grow wheat and prosper."

After the harvest of 1927, William sold his land at Innisfree, persuaded Grandma Platt to sell her home quarter, and the entire family moved to the new land of prosperity—with more money than William had ever had before.

Sadly, a series of disasters followed. William became ill, the winter brought temperatures in the −40s, the green poplar firewood couldn't keep the house warm, and the barn was completely inadequate and had to be rebuilt. By mid-February, Arnold was down to 110 pounds on his five foot-five frame (he claimed that he carried an additional two pounds of dirt, not having had a bath since they left Innisfree).

After a week off in Edmonton, Arnold returned to the farm in early March to begin clearing another 60 acres of poplar bush. So far the hard-ship was but part of the grand adventure.

But then the crop of 1928 was severely damaged by a late August frost. While threshing it, William caught his arm in a belt, and barely escaped with his life. He spent most of the fall of 1928 and winter of 1929 in hospitals in Westlock and Edmonton. Arnold was left with the threshing to complete at their own farm and threshing contracts to fulfill on six or seven neighbouring farms. Arnold hired another neighbour to help, got together a crew in Dapp, and harvested the crops they had agreed to thresh. The income barely covered expenses.

After the harvest, while William recovered in hospitals, Arnold put money in the family treasury by hauling wheat to the elevator, cutting the trees on another 50 acres of poplar bush, and hauling lumber between a sawmill at Pibroch and a planing mill at Clyde. In addition, he tried to manage a crew that his father, from his hospital bed, had contracted to slash and pile the trees that Arnold had not been able to handle. As Arnold said, the crew was

> *frequently drunk, most had venereal disease and really foul mouths. They terrified me. Their piling was poor and my mild remonstrations were met by a stream of oaths and threats that led me to back off with a mild request that they try to do better.*

By the summer of 1929, school seemed a distant memory. Arnold decided to rent and farm a quarter-section of land. The rental agreement split the proceeds from the crop one-third to the owner, and two-thirds to the renter. Arnold divided his share with his father because he was using his father's machinery.

The crop looked good, and in July wheat was $2 a bushel. Arnold had an option to buy the land, should the owner decide to sell, and the owner, Hunter, offered to sell the land to Arnold just as the crop was ready to harvest By harvest time, though, wheat was down to 99 cents a bushel and William advised Arnold to hold onto the wheat until prices improved in spring. He also advised Arnold to buy the land, promising Arnold all the help he could provide in making the purchase.

Arnold sold his wheat and held off on the purchase, thinking it would not be possible to make a living as a grain farmer in that area; he would need livestock as well. His schooling in farm management and finance helped him realize that he would need to make a greater investment than the return on that investment was likely to warrant, so he decided not to buy the land that fall (1929). The stock market crashed in October and, by spring, wheat was selling for thirty cents a bushel. Arnold had had a narrow escape.

Having decided against buying land, Arnold was not sure what to do next. The idea of going to university came back to him, but his diploma in agriculture did not satisfy high school matriculation requirements. There was a program for graduates of the diploma program who wanted to meet matriculation requirements; the Olds college had offered one since 1924. The Vermillion [sic] School of Agriculture sent a letter to its former students indicating that, if they were interested in such a program, the Vermillion school would provide the space and the instructors if at least twenty students enrolled and paid the rather substantial tuition fees. By the late fall of 1929, enough students had indicated they wanted to take the course—Arnold being one of them—and the school opened the program.

The program required the students to take the full equivalent of the core high school subjects in one five- or six-month term. At the end of the term, the Department of Education set special exams for these adult students. Two outstanding teachers drove the group through the courses of study. There was no time for any outside enterprise, such as running a gaming house; indeed, there was hardly time for anything other than school work. Arnold had never worked harder before or since, spending long days in the lecture room and long nights in his room studying.

Yet Arnold somehow found time to edit the Vermilion [sic] School of Agriculture Yearbook for 1929/1930—and to become acquainted with at least one young woman. Donna Oxford, whose parents Silas and Inez farmed near Amisk, attended the Vermillion School of Agriculture that year. Their acquaintance developed into friendship as they worked together on the yearbook and on the literary committee, and by the end of the school year the friendship had developed into something more. They contemplated marriage even as they considered enrolling at the University of Alberta in the fall of 1930.

Once again, Arnold excelled in his examinations, his mark of 98% in algebra being most noteworthy. The school record is notable, not only for its account of Arnold's achievements to date but also for its indication of those that were to come. When he finished his diploma, his classmates correctly predicted botany and civics as the foundation for Arnold's future accomplishments. As editor of the 1929/1930 yearbook, Arnold addressed two causes that were to give meaning to much of his life: the need for "scientific agriculture" and the need for agricultural leadership to encompass the whole range of provincial and federal issues. In his editorial he wrote:

> The great and growing problems that are constantly facing the farmers of Alberta demand that not only the best brains of the Province be brought to bear on the solution to them, but that our young people must be trained so that they may be conversant with the needs of the Province, if she is to acquire and maintain her rightful place in the Dominion of Canada.

> The time is coming when all the farmers on the western plains will of necessity be trained agriculturalists. It will be the duty of the Schools of Agriculture to supply a large measure of such training and a solemn duty rests on the graduates of the Schools; we must prove to the people of the Province that we have received beneficial training, that we have become better farmers and better homemakers, that we have become better citizens by virtue of the training that has done so much to shape our lives and tone our experience.

Arnold was now ready to go to university. But his scheme to make money to pay for his university education failed, and this almost prevented his going. His father William had an opportunity to take on a large job of clearing and breaking land for one of the neighbours at Westlock, a neighbour who was said to be very wealthy. The ingenious contract provided for payment at an agreed-upon rate per acre, payable in two ways. At the end of the summer, the landowner would pay cash for expenses such as gas, oil, and additional labour, but not for William's or Arnold's work. Payment for that would come from the first and second crops along with an additional bonus based on crop yields. Because Arnold did not have a farm of his own and because by the summer of 1930 jobs were becoming scarce, Arnold thought this was the thing to do. He estimated that his share of the proceeds would give him $2,000 with which to pay for his university education. William and Arnold worked hard and kept up their end of the bargain but, by fall, the neighbour was bankrupt. He left the country without paying a cent to the Platts.

This setback did not stop Arnold. He was determined to make his dream of going to university come true. He wanted an education, and he wanted to get it at the University of Alberta, where Donna Oxford had enrolled. He consulted his father, estimating that $500 would see him through his first year. William did not have $500, but he could spare $200 then and promised a little more if the crop could be threshed. Rain and snow had come at the start of September, with the crop standing in stooks in the fields. Classes for the fall of 1930 had already started when Arnold set off for Edmonton with the two hundred dollars in hand.

He mounted the great stone steps of another symbol of the enduring value of education, the neoclassical Arts building in the centre of the University of Alberta campus, and stood before its huge wooden doors. Arnold rehearsed his case for admission before going up to the registrar's office on the third floor and presenting himself to the Registrar, A.E. Ottewell.

Seemingly unaware that the matriculation program at Vermillion was intended primarily for people who wanted to study agriculture at university, Arnold told Ottewell that he wanted to be a chemical engineer and, demonstrating a growing disregard for bureaucratic process, wondered if he would have to fill out any forms. The Registrar assured Arnold that there were a fair number of forms to be filled out, but did not immediately send him on his way to do so. When the Registrar asked Arnold what he thought qualified him to be admitted to the faculty of engineering, Arnold quite proudly presented the official documents from the Department of Education showing both his grade eight departmental examination results and his results on the special exams he had written to satisfy his high school requirements.

As the former Director of Extension at the University of Alberta, Ottewell had visited almost every community in the province, and may well have known the Platt family name as William's house had been the repository for books from the office of Extension. He complimented Arnold on his excellent standing, but pointed out that he lacked the credits needed to enter engineering, being short on mathematics. He suggested that, as classes had already started, Arnold take the winter to concentrate on the mathematics he hadn't taken, perhaps also putting some work into developing his writing skills. But this did not fit Arnold's plans. He felt the need to go to university right away. He was twenty-one, and felt that life was getting on. He also intended to get married to Donna as soon as it could reasonably be arranged.

Ottewell suggested a second possibility: he would admit Arnold to the Faculty of Arts. This idea also held little appeal for Arnold. He wanted to study chemistry and biology, those being his main interests, and Donna Oxford was enrolled in a B.Sc. program in chemistry. Finally Ottewell suggested the Faculty of Agriculture as the place for Arnold to pursue his interests, for the program of studies there would allow him to obtain a B.Sc. in biochemistry. Arnold agreed that this was a reasonable solution, and proceeded to register and enrol in his first-year classes: botany, chemistry, bacteriology, entomology, mathematics, animal husbandry, political economy, and physical education.

In addition to attending lectures and getting caught up on the classes he had missed, Arnold had to find a place to live. He recalled that someone he had met at Vermillion the previous winter, a Scotsman named Ross, had taken a job in Edmonton after leaving Vermillion in the spring. Arnold discovered that Ross was living in a boarding house close to the university. Ross invited Arnold to share the room and its benefits—which included sleeping with the landlady. Arnold accepted the room, but declined the extras, claiming that the fear of disease or unwanted pregnancy suppressed whatever desire he might have. He did not let on that Donna and he were planning to be married.

It's possible that Donna was a distraction in Arnold's first year at university. But there was also another reason that his classes did not get Arnold's full attention: the harvest at Westlock was not finished, and any more money he might receive from William depended on its completion. Ross had a car that he made available to Arnold on weekends and, every weekend until mid-November, Arnold drove to Westlock on Friday evening, threshed grain all day Saturday and Sunday, and then drove back to Edmonton on Monday morning in time for classes. Arnold knew that he was ill-prepared for his mid-term examinations but he did not realize how poorly prepared he was until he was shocked by the results; although he was taking eight courses, he had passed only two or three exams.[4]

The University of Alberta had enrolled about 1200 students that fall (1930) and Arnold's poor performance was noticed. The President, Dr. Robert Wallace, invited Arnold and others with similar examination results to meet with him in his office. Having been raised in the Orkney Islands and educated at the Universities of Edinburgh and Göttingen, Dr. Wallace had no difficulty in playing the stern Scotsman, persuading Arnold and the others that he meant what he said when he said that they could not return to the University after Christmas unless their work improved significantly. He assured them that a fair percentage of the first-year class left prematurely each Christmas.

The harvest over and an additional $100 in his account—the wheat having sold for only 30 cents a bushel—Arnold was able at last to settle down to his studies. He did well enough to be allowed to stay, but his success in first year was not yet certain. His English class was giving him difficulty. In spite of his love of reading poetry and fiction and his skill as a speaker and debater, Arnold seldom kept to the conventions of grammar and spelling in his writing. The first essay he handed in to Professor J.T. Jones came back with a note asking Arnold to please come and see the instructor. Professor Jones, who had come to the University of Alberta from Oxford in the mid-1920s, told Arnold that without a tremendous improvement in his writing he would never get a degree from the University.

But he offered to help Arnold overcome this limitation. Essays were due every two weeks. He suggested that Arnold write each essay a week before it was due, give it to Professor Jones to read, and then go over it with the Professor in a weekly meeting before rewriting it and submitting it for marking. Professor Jones subsequently spent one evening each week tutoring Arnold, and then drinking cocoa with him and engaging him in discussion on topics of every kind. Arnold never forgot the dedication and kindness of this remarkable professor. In later years, whenever Arnold told this story, he always credited Professor Jones with making it possible for him to get through university.

Quite unintentionally, his work with Professor Jones also helped him in his animal husbandry course. The course did not hold much interest for Arnold, and the lectures were less interesting to him than the textbook. Assuming that the textbook would provide more than enough material for him to pass the course, Arnold paid little attention to the lectures. Writing those drafts and revisions of essays for Professor Jones took a substantial amount of time and, in the interest of efficiency, Arnold decided to write these essays during the animal husbandry lectures.

The final examination in that class proved to be much more difficult than Arnold had anticipated; he had obviously missed much of what was said in class and, when he handed in the examination paper, he felt sure that he had failed. He was more than a little surprised to discover that he had passed the course with a mark of 79%. Subsequently, he met the professor of animal husbandry in the hall, and remarked to him that he did not think he had done very well on the exam and that he was surprised at his respectable mark. The professor told Arnold that he hadn't done well on the exam at all, that he really hadn't even passed. But the professor recognized Arnold's diligence, for while everyone else had been sitting in class looking bored, Arnold had been busily writing down every word the professor said. Such effort deserved to be recognized, and he had given Arnold a decent final mark. Not until several years later, over a few beers in the professor's apartment, did Arnold tell the true story of his apparent industry in that class.

Arnold's personal life continued to complicate his life as a student. He and Donna Oxford were very much in love. That they were thinking about getting married when they had just started their university studies is puzzling, as they were both driven to succeed academically and marriage ended Donna's academic career. Some who knew both Arnold and Donna somewhat after this time suggest that they were both very shy and lonely people who clung to each other in the city, but this explanation is not entirely satisfactory. Neither were reclusive social misfits, both having been involved in clubs and societies at Vermillion. Donna had been secretary of the Literary Committee at Vermillion. The 1927/1928 *Vermillion School of Agriculture Yearbook* says this of her:

> *Of a rather shy nature, she does not allow her shyness to interfere with*
> *her fun. Boys can hardly be said to be her pet aversion as—*
> > *"She likes them thin, she likes them tall*
> > *I guess she kinda likes them all."*

And Arnold needed the close companionship of a woman. One of the earliest recollections that he recorded is of his aunt Birdie "a moderately stout motherly type, who, when I was small, took me in her arms and gave me hugs." Later, while William was recovering from the accident that almost cost him his arm, Arnold had come to appreciate William's wife Daisy as a kind of older sister, with whom he could talk about "love, sex, and what made life worthwhile. She had great wisdom—greater than I appreciated at the time. Before going to bed we would give each other a hug." One cannot help but note the association between "wisdom" and "hugs," and their connection to what his mother's house represented.

During the first term, Donna lived in residence, and Arnold shared the boarding house room with Ross, an arrangement neither Donna nor Arnold liked. By Christmas, change was in the air. Ross had decided to move out, and the landlady declared that her plans for the room did not include Arnold. Grandma Platt came to the rescue; she had decided to move to Edmonton. The house that was to have been built for her on the farm at Westlock had not yet materialized, and she felt at loose ends. An old neighbour and friend from Innisfree owned a duplex in Edmonton, and half was available for rent in January 1931. Grandma Platt decided to rent it for herself, and then to rent rooms to Arnold and to his cousin Ted Barber. Another room was available for Donna.

This relatively stable domestic arrangement allowed Arnold and Donna to complete their year's work at the university with some success, Arnold achieving second class standing with his average of 74% and Donna getting the highest marks ever given in biochemistry. Donna's achievement once again demonstrated the Vermillion School yearbook's prescience; it noted that Donna had wondered "why it is not possible to obtain more than 100% on an exam." Arnold's marks were good enough for him to qualify for a summer job with the Department of Field Crops— a job he was very fortunate to get, given the shortage of jobs in 1931 and the university's shortage of funds. With the prospect of summer work for Arnold, he and Donna were married, somewhat secretly, in April.

The summer job also allowed Arnold to develop connections with people who would help him to enter academic life more fully. His immediate supervisor was Hopkins, Arnold's former teacher of English literature at Vermillion, who had been the host of discussions and teas. Arnold also became acquainted with Professor Olaf S. Aamodt, a plant breeder and geneticist who had recently joined the Department of Field Crops. Dr. Aamodt was known internationally; he had studied at the University of Minnesota and Cornell University, and then had worked in plant pathology with the University of Minnesota and the United States Department of Agriculture. Dr. Aamodt's research had taken him to Germany, England, and the Scandinavian countries to study the control of plant diseases.

It was at this point that Arnold discovered his love of plant breed-ing, spending as much time as possible in the plant breeding plots, a pursuit that Hopkins facilitated as much as he could. Dr. Aamodt and Arnold developed a close and continuing relationship. Before Arnold finished his studies for the B.Sc. in 1934, he and Dr. Aamodt published a paper together on frost resistance in wild oats. When Arnold received his B.Sc., Dr. Aamodt encouraged him to continue with graduate studies and supervised his research until 1935, when Dr. Aamodt left the University of Alberta for the University of Wisconsin.

This ability to form relationships with people stayed with Arnold throughout his career. As an undergraduate, although Arnold was a considerably better than average student, his marks were not outstand-ing. His unconventional schooling, most significantly his never having attended high school, had not provided him with the depth of learning needed to obtain the highest marks at university. In addition, his constant struggle to find money to pay for his education and to provide for his family prevented him from focusing single-mindedly on his studies. Yet that very unconventionality gave him perspectives on and approaches to

Four Generations:
Grandma Platt, William,
Arnold, and Wayne,
c. 1938. [Platt Family
Collection]

the disciplines he was studying that drew the attention of some faculty members, who recognized the brilliance that the marks did not show. It is to their credit, credit that Arnold unfailingly gave, that they took the time to work with him.

The second year of university was about to start. Donna was pregnant, due to give birth before Christmas. The young couple needed money for the necessities of life, for tuition, and for the medical and hospital costs associated with Donna's impending stay—there being no universal hospital or medical care insurance at that time. They had saved as much as they could during the summer. They had grown vegetables in a garden at Ross Shepherd's farm near their small house on the outskirts of the city at the east end of 82nd Avenue; and they had restricted their social life to attending a few Sunday baseball games at a cost of ten cents each for admission and ten cents for streetcar fare.

Arnold had developed good relationships within the department of bacteriology and had the promise of part-time work washing Petri dishes, sterilizing equipment, and setting up labs. It wasn't much, but Arnold registered in second year. They managed until their baby Wayne was born, in early December. Although the house they were renting cost very little, it was isolated and too far from town and the university for the safety of Donna and their newborn baby; it did not have running water or an indoor bathroom; and it was impossible to keep warm. They had to move to closer but more expensive rooms.

With the added cost came opportunity. In similarly difficult financial circumstances during the school term of 1926 to 1927 in Vermillion, Arnold had made money by running a gaming house. Nearby, living in a garage behind a house in the Garneau area, Arnold had a friend, Wallace, whom Arnold persuaded to provide space for a game on Sunday afternoons. Arnold let it be known among the wealthy boys living in residence and at the newly established fraternity houses that they were welcome to join a blackjack game. Arnold was the banker; Wallace merely provided the facilities and his imposing presence, being sturdily built and over six feet tall. As Arnold told it,

> Most of these boys did not know much about playing cards and were pretty reckless in their betting. So I, the banker, always came out ahead and some Sunday afternoons made a great deal of money by my standards. The money went to buy the stale bread and all the other things that we needed to keep body and soul together.

That income, the money earned from the part-time job in the lab, supplemented by a gift of half a moose that they kept frozen on the roof of the building they lived in, got them through the 1931/1932 term. Just as importantly, as Arnold remarked, they had the faith and the courage to keep going, and the confidence that they were going to make it. By spring, both the academic and the economic situations had improved.

Arnold's academic record was better in his second year than in his first, his average standing at 77%. He was able to work at the university's plots again that summer and throughout the rest of his time as an undergraduate. He was now determined to become a geneticist and plant breeder, and he continued to work with Dr. Aamodt and several other professors of note. These included Dr. A.W. Henry, a plant pathologist; Professor R.D. Sinclair, a specialist in animal breeding who had organized the agricultural club that Arnold joined; Dr. E.W. Sheldon in mathematics, the only professor at the university who taught statistics at that time; and Professor Macgregor Smith in agriculture engineering, who organized a competition in public speaking. Noting the developing importance of statistical analysis for experimental work, Arnold elected to take Dr. Sheldon's course. The work in statistical analysis would later have significant application in Arnold's work in developing Rescue wheat. While Arnold did not take Professor Macgregor Smith's course, he did win the cup for public speaking in his competition.

The family got by. Arnold continued to work as an assistant to Dr. Aamodt during the summers until he finished his B.Sc., and to find other work at the university during the school term. Though still an undergraduate, Arnold was becoming established as a scholar to watch. Between his third and fourth years, from July 24 to August 5, 1933, the World's Grain Exhibition and Conference, one of the largest gatherings of the world's experts on grains, was held in Regina, Saskatchewan. That Arnold attended cannot be established with certainty, but Dr. Aamodt presented a paper there, and Arnold and Dr. Aamodt were working together on a paper that they published in 1934 while Arnold was finishing his fourth year of undergraduate study. As well, there was a copy of the conference proceedings among Arnold's papers. These facts suggest that Arnold was there, as did his comment to me that his work had taken him to Regina during the middle of the depression.

The list of people who presented papers at the conference is a veritable list of everyone of note in the international wheat research community. Many people with whom Arnold subsequently worked were there. Dr. E.S. Archibald, head of the Dominion Experimental Farm Service

Arnold, B.Sc., University of Alberta, 1934. [Platt Family Collection]

in Ottawa, organized the program. C.H. Goulden of the rust research laboratory in Winnipeg, H.J. Kemp of the Swift Current Experimental Farm, J.B. Harrington of the University of Saskatchewan, and many others whom Arnold came to know presented their research.

His B.Sc. in Agriculture conferred in May of 1934, Arnold went directly into graduate studies. As a graduate student, he qualified for a graduate research assistantship, which paid his tuition fees and also provided a small monthly stipend. The family was growing. His daughter Shirley was born in October of 1935, and Arnold needed to supplement his income. As a graduate student, he spent time in Ottawa as a research assistant, leaving Donna and the two children behind in Edmonton. Family lore has it that Arnold added to his income during that period by bootlegging booze, which he bought in Hull and sold in Ottawa. In the last year of his M.Sc. program (1935/1936), he combined his course and research work with teaching as a sessional lecturer.

With the defence of his thesis "The Reaction of Certain Cereals to Freezing Temperatures" in April 1936, Arnold's time as a student at the University of Alberta came to an end. After years of determination, sacrifice, perseverance, and genius, Arnold and Donna would have to find new opportunities in the midst of an economic and agricultural depression.

Research,
Rescue Wheat,
and Recognition

In Calgary, Alberta, most people who enter the Stampede Grounds from the light rail transit station enter on the second floor of the Roundup Centre. On their right as they walk along, they notice the Grain Academy, a museum that displays artifacts and information related to grain's significance in the development of the provincial and national economy. On the north wall of the Academy, among the twelve "Grain Pioneers"—people such as Henry Wise Wood, George Church, and Charles Noble—Arnold Platt is recognized as one of the three "Crop Improvers of Alberta." He is noted for his development of Rescue wheat, a sawfly-resistant variety that was licensed for commercial production in 1946.

It's a wonder that Rescue wheat was developed, and it's just as much a wonder that Arnold's name is up there. As often as not, his achievements have gone unrecognized. During the time that he worked for the Dominion Experimental Farm Service from 1936 to 1951, Arnold achieved success as a plant breeder, and he originated the use of field plots in southern California, which allowed Canadian crop scientists to speed their research by growing two crops each year. The federal department of agriculture did not publicly acknowledge Arnold's responsibility for developing Rescue wheat while he was working with the department, and his responsibility for the establishment of winter plots in California is not mentioned in public record.

When Arnold finished his M.Sc. at the University of Alberta in the spring of 1936, he had begun to establish himself as a researcher specializing in the effects of environmental stresses, such as frost and drought, on agricultural crops. He wanted to continue that work. From what he had observed at the University of Alberta and at the Dominion Experimental Farm Service in Ottawa and from what he had been told by his supervisors, Dr. O.S. Aamodt and Dr. K.W. Neatby, he knew that the best way to do that would be to go immediately into doctoral studies.

But there were several problems associated with taking that path. No Ph.D. program of substance and reputation was available in his field in Canada. If Arnold wanted to do a doctorate, the family would have to relocate, either to the United States or to Great Britain. Arnold and Donna had already lived the life of poor students for six years and by the spring of 1936 they had three children, the third, Joan, having been born in April of that year (very close to the time that Arnold defended his thesis). Employment was not easy to find, but Arnold had lectured in Agriculture at the University of Alberta in 1935/1936. While the appointment was not a continuing one, the possibility of its being renewed from year to year was quite good. A lectureship was better than the work many other graduates had been able to find, and the temptation to stay in Edmonton was strong. Staying would provide stability, and the work

Reclamation plot near Val Marie, Saskatchewan, c. 1936. [Platt Family Collection]

at the university would mean Arnold wouldn't have to leave the family again to work at the Experimental Farm Service in Ottawa. But Arnold did not like teaching, at least not the formal, classroom kind of teaching, and one year of it was enough. He wanted either a Ph.D. program that was supported by a scholarship or a job that did not involve teaching.

It was the Ph.D. program that Arnold wanted most, and he looked for a university that would give him the opportunity to pursue his research while also supporting him with a scholarship. At the same time, he realized that a Ph.D. program that met those criteria might not be open to him, so he would have to look at jobs that were available. In the depths of the economic and agricultural depression of the mid-1930s, few career opportunities were available—but there was one notable exception. The disastrous circumstances of the time had led the government of Canada to pass the Prairie Farm Rehabilitation Act (PFRA) in the spring of 1935. The *Report of Activities Under the Prairie Farm Rehabilitation Act, November 15, 1935* describes its purpose as follows:

> to remedy the severe effects of continued drought and soil drifting
> which have been experienced for several years throughout Manitoba,

Saskatchewan, and Alberta. Under the terms of the Act, measures are provided to assist farmers in the affected areas to reduce the destructive effects of drought and soil drifting. These measures consist principally of encouraging farmers to adopt improved cropping and cultural practices to prevent soil drifting through the agency of the Dominion Experimental Farms.[1]

While the PFRA program had not been fully implemented in 1935/1936, its appropriation for 1936/1937 was increased by a quarter of a million dollars so that one million dollars was available to support its work that year. The Dominion Experimental Farm at Swift Current was located in the centre of the worst of the damage, and it needed expert help in reclamation work. Arnold, through his research, understood what was needed to reclaim land that had been ravaged by the forces of nature and ill-informed cultural practice. Just as importantly, he had practical experience as a farmer—one of his earliest recollections was of following his father as he walked his pastures, reseeding the bare patches. So Arnold applied for the job in land reclamation at Swift Current. Simultaneously, he sent out applications for Ph.D. programs at universities in the midwestern United States.

Probably because his failure to pursue a Ph.D. so deeply disappointed him, Arnold did not talk about what happened that spring and summer of 1936. None of his children remember him saying anything about it to them in later years, and none of the people with whom he worked at Swift Current and who talked with me about Arnold's work there can recall Arnold ever mentioning this episode. He told the story to his widow, Helen, and he mentioned some of its elements to me, but concrete evidence confirming these events is very limited. The only documentary evidence consists of an envelope from the Department of Agronomy at the Kansas State College of Agriculture and Applied Science (now Kansas State University) in Manhattan, Kansas, addressed to Arnold William Platt at Swift Current, and postmarked June 26, 1936. The envelope contains an official transcript of Arnold's record at the University of Alberta dated May 8, 1936, but the correspondence from Kansas State is lost and no record of it can be found at the College. However, the fact that the correspondence existed suggests that the following, which is our recollection of Arnold's account, has some basis in fact.

Arnold said that he was accepted into a Ph.D. program at a mid-western U.S. university and was granted a scholarship. The offer came after he had accepted an appointment with the PFRA at Swift Current and moved there. He and the family were prepared to relocate again to take up residence at the university in the United States in time for the start of the fall 1936 term. Through the course of correspondence with the university, the university became aware that Donna and the three children would accompany him. The university said that the amount of the scholarship was not enough to support a family; it was only adequate for one. Arnold replied that the scholarship provided more money than the job at Swift Current, and that the family was able to get by on that so he couldn't foresee money being a problem. However, the university was adamant and withdrew the scholarship.

Arnold had connections with several universities in the mid-western United States, and it seems likely that he would have been keen to pursue Ph.D. studies there. Dr. Aamodt had taken a post as Head of Agronomy at the University of Wisconsin in Madison and had close contacts with the leading plant scientists in the country. One of those, Dr. Ernest Sears of the United States Department of Agriculture, was doing significant work in wheat genetics at the University of Missouri in Columbia. He was part of an expanding group of geneticists at the University of Missouri, Barbara McClintock having come there just that spring. As Evelyn Fox Keller reports in her biography of Dr. McClintock, *A Feeling for the Organism*, in the mid-1930s the University of Missouri was establishing itself as a major centre of work in genetics, having received a grant of $80,000 from the Rockefeller Foundation for that purpose. Donna had close connections with Missouri as well. Her parents had grown up and been educated there, and her only sibling, Frank, was attending university there in 1936.

However, as things worked out, Arnold and the family settled near Swift Current, living outside town in a small house on the South Farm, land the Experimental Station had acquired in 1924. The station had built five houses in 1926, and it seems that the Platt family lived in one of these.[2] The tension in Arnold's life between his need to establish a home of his own and what represented his mother's house—which I came to see as associated in his psyche with education, research, and scientific work—was to continue. Once again, Donna found herself somewhat isolated at home (although now in a much better house), while Arnold immersed himself in an environment of scientific work that proved to be quite similar to the environment he had loved at the University of Alberta. These circumstances were unhappily similar to the ones Donna had endured when she and Arnold were first married and lived on the outskirts of Edmonton.

Today, the Swift Current of the 1930s evokes images of the dust bowl and of desperation, such as one might see in the National Film Board's *The Drylanders*, but it was no cultural or scientific desert. No sooner had Arnold arrived than the Experimental Station demonstrated its central place in the community and in scientific research.

The grand opening of the new Soils Research Laboratory on June 22, 1936, was a gala affair that attracted more than a thousand people. For weeks leading up to the great event, the *Swift Current Sun* gave it front page coverage. The opening gala brought together many of the country's leading agriculturalists and political leaders. J.G. Gardiner, the federal minister of agriculture, was there as was former station superintendent and the new Saskatchewan minister of agriculture, J.G. Taggart. Dr. E.S. Archibald, Director of the Experimental Farm Service, was there from Ottawa as well. Arnold met them all. As a scientist, he was part of a select group at the station, and the station had a prominence in the city and region that is hard to imagine if one thinks of Saskatchewan in the 1930s in terms of relief trains, Bennett buggies, and flour sack dresses.

Coincident with the gala, the Western Society of Agronomists was meeting in Swift Current. Seventy-five of the leading agronomists in western North America met for three days and Arnold had the opportunity to meet with them. Dr. K.W. Neatby, Arnold's former supervisor at the University of Alberta, introduced the keynote speaker, Dr. White from the Imperial Experimental Station in Wales.

Arnold started his post before the new research lab opened, and his first duties focused on land reclamation at the Cadillac Reclamation

Station, about forty kilometres south of the Swift Current station. Reclamation work there was to involve a series of experiments similar to those that had been undertaken at the reclamation station at Melita, Manitoba. The PFRA report for the year ended March 31, 1936 describes the experiments as dealing

> *with various aspects of crop production on marginal land, such as rota-*
> *tions under both strip farming and large field conditions, the growing*
> *of cover crops, and the cultural management of light drifting soil. The*
> *value of tractor powered equipment for this work is being determined.*
> *Experiments are also being planned on the use of fertilizers on drifted*
> *soil, on the methods of establishing grasses and clovers for soil binding*
> *purposes, and for the production of hay and pasturage.*[3]

Much of the former grassland in southwestern Saskatchewan had been broken during times of good grain prices and relatively good rainfall in the 1920s. Restoration of this land involved re-establishing grasses on the land, which had by this time been seriously eroded. This proved to be a challenge, and nature did not cooperate. The PFRA report for the year ending March 31, 1937, describes the difficulty of the work.

> *This Station, comprising 1280 acres, was established in 1936 for the*
> *reclamation of an area near Cadillac, Sask. where soil drifting has been*
> *extremely serious. Very dry conditions prevented work being started*
> *during the summer, but autumn rains have enabled some necessary*
> *seeding of grain so as to prevent drifting and to enable spring seeding*
> *being undertaken with some hope of success.*[4]

Arnold soon realized that much of the land, once restored to grassland, should remain as grassland. He joined the Saskatchewan Stock Growers Association, and worked with its members to try to make grazing land the basis for viable agriculture. Without doubt, Arnold applied what he had learned at Westlock: that grain production and livestock production can complement each other; that the nature of the land and environmental conditions should determine which predominates; and that neither are viable if market prices are too low or if markets are not accessible.

Even though the job was outside the immediate field of his scientific expertise, the knowledge Arnold gained and the relationships he established while working with PFRA would serve him well later when he became president of the Farmers' Union of Alberta. He and other PFRA officials worked with the Stock Growers Association in establishing community pastures and instituting water conservation practices. His position as an employee of the government did not allow Arnold to actively participate in addressing the more political aspects that determined livestock prices and access to markets, such as transportation costs, but he listened and learned.

But Arnold's work as a reclamation officer for the PFRA was short-lived. In retrospect, the confluence of events and people in the late fall and winter of 1936/1937 seems fated to put Arnold back on course as a geneticist and plant breeder.

The sawfly was becoming a major problem for wheat growers because, in solving one set of problems, scientists, PFRA officers, and farmers were creating another. New cultural practices were necessary to deal with drought and control erosion of grain land: cultivating so as to leave the remains of the previous grain crop as a trash cover, engaging in tillage practices that barely disturbed the surface of the topsoil, and planting crops in alternating strips of crop and tilled soil all kept the topsoil covered and helped the soil retain moisture. But these same practices created ideal conditions for the wheat stem sawfly, an insect pest that attacked wheat.

Tests on wheat grown in strip-farmed fields near Rockyford, Alberta showed that up to 90% of the crop was being lost to sawflies. None of the varieties of hard red spring wheat could resist the sawfly. Cultural practices that could control it led to drifting soil, there was no known effective insecticide against the sawfly, and the sawfly's life cycle made control with insecticides impractical even if one could be found or developed.

Something needed to be done, but no one seemed to be sure what that something was or how to go about doing it. J.B. Taggart left in 1934, and in the summer of 1935 L.B. Thomson became superintendent of the Swift

Current Experimental Station and was put in charge of all PFRA work in the region. Although he had been with the station at Swift Current since 1926, Thomson hadn't been Taggart's obvious successor. H.J. (Shorty) Kemp had been assistant superintendent with Taggart and had been acting superintendent from the time that Taggart left until Thomson was appointed as the new superintendent.

L.B. Thomson did not take long to demonstrate the abilities that had made him such a good choice. He knew how to identify problems and set priorities, he had an uncanny knack for finding the right people to solve the problems of highest priority, and he knew how to find the resources those people needed to do the job. L.B. Thomson did not let administrative procedures get in the way of work likely to bring desired results. As Stu McBean, a member of Arnold's team and L.B. Thomson's son-in-law, remembers, he was not afraid to act before he had approval from Ottawa, a quality that often got him into shouting matches with Dr. E.S. Archibald, Director of the Experimental Farms Service, when he visited the station. L.B. Thomson got the job done and then worried about permission and accounting.[5]

Thomson had studied agriculture at the University of Alberta, leaving in 1926 before Arnold started there as an undergraduate, but he and Arnold knew many of the same people there and Thomson had remained in touch with them. When he hired Arnold in the spring of 1936, L.B. Thomson knew that Arnold excelled in research and plant breeding—but he had no money to hire a researcher.

It seemed that, for every problem solved, two more appeared. First cultural practices introduced to prevent soil drifting had improved conditions for the sawfly, and then the 1935 introduction of rust-resistant Thatcher wheat had encouraged another major increase in the sawfly population. By harvest time in 1936, the sawfly problem was worse than ever before. Once Arnold joined his staff, Thomson did not hesitate to use PFRA money to support research on how to deal with the pest.

The sawfly damages wheat by girdling the wheat stem close to ground level, causing the wheat stem to fall to the ground. The cycle of destruction begins with the adult female emerging through three to four weeks of early summer from stubble or grass adjacent to a field of wheat, flying to the wheat, and laying eggs inside the developing wheat stem. The larva hatch and begin to feed on the inside of the stem. In order to pupate, the larva move down the stem, cut it so that it falls over, and then go into the ground, waiting there to emerge the following year as adults.

Rust in wheat had helped to control the sawfly population. When rust destroyed the wheat plant, it also destroyed the sawfly larvae in the wheat stem, thus reducing the sawfly population. However, stem rust had reached epidemic proportions and had to be controlled. Farmers planted larger acreages of somewhat rust-resistant durum wheat, which also had some resistance to the sawfly, reducing sawfly numbers. The rust problem also required farmers to practice crop rotation; they included sawfly-immune crops such as oats, barley, and flax, again lowering the sawfly population.

But the development of Thatcher wheat by Dr. H.K. Hayes at the Experimental Station at St. Paul, Minnesota, and its widespread intro-duction on the Canadian prairies in 1935 had recreated ideal conditions for the sawfly. Dr. C.W. Farstad, entomologist at Lethbridge and later to be Arnold's partner, estimated that the sawfly was costing about $20 million annually in lost and unharvestable wheat.

L.B. Thomson knew about the sawfly problem before he became superintendent. The assistant superintendent of the station, H.J. (Shorty) Kemp had observed that solid-stemmed or partially solid-stemmed durum wheat varieties seemed to be able to resist the sawfly. Shorty Kemp reasoned that a solid-stemmed common wheat would also be able to show such resistance, but he did not know of any such wheat.

L.B. Thomson's network of connections included Dr. O.S. Frankel in New Zealand. Thomson put Shorty Kemp in contact with Dr. Frankel, who informed Kemp that he had 38 strains of solid-stemmed common wheat. Two of these had originated in New Zealand and the others had been collected in Spain, Portugal, and Morocco. In the early 1930s, Dr. Frankel had provided Kemp with samples of these strains and Kemp began to grow these in plots at Swift Current. C.W. (Chris) Farstad, an entomologist at the Dominion Entomological Laboratory in Lethbridge, worked with Kemp in testing these strains' resistance to attack from sawflies, and Kemp reported the results in a paper he published in 1934.[6] One line of wheat, called S-615, was especially resistant. However, because these strains were of poor milling and baking quality, they were useless for commercial crops.

This was about as far as Kemp could go. He excelled at devising machines and was a proficient manager of field trials, but he was not a plant breeder. Arnold Platt was the station's plant breeder and, in the fall of 1936 when he reviewed the situation, he thought the first thing to do was to develop some hybrid lines. The hybrids were to be grown in the summer of 1937, but the circumstances of the summer of 1937 forced Thomson to take another course of action: he put Arnold in charge of breeding wheat that would resist the sawfly. As Chris Farstad wrote,

> *In 1937, plots on the Experimental Farm at Swift Current were a complete failure. The failure was so complete that there was no seed even from the carefully tended rod-rows of lines from crosses that had been made by H.J. Kemp.*[7]

Dr. Farstad noted that "it took the vision and drive that has always been most characteristic of Arnold's work to get the project really rolling." Arnold got it rolling in a way that was characteristic of his approach to such problems. At first, he seemed to do nothing. He would hole himself up in his office with his pipe and scientific papers for days before he'd emerge with a plan. But when he emerged, he was ready to go to work.

He'd reviewed all the relevant literature, called everyone involved in similar work in Canada and the United States—and determined that no one had been working on the creation of a solid-stemmed common wheat. The only related work that had been done involved inter-species crosses, such as crossing durum wheat or Polish wheat (*T. polonicum*) with common wheat. In his work with the cereal division in Ottawa, Arnold had learned that crosses between solid-stemmed common wheat and hollow-stemmed common wheat yielded hybrids in which nearly all the stems were hollow, but in 1937 he did not yet know whether this was caused by environmental conditions, genetic conditions, or a combination of the two.[8] He assumed (correctly, as he later learned) that both were responsible.

The low incidence of solid stems in the hybrids, about one in sixty-three, meant that he would need to plant a large number of seeds to get a few hybrids that were solid-stemmed. It would take several years of breeding to produce a solid-stemmed variety. Arnold believed that the sawfly problem was too severe and the economic losses were too great to allow the plant breeding program to be delayed until the spring of 1938. He had identified the varieties *Canus*, Reliance, Coronation, Thatcher, and two as yet unreleased varieties as likely candidates for the breeding of solid-stemmed, sawfly-resistant common wheat with good milling and baking properties. He also wanted to try crosses involving the newly released Apex, which had been developed by J.B. Harrington at the University of Saskatchewan.

Swift Current did not have a greenhouse, but that did not stop Arnold. Having worked in the greenhouses of the Dominion Experimental Farms in Ottawa, Arnold knew that suitable space could be had there. Thomson devised a way for Arnold to spend the winter in Ottawa: he had Arnold designated as a research assistant in the Dominion Department of Agriculture. Arnold packed up his seeds, and was on his way to Ottawa for the winter of 1937/1938.

He went alone, leaving Donna behind with six-year-old Wayne, three-year-old Shirley, and baby Joan. The personal cost of that separation can only be guessed at, for no letters from that time remain. Nor are people with whom he worked that year still alive. Those who knew him a few years later, in the 1940s, report that Arnold was a private person who did not talk about his life at home or about the effects of major absences such as this one. He tended his plants in the greenhouse. He read scientific papers, and he also had time to indulge his love of reading classical and contemporary literature. The National Gallery gave Arnold a place to deepen his appreciation of painting. It is likely that, being in Ottawa, Arnold took advantage of the opportunity to pursue his interest in civics. That year (1938), Parliament was in session from January 27 to July 1, giving him ample opportunity to follow the proceedings from the visitors' gallery.

He came back to Swift Current with 300 hybrid seeds from plants that had exhibited the solid stem characteristic. Because Arnold was not at all sure that these 300 seeds contained the parent material needed, he divided the seed into two lots. The first lot he would increase under conditions as favourable as possible to obtain a good supply of seed. The second lot he back-crossed with the parent variety that was rust-resistant and had good milling and baking qualities.

The second approach did not yield useful results because, as his further research[9] revealed, the three genes responsible for the solid stem characteristic were recessive, and back-crossing took too long to bring about the results he needed. The first lot he sowed individually, resulting in plants that were similar but that contained some characteristics of one parent and some of the other. By the fall of 1938, he had about 30,000 seeds from this lot. In spring of 1939, these were again sown individually, producing what Arnold described as "a veritable maze of different types."[10]

In all the papers Arnold wrote in which he described his work, he passed off in one or two sentences the process of selecting plants likely to be sawfly- and rust-resistant while maintaining good milling and baking properties. But selecting for several traits simultaneously, especially in plants grown in conditions somewhat protected from insect pests and diseases, requires a very keen eye in the field and countless hours of examination in the laboratory, splitting stems and microscopically examining and comparing cells. He must also have spent many tedious days doing mathematical calculations by hand so that he could subject his results to the methods of statistical analysis that he had learned at the University of Alberta and from Dr. C.H. Goulden's book on their application to plant breeding. More calculations were necessary to establish the appropriate design of the test plots. By fall of 1939, Arnold had enough promising plants to allow him to start subjecting the next crop to field-testing for sawfly and rust resistance. The progeny from the cross between the solid-stemmed S-615 and the rust-resistant Apex, which Arnold made in the greenhouse in Ottawa in the winter of 1938, resulted in the wheat that would in 1946 licensed as "Rescue"—but Arnold did not know that yet.

Results from the 1939 crop showed a potential problem in using S-615 as the source for stem solidness. Environmental factors seemed to have a strong influence on the degree of solidness in the stem. In order to test this variety under conditions in as many different locations as possible, Arnold arranged for it to be grown at fourteen substations of the Swift Current Station and at Experimental Stations at Scott, Lacombe, Indian Head, Beaverlodge, and at the University of Alberta. He devised an index of stem solidness and proceeded with the task of splitting stems and evaluating them. The results showed that "the amount of solidness varied markedly from Station to Station."[11] Compared with results from other years, stems grown in 1939 were much less solid than those grown earlier. The amount of sunshine the plants received in June seemed to be the main determinant of solidness—the more sunshine, the more solid the stem. Before he could decide whether to continue using S-615 despite the variability in solidness, other tests would have to be made. Consequently, Arnold experimented with two other crosses. One of these involved the solid-stemmed durum wheat Golden Ball, which had shown almost 100% resistance to sawflies. This he crossed with several varieties of common wheat, making the first crosses in the greenhouse in Ottawa in the winter of 1937/1938.

Another source of sawfly resistance involved a tall wheat grass of Mediterranean origin, *Agropyron elongatum*. In tests that Chris Farstad conducted at the Dominion Entomological Laboratory in Lethbridge, this grass had proven to be completely resistant to sawfly attack. Because the grass was only partially solid-stemmed but completely resistant, it seemed to possess a source of resistance different than the solid-stemmed wheat varieties. This made it interesting as a potential parent in a cross-breeding program. Dr. Sears at the University of Missouri was doing some work in cross-breeding wheat with this grass and Arnold thought the idea worth pursuing. Arnold had had little assistance with the scientific work in the first two or three years of the program, and selecting plants, analyzing data, writing reports, publishing results, and developing further plant breeding plans had strained him to the limit. Nevertheless, he persevered until, just as the depression was ending and more resources were likely to become available to support the program, war intervened.

Canada's declaration of war on September 10, 1939, created a need that seemed much more pressing than the need for sawfly resistant wheat, and

Arnold responded. He was at a football game in Regina with friends from Swift Current when enlistment began, and the group stayed up all night after the game talking about what they should do. By morning, Arnold had decided to present himself to the nearest recruiting office and sign up for service. At thirty years of age, married and with three children, Arnold was on the borderline of eligibility but he passed the first screening and went back to Swift Current to wait for his call. It came shortly, telling him to report to the training camp at Dundurn, near Saskatoon.

His marching was not the best, his inability to distinguish colours was something of a handicap, but he persisted. It took some time for the officers at headquarters to process the papers associated with enlistment, but when they did and when they discovered the research work that Arnold had been doing, they promptly put him into the Reserve 8th Reconnaissance Regiment. He returned to Swift Current, his research, and home.

Again he was working almost by himself on breeding a sawfly-resistant variety of wheat. Many of the people at the station enlisted and left to join the war effort. Not only did the war make it difficult to keep staff at the station, energy and resources also went to support the war effort. The United Kingdom needed agricultural products from Canada. As Britnell and Fowke demonstrate, in 1939, 33% of the wheat, 61% of the flour, and 18% of the bacon that the United Kingdom imported came from Canada. By 1940, the percentages had increased to 48, 71, and 55 respectively; and, by 1941, they stood at 81, 94, and 76.[12]

The breeding program could not be expected to provide immediate results and, as late as February 1941, minutes of the committee on sawfly control show that experimental work on the cultural control of sawflies was receiving more attention than the plant breeding program. Even though he now had a large number of hybrids to be tested, Arnold had to reduce the number of test sites to those at Swift Current and Regina in Saskatchewan, Nobleford and Castor in Alberta, and Tugaske and Melita in Manitoba. He would have to rely on staff at these stations and sub-stations or on individuals in the districts to seed and tend the plots. Fortunately, such individuals, many of whom belonged to the local Agricultural Improvement Associations that L.B. Thomson had created to deal with the problems of the depression, volunteered to assist in the work. Working with these volunteers gave Arnold direct contact with the farmers who were experiencing the problem that he was trying to solve.

L.B. Thomson also did what he could to bring in more people to help Arnold.[13] John Dore, who had been with the Swift Current Station since 1926, provided field support. J.G. (George) Darroch had begun working with Arnold in 1939 or 1940, while finishing his M.Sc. at the University of Alberta. Arnold asked for a full-time assistant, and Stu McBean, who had started in forage crop work in 1940, came to work with Arnold in 1941 but left for the war in 1942. In the spring of 1942, Ruby Larson joined what had come to be known as "Arn's Army" as a summer student responsible for counting chromosomes, the first woman in what later became a predominantly female "army" during the war years. Alice Wall, Jean Watt, Jean MacLeod, and Joan Garissere were the other members of his "army." As Alice Wall wrote in the Lethbridge station newsletter of March 1951, "Arn admires a trim ankle and claims that he has always been able to pick the best looking female staff where he has worked."[14] B.C. (Charley) Jenkins became part of the group early in 1943. Steve Buzinski also provided technical support. Stewart (Stew) Wells joined the group in 1945.

In 1941, L.B. Thomson arranged for Chris Farstad to stay at Swift Current during the entire time that adult sawflies emerged and flew to wheat crops to lay eggs. He also agreed that, in the fall, Arnold and Chris Farstad would visit all the plots seeded in the new hybrids, so that they could assess their resistance to sawflies.

Arnold and Chris Farstad had been working together from the time that Arnold came to Swift Current. Both were scientists and researchers, who believed in the need for scientists to be part of the international scholarly community while also working in the farm fields of their region. In 1929, before finishing his M.Sc. at the University of Saskatchewan, Chris Farstad had started work as an entomologist at the Dominion Entomological Laboratory in Lethbridge. He continued to work on the control of cutworms and sawflies while he finished his M.Sc. (1931) and then a Ph.D. at Iowa State University (1940).

Arnold and the Dominion Cerealist inspecting plots at Swift Current, early 1940s.
[Stuart McBean Private Collection]

He and Arnold worked well together, so well that they subsequently became partners in a major farming operation. Together they introduced the concept of bringing the sawflies to the test plots to test the new hybrids in the most severe infestations possible. As Stew Wells noted during his interview, this approach of bringing the sawfly to the plant was an example of Arnold's genius. Arnold had noticed that in the Rust Research Laboratory in Winnipeg, researchers such as Dr. C.H. Goulden and Dr. R.F. Peterson had tested rust-resistance under conditions much more severe than any likely to be encountered in regular field conditions.

Consequently, in 1941, Arnold and Chris Farstad set up sawfly nurseries at widely separated points in the sawfly area. They minimized the need for additional labour by locating these nurseries in ideal sites in farmers' fields, usually the east side of a large field of infested stubble. Next to these nurseries they planted the hybrid varieties and observed which strains were most resistant. Those strains that stood up to this test were then tested for rust resistance.

The results were so promising that Arnold believed the time had come to increase the number of seeds as rapidly as possible. It was at this point that Arnold made his second major innovation in Canadian plant breeding by establishing a program to increase seeds by growing two crops a year, one in Canada and the other in the southern United States. He needed to continue the breeding program and was prepared to do that with minimal resources.

He planned to use as much local and volunteer labour as possible again in 1942, probably because he knew that asking for more resources would be futile. If more money and help could not be found in wartime, he hoped for at least the kind of support that would let him use his ingenuity to get the job done. This desire is clear in the program outline he submitted to L.B. Thomson, in which he wrote:

> It would seem desirable for individuals and institutions concerned to have the assurance of the Director [of the Dominion Experimental Farm Service, Dr. E.S. Archibald] and the Dominion Cerealist [Dr. L.H. Newman] that their efforts are appreciated and the general program has the approval of these officials.[15]

It's a telling remark, for by this time he had learned to expect little support from Ottawa for his plan to grow a winter crop outside Canada.

From the start of the project in 1937, Arnold had been aware that seed would need to be increased rapidly once a suitable strain had been developed. Now that promising strains had been developed, Arnold, in the outline for 1942, once again mentioned the need to increase seed on a large scale by growing two crops a year. He said that he would investigate possibilities in New Zealand, Australia, and the southern United States. Arnold looked into the possibilities and determined that it would be possible to grow a winter crop in southern California. He summarizes what happened in a report to Dr. Archibald, written in the summer of 1945; this report was occasioned by an accident in California. It shows Arnold's frustration, but also demonstrates his ability to proceed by using his own resources:

The possibility of using this scheme [growing seed in winter plots in California] *was discussed at the inception of the project in 1937. No action was taken. In 1941 the matter was again considered in view of the urgency of increasing certain sawfly resistant lines but it was again felt that no action could be taken. Again in 1943 an effort was made to increase some of the sawfly resistant lines. Finally in the late fall of that year L.G. Goar, Officer-in-Charge of the Imperial Valley Field Station,* [of the United States Department of Agriculture in Meloland, California] *agreed to increase up to ten pounds of one line. As there were at least ten lines, that, at that time, appeared equally good; the choice was a difficult one but by great good fortune 4188 was chosen. Our only obligation was to do our best to see that Goar was properly compensated. From the ten pounds forwarded to him, 14 bushels were received which seeded 30 acres in the Swift Current area in the spring of 1945* [sic; this was the spring of 1944].

The whole question of winter increase was reviewed at the meeting of Western Cerealists in February, 1944. The Dominion Cerealist wished to make further enquiries of the U.S.D.A. before the idea was approved. As a result of his enquiries and previous investigations it became abundantly clear that if we wanted to increase material in the south we would have to do it ourselves.

Accordingly, in the fall of 1944 land was rented from R.K. Mets of Holtville, California. B.C. Jenkins, of this Laboratory, was placed in charge of the project. He was to increase and return the material submitted, to study limiting factors that might be encountered and any other factors that might affect such a project. In other words, not only was material to be increased, but information was to be obtained that would warrant either the setting up of a definite policy or the abandoning of the scheme.[16]

Arnold's report went on to describe how his scheme had involved not only work on plant breeding that he was doing at Swift Current but also work from stations at Ottawa, Winnipeg, and Scott, Saskatchewan. He acknowledged that the idea of growing two crops a year was not his; Dr. Goulden had grown a second crop in Australia. However, Australia was

Revisiting the winter plots, Imperial Valley, California, 1994. [Gerald Schuler Private Collection]

Oats demonstrate sensitivity to daylight in California Winter Plots, 1946.
[Stuart McBean Private Collection]

too far away to serve as a practical seed production site. It was necessary to increase seed fast and get a variety of seed types into commercial
production as fast as possible. The seed grown in Australia could not be
shipped back to Canada in time for spring planting.

Exactly how Arnold became acquainted with L.G. Goar at the USDA
field station in the Imperial Valley is not known, but both Arnold and
L.B. Thomson had good connections with the USDA. Arnold's former
supervisor and mentor, Dr. O.S. Aamodt, had become head agronomist of
the USDA and had been recognized as one of the top ten agronomists in
the country. Arnold would not have hesitated to ask Dr. Aamodt for help
in contacting someone with the USDA in southern California who might
be able to help. The Western Society of Agronomists had met at Swift
Current; Arnold belonged to the American Society of Agronomy, and he
could have used contacts he made at meetings and through newsletters
and membership lists to make the connection. L.B. Thomson himself
travelled extensively, and insisted that the scientists who worked under
him do the same. He had also travelled widely through the United States
in the fall of 1936, so would have been able to provide some contacts from
that trip.

What is clear is that Arnold, with the support of L.B. Thomson but
apparently without the knowledge and definitely without the support
of officials in Ottawa, sent ten pounds of hybrid wheat seed designated
4188, the result of the S-615/Apex cross, to Goar in the fall of 1943. Goar
planted these seeds with considerable space for each, so that the yield
would be maximized. By the spring of 1944, fourteen bushels had been
harvested and were waiting for someone to come and take them back
to Swift Current. L.B. Thomson provided a rather ancient truck owned
by the PFRA, and Arnold drove it to California to collect that load of
precious seed.

Sometime during the winter of 1944, while Arnold was in Saskatoon
at meetings, he got into a conversation with someone who farmed near
Biggar, Saskatchewan. Arnold mentioned that he was experimenting
with increasing seed by growing a crop in California. The acquaintance
from Biggar said that he knew someone who owned and farmed a size-
able amount of land in the Imperial Valley, Keith Mets, and suggested

that, if the experiment at the USDA station at Meloland proved successful and Arnold needed to increase seed on a larger piece of land, he should talk with Mets. Arnold did so, and he and Keith Mets established what became a lifelong friendship.

Arnold arranged to use plots on Keith Mets' farm in the fall of 1944. Coincidentally, B.C. (Charley) Jenkins had joined Arnold's staff at Swift Current in early 1943. He had finished a masters program and was interested in studying for a Ph.D. (It's not known whether Arnold had the foresight to encourage Jenkins to do his Ph.D. at the University of California at Davis so that he could be in charge of the plots on Mets' farm, but if Arnold's method in encouraging Ruby Larson to pursue her Ph.D. with Ernie Sears at the University of Missouri is an indication of his methods, it is quite likely.) They seeded wheat variety 4188 on October 26, having received authorization to proceed in late September or early October. A memo dated October 11, 1944, from Dr. Archibald, Director of Experimental Farms, to Dr. Barton, Deputy Minister, shows that they had authorization to go along with $5,000 to cover expenses, but money to pay Goar had not yet been approved. Two hundred dollars was finally approved on December 5, 1944, supposedly for work yet to be done but more likely for work done in 1943/1944. Once again, L.B. Thomson had proven that, if plant breeders such as Arnold did the work, he would find the money—but it was a constant challenge.

An account of efforts to get a building, a "cereal barn," and appropriate equipment illustrates the challenge they faced in getting funding. It also helps to explain Arnold's later frustration in Lethbridge, when the "cereal barn" he had been promised was not built. L.B. Thomson had convinced the director of the Dominion Experimental Farm Service, Dr. Archibald, that plant breeding was a very important part of the war effort. In early 1942, the Dominion Government established the Dominion Reconstruction Committee and, at its ninth meeting on January 6 and 7, 1943, Dr. Archibald emphasized the importance of plant breeding in his presentation to the committee.[17] By October 1944, Thomson had also convinced Dr. Archibald that the sawfly-resistant wheat program was important enough to warrant proper space and equipment. Ingenuity and adaptation had reduced the original estimate for the facility from

Inspecting California Winter Plots, 1946. Arnold's ever-present pipe figures prominently.
[Stuart McBean Private Collection]

$25,000 to $19,000. The program also required a new truck, because the truck they had borrowed from the PFRA had been destroyed in a fire. The truck, a combine, and other shop and laboratory supplies added another $4,100 to the budget.

The process involved in getting even a portion of the money illustrates why a man with a mission had to act first and then get permission.[18] In a memo dated October 11, 1944, Dr. Archibald asked the Deputy Minister, Dr. Barton, to approve this expenditure from $200,000 that had been set aside under "Vote 468 in the Supplementary Estimates for Agricultural Research Special Projects." The paper trail shows that the amount requested was reduced to $12,000, and that the expenditure of that amount required the approval not only of the Deputy Minister of Agriculture but also of the Treasury Board. Treasury Board informed Dr. Archibald that in this case "since a matter of principle is involved, it will be necessary to have the authority of the Governor in Council."[19] By December 12, 1944, nothing had been done, and Dr. Archibald wrote once again to his Deputy Minister. Finally, on December 28, 1944, the

Clerk of the Privy Council sent a minute of a meeting of the Governor General in Council approving the expenditure of $12,000. All this to get half the money needed to convert an old hangar that had been moved to the station and was being used as a storage shed.

After a motor vehicle accident in California in January 1945, it took nine months of report and memo writing—and the intervention of the Minister of Agriculture, J.G. Gardiner himself—before Charley Jenkins was reimbursed $255.25 for medical expenses. Arnold was known for supporting his staff, and was furious that such elaborate machinations were necessary to pay the medical bills for attending to Jenkins' broken hand. It is not difficult to understand both Arnold's frustration at such bureaucratic obstructionism and his subsequent decision to resign.

As Jenkins' report makes clear, the accident was completely the fault of the driver of the truck that collided with the one Jenkins was driving:

> The accident occurred at about 6:35 on the evening of January 30.... A large diesel truck loaded with produce and owned by Mr. Haase was parked on the left side of the road partly on the highway. I noticed the lights on this truck and swung well over to the right to give it clearance, but at the same time a lettuce truck coming from the other direction crashed into the front of the pick-up. It was at the time of night when some drivers had lights on while others did not. In any case there was no indication that the vehicle was coming toward me until the crash occurred. My pick-up lights were on dim at the time. The impact on the left front wheel must have caused the steering wheel to give a sudden jerk breaking three bones in the back of my right hand. In the investigation which followed, highway patrol officers placed the responsibility on the parked truck. Had it not been parked out on the highway, the lettuce truck would have passed without colliding with me because it would not have been necessary for it to cross the center line.[20]

As part of the process required to reimburse Jenkins, Arnold had to write a complete report of activities in California. The circumstances help to explain the tone of his introductory remarks in that report. Arnold accused the Dominion Cerealist and the Director of the Experimental Farm Service of not having responded expeditiously to his request for

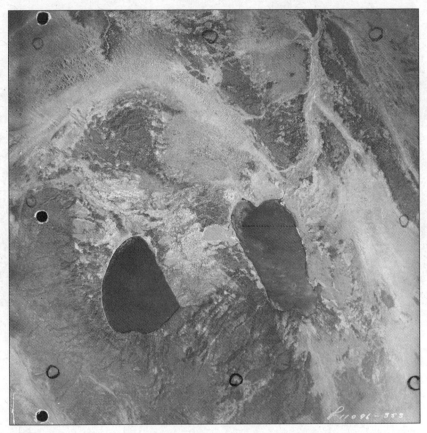

Aerial photo of Platt and Rescue Lakes, Twp 62, Rge 12, W2, Saskatchewan.
[Platt Family Collection]

support in this part of the project. Such an accusation helps to explain the subsequent lack of credit and recognition that Arnold was given for his developing Rescue wheat and for introducing the use of test and increase plots in southern California to researchers in the Canadian department of agriculture.

Tests of variety 4188, now called Rescue, continued in 1945. As Arnold reported,

it yielded just slightly less than Thatcher and considerably more than Marquis or Apex even though sawfly damage was not a factor in these tests. Where sawfly damage was severe Rescue yielded more than any of the other varieties. In maturity it was intermediate between Thatcher and Marquis. The seed was larger than that of Thatcher, brighter, less

Canadian and US Scientists commemorate Rescue Wheat achievement, Havre, Montana, 1946. [Platt Family Collection]

prone to bleach and higher in bushel weight. The most serious defect of the variety is that it is not equal to Marquis in baking quality. For that reason it will not be graded higher than three northern.[21]

The program of increasing seed by growing two crops a year had been so successful that, in the spring of 1946, each applicant received ten bushels of seed. Not only were the breeding and seed increase programs successful, they had been accomplished in record time. In 1951, Chris Farstad wrote that the time from the first cross in 1938 to commercial production in 1946 was the fastest ever achieved.[22]

The economic benefits were substantial. According to J.G. Gardiner, sawfly damage was causing about $30 million in losses each year.[23] Public recognition of Arnold's achievement came almost immediately. The *Free Press Weekly* published an interview with Arnold on March 27, 1946, and in September 1946 the *Canadian Geographical Journal* published Arnold's account of the work. *The Star Weekly* magazine published Montana writer Joseph Kinsey Howard's account of the achievement on April 17, 1948.

J.B. Harrington of the University of Saskatchewan, the developer of Apex wheat, added a tribute to Arnold's work in developing Rescue wheat that was published in the description of Platt Lake in the *Saskatchewan Gazetteer* in 1949.

The Government of Saskatchewan named Platt Lake and Rescue Lake in his honour. Because Arnold had worked so closely with United States Department of Agriculture (USDA) researchers in Montana and North Dakota, where the sawfly was also causing devastation, its officers and scientists celebrated the achievement with a daylong conference and dinner on November 29, 1946, in Havre, Montana. Arnold was invited to present his work at conferences and meetings including the 17th Annual Spring Wheat Improvement Conference in St. Paul, Minnesota in February 1948 and the University of Saskatchewan Agriculture Conference's Tenth Series of Graduate Lectures in January 1949. And in 1950 the Agricultural Institute of Canada gave him its most prestigious award, naming Arnold a Fellow.

But no recognition came from government of Canada officials in Ottawa. As Lilian McBean, daughter of L.B. Thomson and wife of Stu McBean told me, the government of the United States celebrated Arnold's achievement before the Canadian government even said thank you. Chris Farstad made a similar observation in his remarks in 1951:

> *During those early years of the programme and throughout the war years when staff, transportation and appropriations were not what they might have been, the main objective was to get the job done....without too much worry as to whose Division or Section was actually responsible or to whom credit should be given. The latter problem* [crediting the persons responsible for an accomplishment] *arose after the job had been fairly well complete and sawfly resistance was accomplished.*[24]

More than forty years later, a Department of Agriculture publication, Dr. T.H. Anstey's *One Hundred Harvests*, at last gave credit to Arnold as the plant breeder responsible for developing Rescue wheat.

Arnold was the first to insist that he had not done the work by himself. Although he developed the research plan, made the initial cross, planned

At Lake Deschambault, 1969, on the way to Platt and Rescue Lakes.
They drain into this lake. [Platt Family Collection]

each year's crosses and tests, supervised the operation, and made the selections, he valued very much the contributions of those who worked with him. Arnold had the highest regard for L.B. Thomson, who got things done in spite of shortages caused by the focus on the war effort. Thomson had done what he could to provide Arnold with the best people. Arnold provided the genius, determination, perseverance, and leadership that made the team succeed.

THREE

Never a Bureaucrat

Becoming a Master of Organization and Administration

Arnold's third major achievement during the time that he worked for the federal department of agriculture affected the organization of research conducted under the department's auspices. He laid out the basis for a plan of reorganization, which evolved as Arnold's experience as an administrator deepened, from a first version in 1944 to a more substantial one in 1947. The plan was so far-sighted that, although implemented in large part in late 1948, it was not fully implemented until 1958. (It was this genius for organizational structure that Arnold drew upon in his work with farm organizations that led to the creation of Unifarm.)

Arnold was noticed not only as a leader in plant breeding but also as an organizer and planner almost as soon as he arrived in Swift Current. The Director of the Dominion Experimental Farms, Dr. E.S. Archibald, wrote a memo to the Deputy Minister of Agriculture, Dr. Barton, on November 23, 1937, informing him of a seminar series that Arnold initiated at the Swift Current Experimental Farm.[1] The first paper in the series was Arnold's "Recent Advances in Plant Breeding."[2] Prior to Arnold's arrival, members of the staff had published few scientific papers—Baden Campbell mentions two that had been published in the 1930s.[3] During the 1940s, while Arnold was at Swift Current, the Station staff published about twenty papers in scientific journals; Arnold was principal author or co-author of half of these. In October 1941, together with Chris Farstad, he published an annotated bibliography, *The Resistance of Crop Plants to Insect Attack*, which reviewed research as it applied to wheat, corn, sorghum, oats, onions, clover, soybeans, canning peas, alfalfa, apples, potatoes, raspberries, and other crops. He was demonstrating the truth of Grisdale's observation at Olds that he would make a good academic, and he was establishing himself as a very capable administrator.

His ability to plan, manage, and execute a multi-year research project in plant breeding suggested his ability to apply these skills in other areas. It is not clear exactly when Arnold became responsible for the cereal grains program at Swift Current but, by January of 1944, he was in charge of research programs for wheat, barley, oats, and flax, and for the administration of these programs at Swift Current.[4] He also made recommendations about the cereal crops breeding program and its administration for all of Western Canada. The Dominion Cerealist, Dr. L.H. Newman, called a meeting of Western Canadian Experimental Farms members involved in cereal crop improvement in February 1944, in Winnipeg. The purpose of the meeting was to develop an administrative plan for "The Organization of Cereal Work Under Dominion Experimental Farms System." This was the meeting to which Arnold referred in his report on increasing seed in California and at which he concluded that he would have to proceed on his own.

Before the meeting, Arnold wrote a detailed memo to Dr. Newman, outlining a plan for research and crop improvement at the experimental farms. While it is likely that the battle behind the scenes, between Arnold and Dr. Newman, over the urgency of establishing plots in California prevented the adoption of Arnold's recommendations for organizing the research work, it is also true that his plan and Dr. Newman's differed on matters of principle. Arnold's plan[5] focused on solving problems at the regional level, while the plan Dr. Newman presented at the meeting focused on ensuring accountability through the hierarchical structure. Dr. Newman's plan set out the following principles:

(A) *The Director of the Dominion Experimental Farms System is responsible to the Minister for the work done by each Division.*

(B) *The Dominion Cerealist is directly responsible to the Director for all Cereal Work on Dominion Farms.*

(C) *In view of items A. & B. it is essential that the Dominion Cerealist be kept in close and constant touch with all work in their respective fields.*

Arnold's plan began with a list of problems that needed to be solved in the production of wheat, barley, oats, and flax, and then set out the main objectives of the administrative system necessary to solve those problems. Chief among these was:

(1) *To see that all problems are fully met to the extent that facilities and funds are available, as the latter is always limited to see[ing] that first things come first.*

Arnold's plan was at odds with Dr. Newman's in the matter of deciding who should lead the project. Arnold's plan recommended solving problems on a regional basis; regions would be determined by the nature of each problem. A regional meeting would determine the general approach and would select the project leader, who "would normally be the person responsible for the major portion of the work, but would not normally be a headquarters official."

Dr. Newman believed that his objective of keeping in close contact with field work could "best be accomplished through the various crop specialists, located at Ottawa." Arnold advocated creating project teams coordinated by the project leader; structures would be flexible, with certain problems requiring teams of specialists from a number of stations in the region and other problems requiring input from only one or two stations.

(It is tempting, from the vantage point of the twenty-first century, to see Arnold as a visionary advocate of an approach to management that has since become an accepted standard, and Dr. Newman as a representative of the old military model of control and command. Such an assessment may or may not be valid.)

Dr. Newman's ambivalence about the work in cross-breeding at regional stations suggests that he struggled with the choice of models:

> Until comparatively recently...practically all new material was created at or obtained through the Cereal Division at Ottawa, and sent on to the various Branch Farms for testing. A few years ago, it was decided to increase the scope of the work on the Branch Farms so as to include selection work as applied to hybrid material. Bulk populations resulting from crosses made at Ottawa were sent out to the Farms for exploitation. It was felt that not only would this plan make it possible to expand the work substantially but that it would provide Branch Farm people with an incentive to do work of value on their own. In a few cases, the Branch Farms have gone even further and have engaged in crossing work. This however, has been found a time-consuming business, especially in view of the importance of making a sufficiently large number of crosses to produce a worth-while F2 population. As a result of this policy, we now have at a number of Branch Farms some very promising material, some of which is already in rod row tests.[6]

Newman's comments reveal both a note of paternalistic condescension, in his comment about providing an incentive to people at the regional stations to "do work of value on their own," and a hint of paternalistic pride in the results that the innovative but rebellious sons have achieved.

With strong leadership from Ottawa, Dr. Newman developed his plan for the administration and organization of work on cereal crops, dividing responsibilities between the levels of the region and the individual station. He tried to provide for flexibility, noting that

> *it should be understood, however, that should any cerealist suitably situated, find himself in a position to do work along the line in which some other station is more or less specializing, he should have every opportunity of so doing.*

Dr. Newman's idea of organization and administration prevailed. The minutes of the Winnipeg meeting record that Arnold supported elements of Dr. Newman's plan that "favoured the regional idea of the development of the programme," while H.J. Kemp "emphasized the fact that the programme should be truly national." The thoroughness of Arnold's development of a model for administrative structure was noted, even if his model did not fit the ideas of organization then prevalent in Ottawa.

Circumstances changed. The success of Arnold's work in California demonstrated that his model could work. In the seed he sent to Holtville, California, he included seed from a number of projects being carried out at experimental farms in the region; to Ottawa, and in his report to Dr. Archibald, Arnold demonstrated the value of coordinating work on a regional basis. Dr. Archibald's covering memo to the Deputy Minister, Dr. Barton, concluded that "it is probably a good thing that this was done."[7]

Dr. Archibald could not baldly state that Arnold had been right and Newman had been wrong, but the implication is clear. In 1947, when Arnold presented his revised plan, Dr. Newman's retirement as Dominion Cerealist must have been imminent, as Dr. Goulden was appointed to that position in 1948. In 1947, when Arnold had another opportunity to present a "Proposed Plan for Cereal Plant Breeding in Western Canada,"[8] the plan found favour—but in a way that gave Arnold no credit for it. The plan was implemented, not through the Experimental Farms Service, but through the Science Service that since 1945 had been under Dr. K. W. Neatby.

Arnold developed his revised plan for organizing the cereals program for Western Canada for the meeting of Western Cerealists at Winnipeg in 1947. He advocated the establishment of a cereal breeding laboratory for Western Canada.

> It cannot be over-emphasized that future progress in plant breeding depends upon research in plant pathology, entomology and chemistry as well as in such fields as genetics. For this research to be most effective it should be conducted jointly by the pathologist, entomologist or chemist and the plant breeder. The plant breeder can facilitate the researches of the above by providing a wealth of material for experimentation that is positively identified, providing facilities for widespread tests under varying environmental conditions and keeping in the foreground the plant breeding point of view. The pathologist, entomologist and chemist provide the basic information upon which plant breeding programs are planned and carried out. For this team to function efficiently all members should be in the same or adjacent laboratories. If they are, the work becomes closely coordinated without any great effort, results of research can be utilized in breeding without loss of time and the different workers mutually stimulate each other. This mutual stimulation is of very considerable importance.[9]

In support of his argument, he illustrated the success achieved in breeding rust-resistant wheats using this organizational model. He also cited work being done in the United States, pointing out that "in the United States, emphasis is now placed on joint regional research laboratories. The recent Flannigan-Hope Bill places great emphasis on cooperative team research on a regional basis."[10]

The implications of Arnold's proposal become clearer when considered in the context of the existing organization. He was advocating an organizational unit that would be responsible for all research. Dr. Anstey's account in *One Hundred Harvests*[11] of the rationale for the organizational structure created in 1937 explains its intention and its effects:

> *In forming Science Service and restructuring Experimental Farms into a Service, both of which had an agricultural research function, the principle said to have been followed was to separate the scientific aspects from the experimental aspects and place each under a different administration. A separation into basic and applied research is probably what was meant. Science Service staff was encouraged to delve deeply into the problems they studied. In doing so, they built a firm data base in many areas of biology associated with agriculture. Scientists today still use these basic data upon which to build their theories and develop technologies in production, protection, and utilization of crops and livestock.*
>
> *Both services were restricted in their hiring practices with respect to the disciplines they could employ. Neither could recruit agricultural economists [as] these were the sole responsibility of Marketing Service. Experimental Farms could hire neither taxonomists nor chemists; these were the jurisdiction of Science Service. Finally, Science Service was not permitted to hire plant breeders, for they fell within the jurisdiction of Experimental Farms.*[12]

At the Winnipeg meeting in February 1947, Dr. Newman asked Dr. C.H. Goulden, then of the Dominion Rust Research Laboratory in Winnipeg, to speak to the subject of organization. The minutes indicate that Dr. Goulden advocated a model similar to the one Arnold had described in his memo, and it is reasonable to think that Dr. Goulden had received a copy of that memo. The idea for this new organization found its way to Dr. K.W. Neatby, Director of the Science Service of the Dominion Department of Agriculture, Arnold's mentor and supervisor at the University of Alberta and President of the Agricultural Institute of Canada in 1943/1944. Dr. Anstey hints at this in *One Hundred Harvests*:

The viable seed of an idea to unite Experimental Farms and Science Service was present in 1947 when Neatby, who had been appointed only 2 years earlier and van Steenburgh formulated a new Science Service policy. The seed may well have developed further in 1948 when Dr. Cyril Goulden moved to Ottawa from Winnipeg as chief of the Cereal Crops Division.[13]

Dr. Neatby saw the merits of the proposal and took the first steps in the creation of Canada's first Science Service Laboratory. Dr. Anstey describes what happened:

In the fall of 1948, Neatby made a 6-week tour of agricultural research organizations in and around Washington, D.C., and eight northern states in the United States. He then prepared a voluminous report (58 pages) and a summary comparing the American organizations with the Dominion Department of Agriculture. He observed to Deputy Minister Barton that "consideration might well be given to radical changes in our administrative setup." He pointed out, as an example, that in Canada livestock research was distributed among the divisions of Animal Pathology and Chemistry in Science Service Health of Animals in Production Service, and Animal Husbandry in Experimental Farms Service. He advocated for Canada something "comparable to the Bureau of Animal Industry." Without doubt Neatby was unhappy with the organization of agricultural research in the department, but because Deputy Minister Barton had agreed to the system devised by Swaine, Neatby probably was not going to change it until a new deputy minister was appointed, although he had planted the seed.[14]

Although the seed described by Anstey did not grow to maturity until 1958, when Science Services and Experimental Farm Services were joined, the new plant was established in Lethbridge. As the *Lethbridge Herald* reported in its 48-page special section marking the opening of the Science Service Laboratories on September 17, 1949:

History of major importance has been registered in the scientific investigation of agricultural problems in Canada by the establishment of

the new Science Service Laboratories just east of Lethbridge by the
Dominion Department of Agriculture.

Born out of a burning desire to assemble agricultural scientists
engaged on every phase of research, experimentation and production
so that they could launch and maintain a smooth and combined attack
against any problem on the agricultural front of the prairie provinces
and together study all its aspects thoroughly and efficiently, the new
establishment here is the first of its kind in Canada....

Conceived at Ottawa by the brain of Dr. K.W. Neatby, the director of
Science Service of the federal department of agriculture, as an idealistic
objective in which the skills, ingenuity and efforts of scientists could be
pooled and coordinated in seeking solutions to agricultural problems,
the new establishment here represents the achievement of that objective
and heralds a new method of approach to problems tackled by Science
Service.[15]

Arnold's hand as the originator of the proposal is evident in the next
paragraph of the *Herald* article. The article went on:

In the past the various units of Science Service were scattered about
various points in the prairie provinces, resulting in much loss of valu-
able time by skilled technicians in traveling about to consult each other.
Often scientists from several scattered laboratories were needed on a
single project and, because they had headquarters far removed from each
other, their work was made cumbersome, difficult, and often slow.[16]

In 1947, Arnold had written:

If the personnel are not situated together they must resort to so-called
co-operative projects. If these are formally organized it results in much
wasted time and expense in conferences, preparing reports, etc. If they
are not formally organized much time and expense are wasted in travel-
ing and they become unworkable as personnel become more numerous
and problems more complex. Furthermore if personnel are not working
together individual workers are more likely to go off on tangents, misun-
derstandings arise and personnel changes seriously disrupt the work.

The *Herald* article concluded by tracing the origin of the idea of a combined Science Service Laboratory to two projects, one on bacterial wilt in alfalfa, the other on sawfly resistant wheat:

> *There were already two important co-operative projects involving Lethbridge entomologists underway, both projects being of a nature also demanding the attention of other units of Science Service and both lending themselves to intensive investigation in the Lethbridge area.*
>
> *One of these projects involved bacterial wilt in alfalfa, a crop which is extensively grown about Lethbridge.*
>
> *The other called for the development of a variety of wheat which would offer resistance to sawfly, a pest common about Lethbridge and one on which research work had been conducted by the entomological laboratory here in co-operation with plant breeders at the Swift Current Experimental Farm.*
>
> *The need of having teams comprised of scientists from various units of Science Service tackling these two projects simultaneously readily suggested the advisability of concentrating Science Service facilities.*[17]

It seems clear that Arnold did not receive credit for planting the seed that eventually became the Science Service Laboratories. That in itself would likely not have troubled him greatly, as he was more interested in developing a structure that would facilitate research and its application than he was in getting credit for an idea. What did trouble him—and subsequently contributed to his decision to leave research—was an administrative conflict between Dr. Neatby's division and Dr. Archibald's Experimental Farm Service.

Because, under the old division, Science Services could not hire plant breeders, Arnold and his group in the cereal breeding laboratory would continue under the Experimental Farms Service while the other three groups—Dr. Chris Farstad's field crop insect laboratory, Dr. M.W. Cormack's plant pathology laboratory, and Dr. W.A. Roberts' plant physiology laboratory—would come under Dr. Neatby's Science Service. A compromise resolved the conflict—Arnold's Swift Current team was relocated to Lethbridge—but with that solution came the need for Arnold's laboratory to engage in an additional layer of reporting; the other laboratories in the Science Service Laboratories did not have this extra work.

While the move from Swift Current to Lethbridge was still in the planning phase, a personnel matter illustrated the kind of difficulty that the split administrative model could create. All of Arnold's group except Stu McBean were to go to Lethbridge. The group included Ruby Larson, who was just finishing her doctorate. Resources at Swift Current, especially during the war, had not allowed her appointment as a scientist, and L.B. Thomson had exercised his customary talents by having her appointed as a "herdsman" with the PFRA so that she could count chromosomes in various hybrid wheats. Arnold believed that at Lethbridge she should have an "appointment," departmental code for being classified as a professional and a scientist, and he presented the case to the "Head"—to either the Head of the Experimental Farms, Dr. Archibald, or the Head Cerealist, Dr. Newman. In Larson's recollection, the "Head" told Arnold that no woman would get an "appointment" to a research position as long as he was head. Arnold then talked to Chris Farstad about whether or not he would accept her as an "entomologist." Chris agreed to do so, and they talked with Dr. K.W. Neatby. Dr. Neatby respected Ruby Larson's work, and he talked with his head of entomology in Ottawa, Bob Glen. Dr. Glen had a vacant position in entomology in Nova Scotia that he could transfer to Lethbridge; Larson was thus appointed a taxonomic entomologist in Lethbridge, and reported to Farstad while working closely with Arnold.

Arnold's life and work in Swift Current had led to the achievements already noted, and had provided opportunities for him to develop abilities that he would put to significant effect after he left the federal government's employ. He developed as an agricultural economist, a colleague, and a manager, and he grew personally and professionally through his involvement in community and professional organizations. All these public domains of activity affected and were affected by the more private one of life at home.

L.B. Thomson was Arnold's role model and mentor. The two were very close, kindred spirits in that they were both "doers," in Stu McBean's words. Both knew how to set priorities, and both had a knack for using the official system, or circumventing it if necessary, to find resources to deal with the most urgent matters. More importantly, both realized that they could not solve problems or achieve much by working alone; they needed others to work with them, and they both knew how to select the right competent, intelligent people for the job that needed to be done. They then gave those who worked with them the room they needed to get that job done.

Stew Wells remembers Arnold as a leader, not a driver. Arnold led by listening, by putting others ahead of himself, and by challenging and stimulating those he led. Stu McBean remembers Arnold as a listener:

> Everybody was always impressed with Arn because he had the knack of being a listener. Most of us aren't good listeners. We'd sooner talk. But he would listen and then say the right thing or build a person's ego up. I can remember discussing things with him in his office and then going back to my office and thinking, "I was pretty good in there" and then it would suddenly dawn on me that it was his idea, really. He had the knack of having the conversation lead me to the right answers.

The people Arnold worked with at this time invariably comment on Arnold's brilliance; they also remark on his way of putting others in the spotlight. Ruby Larson illustrates this quality in her account of a USDA official's visit to Swift Current:

> At Swift Current we had a visitor from the USDA, Dr. Laudermilch, whom Arnold introduced. He used the visitor's name often and noted the significance of the occasion of this visit. He did not put himself forward but always put the other person or the event in the foreground. So people were not aware of the work behind the scenes of the person who was manipulating all this. Arnold had the ability of making others feel that they are at the centre while it was really he who was "pulling the strings." This is why his name doesn't come up very often.

Arnold couldn't abide ill-preparedness or stupidity, and he created an environment in which his staff were stimulated to show their knowledge and to gain new knowledge. He used the model of work teams that he had proposed to Dr. Newman in his work with his own staff. According to Stew Wells, everyone on the team worked on everything. Each person had an area of responsibility but all contributed to everything, thus ensuring that all members of the team had more than just a narrow focus on their area of specialization. Arnold also encouraged his team to continue their education. While none had Ph.D.s when they started working with him, at least four completed doctorates while they were employed there: Charley Jenkins, Stu McBean, Ruby Larson, and Stew Wells. Ruby Larson's account shows how Arnold hinted and encouraged but did not push:

> *Arn had started the seminar series. We met every two weeks, often in people's homes. He said to me, "Ruby, have you ever heard of Sears?" I said yes so he suggested that I do a seminar on Sears' work so I said ok. Sears had crossed wheat with rye. The result was usually sterile but some came through fertile. Those that came through fertile were wheat but the plants were missing some chromosomes. They were still viable monosomics or nullosomics. He had built up quite a few viable ones. So I did the seminar. Then Arnold said that someone should go down there and see what Sears was really doing—and he looked right at me. Sears was with the USDA but on campus at the University of Missouri. I wanted to investigate chromosomes affecting the solid stem in wheat so I applied to do a Ph.D. at the University of Missouri. It was war time, the men were away, so women took over.*[18]

Arnold led by example, by being a model of forethought and preparation. Stew Wells attributes Arnold's being so far ahead of everyone else to his making the effort and taking the time to study a problem and plan an approach to solving it. For example, when he took on the sawfly resistance project in 1937, Arnold anticipated the need to increase seed by growing two crops a year. Ruby Larson says that he was often unorthodox in his approach and could appreciate similar behaviour in others. Reasoning that sawflies could select susceptible wheat more effectively than he could, he, along with Chris Farstad, created "sawfly nurseries." They bred sawflies at their test plots so that they could be assured of a population to do the testing.

Arnold worked very hard. The statistical modeling that he did in planning his test plots took at least a day of complex and tedious manual mathematical calculation using a hand-cranked calculator for each test; at first Arnold did not have a calculator, and it's doubly amazing that he did this kind of preparation. As will become evident, the absence of a calculator was to become a serious issue. Because he worked so hard and because he was always short of help, he grew frustrated when he had to justify a budget in which he asked for more assistance. In his budget for 1945, for example, he asked for an additional plant breeder and an assistant for that breeder.[19] L.B. Thomson sent the request back with a note asking "Why is extra help needed in comparison to other cereal breeding…? I want to get at the crux of the extra expense in staff & labour & why it is needed." Arnold understood that Thomson had to make the case to officials in Ottawa and added detail to his proposal. He concluded the revised budget by saying that more staff was needed so that, at some future time, those in charge of projects would have time to:

(D)   *Fully analyse data and prepare it for publication*
(E)   *Keep up with the literature*
(F)   *Quit working seven days a week and take a holiday.*[20]

Arnold added a handwritten note addressed to Thomson:

If this meets with your approval I would suggest you send the third copy to Newman for his information. This could be elaborated and made much longer if you think it desirable. AWP

Even though he might be working seven days a week, Arnold knew how to have fun with his staff and with others at the station. As Alice Wall wrote:

he loves a good party, particularly if it is a poker party…. In fact he was one of the instigators of such an institution in Swift Current. He says his

*chief claim to fame in his Swift Current days was that he was very much
in demand as a bartender.*[21]

Stu McBean says the poker party at the Swift Current station is still going
fifty-seven years after Arnold left, with some of the original participants
still sitting in.[22]

Having fun and serving the community came together in Arnold's role
in the Kinetic Club of Swift Current. The club gave Arnold the opportunity to pursue his interest in "civics." Arnold joined this club rather
than the Kiwanis or the Rotary because the Kinetic Club did not cost
any money to join.[23] The club had formed in 1935, about a year before
Arnold came to Swift Current. It took on various community projects.
In the summer of 1936, when the temperature hit 104 Fahrenheit in July,
the club began to raise money to build a swimming pool. The club also
believed in the need for community festivals.

As Hoffman J. Powley writes in his history of Swift Current, Frontier
Days came into existence in 1938 and the Kinetic Club was responsible:

> *For the last 10 or 12 years previous there had been no July 1ˢᵗ activities to
> mark the occasion. People either were not in the mood or couldn't afford
> the expense to put on any kind of celebration, especially during the last
> few years. This year* [probably 1935] *though, a group of the younger
> citizens around town got together and formed what became known as
> the Kinetic Club. When I say younger citizens, I mean those in the 25 to
> 40 or so. The name "Kinetic" suggested energy, and those first members
> of the club certainly had loads of that commodity. They chose, as their
> first project, what later developed into Frontier Days.*[24]

As a publicity stunt, the club promoted the idea that every man in the
city should grow a beard. They did, and Swift Current became known as
the "bearded city." Twenty-five thousand people showed up for the celebration—in a city of between 6,000 and 7,000. As Powley says, the city
was swamped. Alice Wall notes that Arnold was on the board of Frontier
Days for four or five years, helping to organize other July 1 celebrations,
with themes that included "The International City" and "Home Front
Frolics."

But the club's activities were not limited to carnivals and July 1 celebrations. It also sponsored debates, brought in educational speakers, and promoted the literary arts. Arnold was convenor of the literary committee and served as the club's treasurer. The club gave Arnold the opportunity to make contacts with many people other than his colleagues; these contacts were to be very important in his subsequent career as a farm leader and shaper of public policy. For example, at a dinner and debate the Kinetics held in Vanguard, one of the participants in the debate was Woodrow S. Lloyd, who would go on to become Premier of Saskatchewan.

The war years also gave Arnold an opportunity to take a "civics" role in addition to his weekly donning of the uniform and marching with the reserves. Circumstantial evidence seems to support his claim that during the war years he became involved in planning for the post-war economy, especially in the agricultural sector.[25] This would have been the first occasion for him to become involved in agricultural economics and government policy.

After the declaration of war in September 1939, the Government of Canada created the Agricultural Supplies Committee, which less than a year later became the Agricultural Supplies Board. On February 11, 1940, shortly before the Board was officially established by Order-in-Council, Dr. E.S. Archibald came to Swift Current to talk about the board to a joint meeting of the Rotary Club and the Canadian Society of Technical Agriculturalists (CSTA). L.B. Thomson was President of the Rotary Club and chaired the meeting. As Alice Wall reported, Arnold had been president of the local chapter of the CSTA in 1938 and it was likely he also attended the 1940 meeting.

The *Swift Current Sun* reported that Dr. Archibald "gave a very clear outline of the work of the Agricultural Supplies Committee set up to deal with the problems of distribution and supply of foods."[26] Archibald went on to say that "the program would be designed to look ahead into the post-war period when a greater British market could be obtained." Almost immediately after Dr. Archibald's visit, says Baden Campbell in his account of the research station, L.B. Thomson outlined a program for the Swift Current Experimental Station that would run through the war, saying that "the theme for many seminars for the duration [is] to be the rehabilitation of agriculture and related industries after the end of the war."[27] Arnold had started the seminars and was therefore closely involved with them.

As the war went on, the emphasis on post-war reconstruction warranted the establishment of the Committee on Reconstruction in January, 1942. A year later, in January 1943, Dr. Archibald attended the Committee's ninth meeting to review the work of the Dominion Experimental Farms. He noted particularly the work that was being done in plant breeding, although he did not specifically identify Arnold's work or his name. Archibald talked about the work of the Experimental Farms Service in agricultural policy research.[28] W. Burton Hurd, Professor of Economics at McMaster University, had been seconded to the Committee on Reconstruction and was planning to travel to Western Canada in the summer of 1943. J.F. Booth, Associate Director of Marketing in the Agricultural Economics Division of the Dominion Department of Agriculture and a member of the Committee on Reconstruction, wrote to Professor Hurd, saying "that if you are in the vicinity of any of the Experimental Farms it would be desirable to establish contact with the Superintendent."[29] (This makes Arnold's claim that he was involved in work related to post-war economics seem credible. Arnold's claim that the work was mostly useless also seems to be borne out by the evidence.)

Arnold said that the committee's work was headed in the wrong direction because it assumed that there would be another depression after the war. This was indeed the framework within which the committee began its work. At one of its earliest meetings, on February 25, 1942, the committee received the summary of a paper entitled "The Rehabilitation of Canadian Agriculture." The paper set out the post-war problems of depression and surplus, the depression created by diminished demand and the surplus created by returning soldiers taking up farming:

Agriculture will present a two-fold problem during the reconstruction period. In the first place, it is probable that there will be a severe slump

when heavy war-time demands for Canadian agricultural products
come to an end, although this may not be the case if effective plans are
developed for such a restoration of the world economy as will permit the
export of Canadian products to the devastated areas of Europe....In the
second place, it is probable that a number of returning soldiers will wish
to settle on the land if the government gives them an opportunity.[30]

Because of the close connection between Canadian and United States agricultural production, the governments of the two countries established the Joint Agricultural Committee of Canada and the United States in 1943. Arnold's work on the post-war economy involved working with people in the United States.[31] Given L.B. Thomson's strong connections with the Federal Minister of Agriculture, J.G. Gardiner, and the senior officials in the Department of Agriculture, it is quite likely that Arnold used the seminar series at Swift Current to provide material to this committee. His connections with agriculturalists in the United States would have given him access to information and perspectives that would have been relevant to the work of this committee. Britnell and Fowke assess the work of this committee as having been of little use;[32] this was also Arnold's assessment of the immediate impact of the work he was involved with.

In the longer term, the work had a significant influence on Arnold's career as he shifted his focus from genetics and plant breeding to agricultural economics and policy. He observed that only the exigency of war was able to create the conditions necessary for the agricultural economy to be managed; people would not tolerate such control in peacetime. This lesson certainly influenced his dealings with that faction of the Farmers' Union of Alberta that believed that farmers' circumstances could be improved through government management of supply and prices. It would also certainly influence his advice to Beryl Plumptre later as she tried to regulate prices as chair of the Canadian Food Prices Review Board established in 1973. During the war, such work gave Arnold the opportunity to develop and demonstrate his understanding of the processes of policy-making on a national and international level. These abilities were recognized when his plan for organizing Western Canadian cereal grains research was adopted and he was appointed to head the organization. His abilities were also honed by his work in the agricultural professional association, the Canadian Society of Technical Agriculturalists, later called the Agricultural Institute of Canada (AIC).

Arnold was active in both the provincial and national bodies of what became the AIC. At the national level, he was on the Board of Directors in the mid-1940s. At this level, the Institute brought together professional agriculturalists from universities and agricultural schools, government service, and agricultural business. Presidents of the Institute included people whom Arnold knew very well: Dr. E.S. Archibald; Dr. R. Newton of the University of Alberta; Dr. K.W. Neatby, Arnold's former supervisor at the University of Alberta and subsequently with the federal Department of Agriculture; and L.B. Thomson, who became president in 1945/1946.[33]

The AIC's work focused on four areas: research, marketing education, agricultural policies, and post-graduate work; these were also the themes that found their way into much of Arnold's later work. In the matter of marketing education, for example, the AIC discussed the relative merits of providing courses in farm management, farm business, marketing, and general agricultural trade, through existing departments such as animal husbandry and agronomy or by establishing new departments of agricultural economics.[34] These discussions would inform Arnold's thinking in the early 1960s, when he helped to establish the department of agricultural economics at the University of Alberta.

At the provincial level, the CSTA became the Saskatchewan Institute of Agrologists, which the Agrologists Act of 1946 established as a legally recognized professional society. Arnold's commitment to having agriculture regarded as a profession can be seen early, in his editorial in the *Vermilion School of Agriculture Yearbook* for 1929/1930. (He kept the certificate showing him to be a charter member of the Saskatchewan Institute; it is now in the Platt Family Papers.) The AIC also provided occasions for humour and silliness. When it met for its national conference in Lethbridge, in the third week of June 1947, the *Lethbridge Herald*

Arnold and Donna with Joan, Shirley, and Wayne, c.1939. [Platt Family Collection]

provided extensive coverage and published numerous pictures. One picture that was not published shows a chorus line of leading agriculturalists in make-up, wigs, and tutus, hairy legs kicking high; Stu McBean has a picture of this, showing Arnold playing to this august national assembly, his back to the camera but unmistakably the shortest dancer in the line.

Arnold's work as a scientist, the way he worked with his colleagues and team members, his involvement with his community and with his profession, combined with his insights into organization and administration were marking him out as a leader. And yet, as early as 1946, in private conversation referred to in a subsequent (1947) letter from a friend, reporter Claire Taylor, Arnold talked about leaving the Dominion Experimental Farm Service.[35] His frustration with bureaucracy made the life of an independent farmer seem appealing.

It was at about this time that his father-in-law, Silas Oxford, offered Arnold and Donna the opportunity to make a change. While Silas had been less than pleased with Arnold for stealing away his daughter in a secret marriage, over the intervening years Silas and Arnold had become close friends.[36] Wayne regularly spent summers at the Oxford farm near Hardisty in east-central Alberta, where Silas had become a very successful farmer. Silas offered Arnold and Donna a section of land, complete with buildings, to farm as their own. Arnold was ready to go, but Donna was not. She remembered too well the isolation and privation she had endured in her early years on a farm in that district and had no desire to return to it.

Arnold and Donna had just come through the most harrowing experience parents can have. Powerless to help, they had watched their youngest child, Joan, die of leukemia. She died on July 3, 1942, Arnold's birthday. Joan had been born in 1936, almost at the same time that Arnold and Donna began their new life in Swift Current. When Joan's leukemia was diagnosed, there was no effective medical treatment. Donna and Arnold searched for whatever might afford some hope. They took Joan for experimental treatment in Winnipeg, but it did not help. Arnold repeatedly gave blood for the transfusions that kept Joan alive but could not cure her.[37] During Joan's last months, her parents hired nurses to be with her at all times, so that she could be as comfortable as possible at home.

Joan's illness and death affected both Donna and Arnold profoundly, but the effect found expression in very different ways. I speculate somewhat when I suggest that Arnold showed a peripatetic Platt trait for moving on while Donna wanted to stay and devote herself to the future of her other children, Wayne, Shirley, and the newborn Margaret, who had

Donna, Margaret, and Arnold, c.1950, in Southern Alberta. [Platt Family Collection]

arrived in 1944. Donna wanted to stay in Swift Current when Arnold's position required a move to Lethbridge. Shared adversity either brings people together or it separates them; in this case, it separated them.

In the background, then, while Arnold successfully led the group responsible for developing Rescue wheat, managed the entire cereal crop program at Swift Current, participated in seminars on post-war economics, and contributed to the social and cultural life of the community, was Joan's suffering and the family's grief. Those who knew Arnold then speak of him as a private person; he did not speak to his associates about his personal life. Those who knew the family believe that Donna and Arnold internalized their grief without fully expressing it or sharing it. Work distracted Arnold from that grief, but could not fill the absence.

The post-war environment gave Arnold the opportunity to take on growing responsibilities, both as plant breeder and as administrator. The move to Lethbridge brought with it responsibility for the entire cereal grain program for Western Canada. The wheat breeding program included further work on sawfly resistance, on developing varieties of durum and winter wheat suitable for the region, and on adapting the best varieties of common wheat. Rescue wheat needed better resistance to root-rot and better milling and baking qualities. Work on barley, oats, flax, and rye also came under Arnold's supervision. The new administrative structure facilitated working with the members of the Science Service, but it also brought a new set of challenges mostly having to do with lines of reporting and budgeting.

The incident of Ruby Larson's classification illustrates Arnold's concern that his staff be appropriately classified and paid. As he prepared to transfer his staff to Lethbridge in late 1948, Arnold wrote a memo to A.E. Palmer, Superintendent of the Lethbridge Experimental Farm, setting out four things that needed to be done if the new Cereal Breeding Laboratory was to be successful:

1. *members of his staff would have to be reclassified from their present positions as assistants and laborers to scientists, technical officers, and assistant technical officers*
2. *a new position for a plant breeder at the "scientist" classification would have to be created*
3. *plant breeding equipment (including a non-automatic calculator) would have to be purchased*
4. *a "cereal barn" for housing seed and supplies would have to be built.*[38]

In another memo, Arnold names the staff members to be transferred and asks Palmer's advice on how to compensate staff members for moving expenses, saying, "I presume that the Department will pay for the travelling expenses of the people concerned, and their families, together with the movement of personal effects."

Palmer's reply, in a memo dated November 10, 1948, outlining the do-it-yourself model of moving was indicative of things to come:

Regarding the move from Swift Current I find that the carload rate on furniture is 61 c from Swift Current to Lethbridge. The minimum car lot is 20,000 lbs., which would cost $122.00 for a car. I would suggest that you enquire of your Station there regarding this matter, and see if it would not be less expensive to transport household equipment by *railway. We could place our truck at your disposal for unloading the car here, and I suppose the Station there would help in the loading. Even if Transport service is required I believe it would still be cheaper to ship by railway.*

The details of the move are not clear, but it was made, people settled in to their new homes, and work proceeded.

As an administrator, Arnold wanted to take full advantage of the new Science Service environment. While he could share some resources, he still needed the items he had requested earlier. Now at Lethbridge, Arnold's request competed with other requests from the Lethbridge Experimental Farm staff. If a request was successful, Palmer would pass it on to Dr. Archibald in Ottawa. The other three Science Service Laboratories dealt directly with Dr. Neatby in Ottawa.

Almost a year after the move, on October 7, 1949, Arnold wrote again to Palmer, noting that no action had yet been taken on his original requests. Because the memo sets the scene for Arnold's resignation, it is worth quoting in its entirety:

There are three matters pertaining to the proper functioning of this laboratory that have been hanging fire for a long, long time that I feel should be cleared up.

1. Re: Technician Appointment

> *According to my information a position of Assistant Technician grade 2 was authorized for this laboratory as of December 1, 1948. This position has not been filled. As you will recall I have enquired about this several times. There are at least two men available locally who would be interested and have the qualifications to fill this position. I would like to know why this position has not been filled. Such information would guide me in making plans for the staff we are to have at this laboratory.*

2. Re: an additional assistant in spring wheat breeding

> *I will recapitulate this situation briefly. When at Swift Current,*

Jenkins was devoting full time to this project, McBean and Miss Wall were each devoting about 80% of their time to it and I was spending what time I could. The reason for this emphasis on this project was that the Board of Grain Commissioners, the Associate Committees and others felt it was a matter of some importance to get out a variety to replace Rescue. It was also felt that it was desirable to obtain other sources of resistance than that possessed by Rescue. There is evidence that the Rescue type of resistance may break down. Competent authorities regard this last project as likely to be difficult. We had also accumulated some evidence that progress on breeding for drought resistance could be made if time could be devoted to it.

Since coming to Lethbridge Miss Wall has been alone in spring wheat breeding with what assistance I could render. In addition we took on the soft white wheat project which in itself is a full time job. At least a year ago I asked for a new assistant in this work. I was promised that a position would be made available as soon as I found an applicant. This proved difficult but in April 1949 a suitable applicant was found and I asked that the position of Agr. Sci. grade 2 be established at once. In August I received word that as the proposed applicant was no longer available the position was not being processed.

As it seems to me that it may take some time to obtain help following that technique I would recommend that a position of Agr. Res. Officer grade 2 be established as soon as possible. I would like to know whether or not this recommendation is accepted and if it is whether or not the Department thinks it would be possible to have this position filled by April 1950. I will be needing this information to plan our program for next season.

3. Re: calculating equipment

It would take too long to go over my efforts during the last 15 months to secure calculating equipment for this laboratory. My present information is that the Department has no money with *which to make purchases. The present situation is that we have on hand data from all this year's experiments plus other data to be summarized and used for scientific publications. We are able to borrow a hand operated adding machine from time to time. We propose to try and average results from this year's varietal tests for our annual report. These will not be strictly accurate because they are lattice designs but it is the best we can do. Possibly the Cereal Division will undertake to do this work for us. As to the data from our research projects this will have to be filed until we get equipment to handle it or can arrange for one of our staff to go to some institution where equipment is available. If there are any other suggestions I would be glad to have them.*

I would again like to emphasize that it would facilitate our work greatly if calculating equipment were available. As a visitor remarked recently, "we are unique among plant breeding establishments in that we have neither calculators nor a cereal barn."

Arnold sent a copy of the memo to Dr. C.H. Goulden, who in 1948 had replaced Dr. Newman as head of the Cereal Crops Division. Dr. Goulden and Arnold were well-acquainted, Dr. Goulden having authored the book on applying statistical analysis to genetics that Arnold used and cited in his work, and Dr. Goulden having been head of the Rust Research Laboratory in Winnipeg when Arnold was testing his hybrids for rust resistance. Goulden was likely sympathetic to Arnold's situation, but an administrative solution would take time.

According to Anstey, Dr. Neatby had proposed the amalgamation of the Science Services Division and the Experimental Farms Service in his 1948 report to the Deputy Minister, Dr. Barton.[39] Dr. Barton was not prepared to reorganize again, having just done so, and Dr. Neatby believed that a new deputy minister would need to take office before anything could be done. The amalgamation finally occurred ten years later, in 1958. Once again, Arnold was ahead of his time; although the genius of his scheme was recognized in Ottawa, this time Arnold lacked the support of an L.B. Thomson that would allow him to proceed on his own.

Arnold had to consider his options. Accepting the reality of administrative structures and accommodating himself to bureaucracy might have been a choice for some, but for Arnold the prospect of such a life was unimaginable. The only real choice was to leave. To do so he needed an opportunity and he needed money.

He was able to raise a little money through a combination of luck and strategy; in 1950, he won a car in a bonspiel. In keeping with the story line that Arnold financed his education by running a gaming house and supported his family by bootlegging while in Ottawa, it makes a good story to suggest that Arnold curled his way to freedom from the Experimental Farms Service. In 1949/1950, his son Wayne was an engineering student at the University of Saskatchewan, and the students' association ran a raffle. The prize was a car, one of four prizes to be won. Wayne sold Arnold a ticket while he was home for Christmas. Initially, eight tickets would be drawn, and the four winners would be determined in a curling match. Arnold's ticket was one of the eight drawn in February 1950, and he was off to Saskatoon for the match. The eight divided into two teams, curled the required number of ends, and Arnold's rink won. Both Stew Wells and Alice Wall attribute the win more to strategy than to skill, but it resulted in Arnold owning a new car.

He promptly sold it and used the money to farm. He resigned from the Experimental Farm Service on February 24, 1951. That day's issue of the *Lethbridge Herald* carried the headline "Arnold Platt Quits Dominion Service—Disagrees Over Policy." The article read:

> *Arnold W. Platt, head of cereal breeding at the Dominion Experimental Station here, "officially" ended his employment with the federal department of agriculture at noon today.*
>
> *Mr. Platt is leaving the government service because he does not agree with the federal department of agriculture on matters of policy, he told The Herald this morning.*
>
> *The cereal plant breeder headed a group of agricultural scientists who gave the world sawfly-resistant wheat and saved western farmers millions of dollars. He stated he has several possibilities of employment but does not know as yet what he will do now that his government service has ended.*

"I disagree with the federal government on the adequacy of its cereal breeding program in this area," the cereal plant breeder declared. "The government program is not large enough. We need at least one more professional man for a bare minimum," he said.

"Members of my staff have not been adequately compensated," Mr. Platt said. "That does not apply to me. I have no kick on my salary but my staff are not paid highly enough," he stated.

NO SUCCESSOR NAMED

No announcement of a replacement has been made by the government, Mr. Platt said.

Mr. Platt was recently made a fellow of the Agricultural Institute of Canada for his work in the development of Rescue wheat.

That signalled the end of Arnold's career as a research scientist. (Some family members believe that Arnold's colleagues in Ottawa were prepared to offer him a position there; however, I have not found any indication of this.) For him to stop doing the research that he loved must have saddened him deeply. However, he was not one to look back; he was more interested in the future.

He could not yet know the implications of his work on breeding sawfly-resistant wheat but, in February 2004, an article on Dr. Owen Olfert's work (a research scientist with Agriculture and Agri-Food Canada in Saskatoon) reported that "the first survey in 40 years of wheat stem sawfly populations reveals most wheat growing areas in Saskatchewan will face problems with the pest this year" and quoted him as saying "There is no insecticide for the sawfly, so producers should be aware of their options now." Dr. Olfert explained that the use of Rescue wheat had almost eradicated sawfly damage and that

with the decline in sawfly populations, farmers started growing varieties with higher yields but no resistance, so they were caught by surprise. Fortunately, wheat breeders had produced newer resistant varieties the solid-stem AC Eatonia [1993] and AC Abbey [1998]—that had higher yields and quality than Rescue. Under pressure, these varieties are not 100 per cent resistant but they are better than hollow-stem varieties.[40]

Both these solid-stem varieties are descended from the original S-615/ Apex cross that Arnold made in 1937, as the chart tracing the ancestry of bread wheats grown in Canada, prepared by Dr. Ron DePauw of the Research Station at Swift Current, shows. Dr. DePauw describes Arnold as a real visionary,[41] in that the cross he made and his subsequent selections resulted in a wheat that would become the ancestor of all solid-stem bread wheats. Its resistance has not broken down.

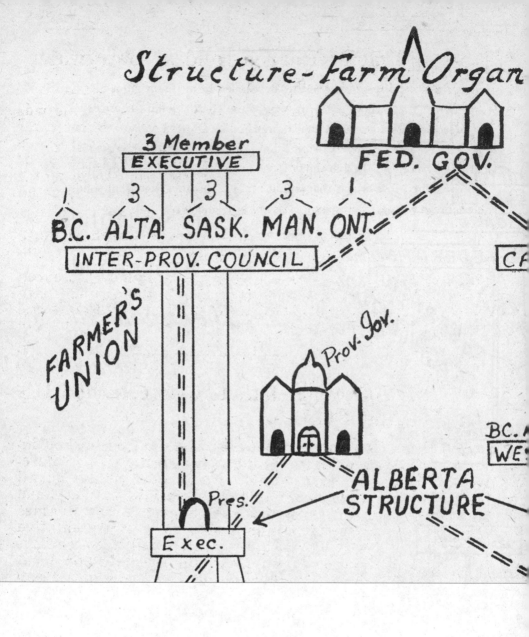

Structure-Farm Organ[ization]

3 Member
EXECUTIVE

FED. GOV.

1   3   3   3   1
B.C. ALTA. SASK. MAN. ONT.

INTER-PROV. COUNCIL

CA[...]

FARMER'S UNION

Prov. Gov.

BC. [...]
WE[S...]

ALBERTA STRUCTURE

Pres.

Exec.

FOUR

The Scientific
Farmer and
The Organized
Farmer

When Arnold resigned from his position with the federal department of agriculture at Lethbridge in February of 1951, he wasn't entirely
sure what he would do to earn a living, and there's no indication that he
was interested in pursuing a career in farm policy and politics. While
still in Swift Current, Arnold had considered a return to farming. His
father continued to farm a half-section near Westlock, Alberta, on barely
enough land for one family, but Arnold had left that house behind more

than twenty years earlier. Farming land owned by his father-in-law, Silas Oxford, near Hardisty was no more an option now than it had been before Donna and Arnold left Swift Current.

In Lethbridge, another opportunity presented itself. When the opportunity came for Arnold to go into a farming partnership with his friend and colleague, Chris Farstad, cannot be precisely determined. Chris Farstad and his brothers, along with another employee of the Lethbridge Research Station Experimental Farm, Herb Chester, leased land to farm on the Blood Indian Reserve, about thirty miles west of Lethbridge, when it became available in the spring of 1949.

Arnold was intrigued by the nature and scale of the farming operation that his friends and former colleagues had started. To him, their farm was another laboratory, on which hypotheses could be tested. He wanted to investigate the feasibility of a system of grain farming in which capital investment and ownership were separated and in which mechanization was pushed to its limits. He had been unofficially involved with the group, N.B. Farstad and Associates, while he was still employed at the Research Station, and in February or March 1951, when the Farstad brothers—Norrie, Alfred, Aksel, and Chris—and Herb Chester invited him to join them formally, as the managing partner of the 5,120 acres they had leased, Arnold agreed.

It was a mutually beneficial partnership. When Arnold officially resigned from government service, in February 1951, Herb Chester and the Farstads welcomed him as partner and manager because they respected his managerial ability as well as his willingness to work along with the rest of the field crew. For his part, Arnold had always loved farming, he would be able to test theories, and he and his family could continue to live in the city of Lethbridge.

The land that Farstad and Associates leased on the Blood Reserve was part of an unbroken grassland block of 28,800 acres, which the Band made available to non-Indian farmers starting with the 1949 crop year. As Hugh Dempsey records in his biography of the senator from the Blood Reserve, James Gladstone was responsible for the plan.

In the summer of 1945,…he [James Gladstone] learned that Ottawa officials were encouraging the cancellation of Blood grazing leases so that the land could be used for farming purposes. The theory was that the land could be worked by young Indian farmers but upon investigation, Gladstone determined that neither the tribal council nor the Indian Department had any money available to get them started.[1]

At first Gladstone opposed cancelling the grazing leases because, without money to get started, the young Indian farmers would fail.

Later, one of the government officials spoke privately to Jim, asking why he had opposed cancelling the leases; Gladstone responded by questioning how young farmers could start to work without financial help. When no answer was forthcoming, Jim made an alternative suggestion that the horse range at the north end of the reserve be leased for farming purposes and that the income from it be used to launch new farmers. He later expressed this idea to members of council and the new superintendent, Ralph Ragan, and was gratified a few years later when the lease was made.[2]

The Regional Supervisor of Indian Agencies, G.H. Gooderham, invited tenders for the leases in early spring of 1949, and tenders closed on April 20. Timelines were tight, and competition was intense. Bidders had to provide evidence of their success as farmers and of the soundness of their finances. They also had to indicate the amount per acre that they were prepared to pay as a "cash bonus" in the first year of operation in addition to agreeing to give the Band one-fifth of the crop in 1950 and 1951 and one-third of the crop in the years following. The Band Council and the Superintendent of Indian Affairs had to approve each lease. The terms of the lease required that, in the calendar year 1949, successful bidders "break, prepare and make ready for crop to cereal grains not less than one-half the total acreage covered by this lease and subsequently seed the same to cereal grains for harvesting in the year 1950."[3]

Superintendent Ragan noted that theirs was a "very fine application" and Farstad and Associates received notice on April 28, 1949, that their bid on 3,840 acres with a cash bonus of $0.55 per acre was successful.[4] Because no acceptable offer had been received on an additional 1,280 acres, the group was offered that parcel as well. They proceeded to break the grassland using two caterpillar-tread tractors, one D8 at 120 horsepower and one T.D. 14 at 60 horsepower, pulling Noble blades. Charles Noble, farming about thirty miles north of Lethbridge, had in 1936 invented the blade as a cultivator that would leave soil almost undisturbed, preventing erosion, and the Associates reported great success in using it for breaking.

By June 11, 1949, the Associates had seeded 300 acres of wheat, more than any other leaseholder and a year before the lease required seeding. By the spring of 1950, they had 5,000 acres ready for seeding to wheat. They harvested almost 80,000 bushels that first year, with wheat selling at about $1.22 per bushel.

Grain farming on such a scale required management, machinery, and labour, but it did not require much money because the crop-sharing arrangement with the Band meant that farmers did not have to put capital into owning the land. This arrangement suited Arnold's circumstances; his modest salary had not allowed him to accumulate capital to buy land and he did not have sufficient assets for a bank to lend him the money he would need. As I often heard Arnold say, "the banks would only lend you money if you already had enough so that you did not really need the loan." This experience in farming with little capital investment undoubtedly influenced Arnold's thinking in later years.

Arnold knew the importance of a good crew. He also knew that keeping a good crew required that the men be treated well. Decent wages paid on time, comfortable accommodation, and palatable food went a long way toward ensuring the loyalty necessary for people to work the long hours required during the critical times of seeding and harvesting. To the extent possible, Arnold hired young band members to be part of the crew. He made sure that the men were paid on time, sometimes even ahead of time. Arnold's daughter Shirley (Platt) Deneka recalls that employees often called at the house in Lethbridge on a weekend, asking for an advance. Donna or Arnold usually obliged.

Accommodation and meals were provided to those working on the farm, but typical bunkhouse living was a dubious benefit. Farstad and Associates had acquired two of the Royal Canadian Air Force huts that had been built on the Reserve during the war and had converted them to a bunkhouse and kitchen. The bunkhouse lacked running water, and Arnold thought the men needed a shower. He constructed a gravity system, which used waste crankcase oil to fuel a burner to heat the water.

A good cook was also essential, but sometimes a cook needed some cooking lessons to become better. Arnold recalled that, regardless of the quality of the meat he provided, one of the cooks turned it into a tasteless mass of grey substance. Pork was indistinguishable from beef. He discovered that the cook was overly fond of her pressure cooker, and tried to introduce other methods, but without success. Finally, he went into the kitchen at night and cut the sealing ring of the pressure cookers; he claimed that the food improved considerably.

Arnold also believed in the crew having a good time. Nobody I talked to mentions him starting a bunkhouse poker game, probably because that game did not need anyone to start it; it had been going on since the first bunkhouse was built in the West. Given his love of baseball, it is likely that he organized a few baseball games. Rodeo was also a popular sport; Arnold enjoyed it and cheered on the employees who participated.

The farm applied the latest technological advances that suited the scale of their operation. Historians of agriculture might wish to investigate the theoretical assumptions underlying the mechanization and industrialization of agriculture in the model Farstad and Associates adopted. Arnold was well informed, and was enough of a philosopher to be aware of what he was involved in. He did not think that technological development could be stopped by decree or that natural disaster would stop it—as his sarcastic dismissal of the views of the former federal minister, J.G. Gardiner, shows:

> *Gardiner repeatedly assured us that sooner or later drought and pestilence from Heaven would solve all our problems, and then we could return to horses and the walking plows and all be better off than we had ever been before.*[5]

Arnold had farmed with horses and his experience told him that, whenever possible, people would substitute gasoline or diesel-powered machinery for human labour and horsepower. He wanted to find out for himself how efficiently grain could be produced in the circumstances of the present and the future, not the past. Consequently, he experimented with the economics of using chemical fertilizer. As Superintendent Ragan noted in the Blood Agency Collection Report for 1952, Farstad and Associates were the "only one of the Prairie Blood group to take advantage of Fertilizer Clause."[6] Arnold tried continuous cropping and summer fallow, eventually developing a crop rotation that involved wheat, barley, flax, mustard, and crested wheat grass for seed and left 1,280 acres or one-quarter of the land fallow.

Arnold also pushed the mechanization of the harvest by using several self-propelled combines running in series on the field, each accompanied by a grain truck running alongside, loading continuously so that the combines did not have to stop until the field was done. He discovered that the combines were quite capable of such continuous operation, but that the trucks had difficulty operating slowly enough, especially when dealing with a heavy crop and abundant straw. Drivers had to "ride the clutch" to slow down the trucks, and Arnold became expert at changing clutches in the field. Arnold was frequently seen in Lethbridge, dust-caked and in dirty coveralls, getting parts.

Having invested capital in machinery instead of in land, the group was able to seed and harvest their land much more rapidly than many of their neighbours. As the saying goes, the difference between a successful grain farmer and an unsuccessful one is about two weeks—the seeding needs to be finished before the rains of late May and June, and the harvest must be complete before the rains of September. Rather than have their large and expensive equipment sit idle after finishing their own field work, Arnold and the associates saw an opportunity to put it to use by seeding, cultivating, and harvesting their neighbours' fields. They established a separate company, Red Crow Limited, to do this. In setting up the separate company, they demonstrated another emerging truth about farming: financial success depends on understanding tax law and accounting, not only on growing grain.

Grain farming, even on the scale Arnold managed, was not a year-round occupation and it was not enough to absorb all of Arnold's mental energy. One of the Farstad brothers, Alfred, owned a logging and lumbering operation in the West Kootenay region of British Columbia. Before Arnold became involved in the leadership of the Farmers' Union of Alberta, he had spent some of his time in the winters helping to manage that business, which was based in Creston, British Columbia. Just as he had learned the use of stumping powder and become acquainted with the rough life of the logging crew in the bush at Westlock, he now came to know the world of timber-cruisers and chokermen, donkeys and high-line leads, booms and tugs on Kootenay Lake, shuttling between the camps in the Kootenays and his home in Lethbridge.

In Lethbridge, he had become involved in the Farmers' Union almost as soon as he resigned from the Research Station. Harry Patching, who together with his brother Del was farming south of Lethbridge at the time, recalls the first Farmers' Union meeting that Arnold attended in late February 1951. By his own account, Arnold joined because he was a grain farmer, because most of his neighbours belonged, and because of family tradition, his father having been active in the United Farmers of Alberta before 1921, when it formed the provincial government.

In 1951, the Farmers' Union of Alberta (FUA) was only two years old, the United Farmers of Alberta (UFA) and the Alberta Farmers' Union (AFU) having amalgamated to create the FUA in 1949. As a new orga-nization, the FUA carried the history and the baggage of its founding organizations. Carrol Jaques encapsulates and symbolizes the difference between the two by pointing to two major events: the forming of the government by the UFA, which was in office from 1921 to 1935, and the 1946 strike led by the AFU.

The AFU had supported radical direct action as a means of influenc-ing government whereas the UFA, recalling itself as the government, had favoured negotiation and consultation with government.[7] Norman Priestley and Edward Swindlehurst document the series of compromises that led to the amalgamation of the two. It was agreed that "direct action" or strike action would be implemented only "when all other means have failed to accomplish the desire of the association, [and is] only to be implemented after a plebiscite of the membership has been taken and carried by a two-thirds majority of those voting."[8] Even though the UFA at its 1939 convention had decided to stop direct political activity, the terms of amalgamation included a statement in the FUA constitution "that any executive officer shall cease to hold office immediately he becomes a candidate for, an organizer of, or officer of any political party."[9]

By 1951, Arnold believed that mechanization was changing agriculture, that agricultural policy needed to recognize such change, and that farmers needed to work together to influence policy. He believed that such influence should be based on objective and disinterested analysis of the situation rather than on partisan politics—a view derived from his training as a scientist and confirmed by his observation of the experience of others. He knew of the sorry experience in politics of L.B. Thomson, his mentor and friend, whom Jimmy Gardiner had persuaded to seek the Liberal nomination in a Saskatchewan riding for the 1949 federal election.[10] At the last moment, Gardiner had withdrawn his support, leaving L.B. Thomson disappointed and embittered.

Consequently, for Arnold, the FUA position on political action was the right one. Arnold's understanding of human nature led him to believe that "direct" actions such as strikes tended to polarize groups and that such polarization was detrimental to civil society. His moral sense made repugnant the idea of withholding or destroying food while people went hungry. He believed that he could help the FUA find ways to affect policy-making that would be more effective than any strike. So, when Harry and Del Patching invited him to come to a meeting to organize an FUA local in their district, Arnold was ready to accept the invitation.

At this time, the FUA was torn by controversy and conflict, four members of the board having resigned on February 5, 1951, three of them citing "communist influence" in the organization as the reason for their resignation.[11] Carl Stimpfle, who had just retired as founding president of the FUA, having previously been president of the Alberta Farmers' Union, addressed the meeting. Harry Patching remembers that people were surprised when Arnold showed up at the meeting. As was his manner, Arnold did not have much to say in the course of discussion, but he made himself acquainted with those present and continued to come to other meetings.[12]

Gradually he began to contribute to discussions, impressing his fellow-farmers with his knowledge and his wisdom. They began to rely on Arnold as a source of information connecting local agricultural concerns to national policies, international production, and trade in agricultural commodities. All of these insights would be of little more than academic interest, however, unless the FUA could shake its image as a group of extremist subversives. The local was organized, and Harry Patching was elected district president.

The group was meeting at the McNally School south of Lethbridge when Arnold took the floor. "Why don't we organize a bonspiel so that people will know that we don't spend our time making bombs in the basement," he suggested. The group agreed that Harry Patching and Arnold should proceed. Patching had contacts in the district, but had no experience with running bonspiels. He deferred to Arnold's familiarity with such events, including his recent victory in the car bonspiel in Saskatchewan, and the two became co-chairmen of the first annual FUA bonspiel in District 14.

That first bonspiel brought forty rinks together in the winter of 1953. Each rink curled two games, the winner being determined by a scheme of points, and the event concluded with a banquet, speeches, and socializing. The annual event grew to include ninety rinks but, after June of 1954, when Arnold became director for District 14, he involved himself less in organizing the bonspiel and spent more of his time giving after-dinner speeches at bonspiels all over southern Alberta.

Arnold's account of how he became director suggests that he took on the job because no one else wanted it and that he was offered a cold beer if he took it. The District 14 Convention in June 1954 had to elect a director because L.E. Pharis, who had held that position since the formation of the FUA, had decided to retire. Some suggested that Harry Patching accept the nomination because he was already president of the district and L.E. Pharis had held both positions. The FUA constitution required that the person elected district director also be on the governing board of the Association, while the district president was responsible for local matters. Arnold remarked that doing both jobs was too much for one person.

No nominations were forthcoming. Harry Patching noticed that Del and Arnold were having a little tête-à-tête at the back of the very hot meeting room. Del rose to nominate Arnold as director, somebody else promptly moved that nominations cease, and Arnold was declared elected. According to Gerald Schuler, who came to know Arnold in the late 1950s when Arnold was president of the FUA and Gerald was on the executive of the Junior FUA, in that tête à tête, Del had strategized that he could end the meeting and force an adjournment to the nearest bar if Arnold would agree to accept the nomination for director. The beer was welcome and the responsibility was one for which Arnold was ready.

Arnold's sense of social responsibility owed much to his father's sense of social justice. His own experiences of the 1930s had taught Arnold that the economic system, if left to run by rules of its own making, would impoverish many more people than it would enrich. Two incidents in the 1930s had impressed this lesson on him, one at a Christmas dinner for the homeless in Edmonton in 1930, the other in Regina at the On-to-Ottawa trek's conclusion in what came to be called the Regina Riot of July 1, 1935.

In his first year of university, Arnold was alone in Edmonton at Christmas time. He had become acquainted with the owner of Mike's News Agency; Mike mixed Arnold's pipe tobacco and supplied him with old magazines and unsaleable books. Every Christmas, Mike put on a turkey dinner for the street people of Edmonton. Arnold accepted Mike's invitation to help with that year's dinner:

I remember helping, with a lot of other people, to set up tables and chairs and whatnot for the 200 to 250 people that we were expecting. They were all men off the street—it certainly wasn't one of the prosperous periods in Alberta's history and there were lots of people who were out on the street through just their inability to get work. And to see these people come and even get warm was a great thing and then they sat down and I was one of the waiters that carried the loaded plates to each of those men who took everything off it including any flowers that might have been on the plate. We provided them with some cookies and Christmas cake afterwards with lots of coffee. It was a great reminder of the kind of things that go on in the world at Christmas time. While Christmas is a time of great joy and pleasure for a great many people, it's a time of loneliness and despair for a lot of people who don't have family

and friends or resources to have a decent Christmas on their own. It's a
lesson that I don't think I will ever forget.[13]

Arnold told me about the second incident sometime in late 1973, as we
were discussing the October 1970 implementation of the War Measures
Act. He recalled a social occasion in Edmonton shortly after the declaration of that Act at which he was chatting with George McClellan, former
Commissioner (from 1963 to 1967) of the Royal Canadian Mounted
Police. The conversation turned to other events, and the Regina Riot
came up. McLellan spoke of his experience as a young officer on horse-
back trying to control and contain the mob. Arnold, much the shorter
of the two, took out his pipe, looked up into McClellan's eyes and said,
"George, I was one of those down on the ground."[14]

In the 1930s, the unchecked economic effects of industrialization
were ruining people's lives as machines replaced labour. In the early
1950s, mechanization was changing agriculture. For farmers like Arnold,
mechanization was the only way to prosperity—but for many others,
it was not; their land base was too small to warrant the investment in
machinery needed to farm efficiently. Some lacked the knowledge
necessary to change the way they farmed. All were affected by the low
prices that resulted from the surpluses produced by the new, mechanized,
and efficient operations, but few understood what was happening.

Arnold did. While he wasn't entirely certain about what needed to be
done, he believed that both farmers and government should be involved
in the solution. He believed that farmers had an obligation to be as efficient as possible—the maintenance and improvement of the world's
supply of food required that. He also believed that the government had an
obligation to develop and implement policies that would simultaneously
encourage efficient production through mechanization and manage the
transition to mechanization.

Such management would require new economic and social policy.
Arnold's farming operation was his laboratory for exploring the most efficient means of production; the Farmers' Union would be his laboratory
for developing policies. By holding office as a director in the organization, he would also have a role in persuading governments to implement

those policies. The persuasive force would be directly proportional to the number of farmers that the FUA represented; consequently, the first priority was to sell memberships.

Arnold had demonstrated his genius for organization when he worked for the federal department of agriculture. The challenge of raising the FUA membership to numbers that would make good its claim to represent most of the farmers in Alberta stimulated him to apply that genius to farm organization. Arnold met with Harry and Del Patching at the Patching farm for a strategy session over lunch. Arnold presented the idea that organizers should target the locals that had no current officers. The excitement of electing new officers would get people involved. The three agreed that they would focus on such locals, not spending much time on those with long-serving officers who had become inactive. The strategy succeeded. Arnold reported that membership in District 14 doubled the first year he was director,[15] contributing significantly to the 61,147 FUA memberships sold in the province by April 1955.

As he went from farm to farm talking about the merits of membership, the living conditions he saw told the story of the farmers' impoverishment. He did not need reams of data to persuade farm people that the cost/price squeeze was real; the view from the kitchen table presented the reality of it. Too often, he would see new farm machinery outside while inside he saw no electricity, running water, telephone, modern appliances, or decent furniture. The available cash and everything the farm family could borrow had gone to buy the machinery essential to operating the farm. Field work, worry, and deprivation—this was not a model of efficiency that could sustain family life.

In July 1954, Arnold was in Edmonton to attend the summer board meeting of the Farmers' Union of Alberta (FUA). Having been elected FUA Director for District Fourteen (the Lethbridge region) in June, Arnold was invited to call on the president of the FUA, Henry Young, for lunch. Arnold arrived at the appointed time before noon and they engaged in the usual exchange. Arnold talked about the condition of the crops he had passed on his drive from southern Alberta, the sorry state of wheat prices, and the difficulties of the hog business. Lunchtime came, but Young made no move to leave and no suggestion of where they might be going for lunch. Time passed, the chitchat continued. Arnold hesitated to engage seriously in farm union issues only to interrupt the discussion when they left for lunch.

Eventually Young opened his desk drawer, extracted some bread and salami, and offered to make Arnold a sandwich. Arnold graciously accepted but, as he chewed, his thoughts kept running to agricultural policy and how to influence its development and implementation. He was not given to extravagant self-indulgence, he respected his president's concern for not spending members' money, and he knew that the federal minister, J.G. Gardiner, and his deputy, Gordon Taggart, were down-to-earth people from Saskatchewan. He knew that much that gets done in Ottawa is accomplished over lunch—but not over that kind of lunch.[16]

So Arnold had that lunch in Henry Young's office and wondered if thrift and deprivation were too much the unconscious determinants of farmers' thinking. Maybe the circumstances required expansive thinking instead of a narrow focus. The results of that thinking would need to be expressed in resolutions that the provincial and federal governments could realistically be expected to implement. Policies advocated by the Farmers' Union needed to be developed in the context of, and with an awareness of, the country's competing interests, both at home and in international trade. Arnold believed that, to be heard, policy proposals would have to come from an organization that conducted itself with decorum and that presented its ideas with dignity. As he undertook the responsibilities of director, he determined to lead by example.

In words that echo those of Stu McBean, Harry Patching described the way in which Arnold conducted himself:

He was highly respected by the other directors. He was the sort of fellow who could sit back, smoke his pipe, listen to the discussion and then after the discussion got to a certain point he would be able to summarize it and say, "this is what I think we want to do." He just seemed to have that knack, that skill. He wasn't very vocal but was a very good person for summarizing and winding up a discussion and reaching a conclusion. He was also obviously well-educated.[17]

The district director's job required Arnold to travel to Edmonton for board meetings and other consultations. As he came to know the inner workings of the Farmers' Union, his initial assessment during that lunch with Henry Young was confirmed. His experience with the federal department of agriculture had given him opportunities to observe and study the qualities of leadership, both effective and ineffective. Now his analytical mind began to assess the leadership that the Farmers' Union was providing.

The organization was very effective at attracting members, having grown from 26,060 in October 1954 to 62,445 a year later.[18] New members were attracted by the range and comprehensiveness of the issues that the Farmers' Union took up. In January 1955, the Farmers' Union presented thirty-five resolutions to the government of Alberta, covering almost everything that might be part of the daily life of a farmer: roadside parks, grants to municipalities, road costs, roads to oilfields, rural electrification, the shooting of ducks, compensation for losses caused by rabies, daylight saving time, and farm fertilizer.[19] However, this plethora of issues did not include any resolutions addressing the major changes underway in agriculture. The FUA convention in December 1954 was the first Arnold attended as a director, and he observed the process closely and listened to the discussion. He was too aware of his being a newcomer to suggest that the resolutions and their presentation to cabinet would do little to improve farmers' economic circumstances; he would wait until he was president before showing a better way.

The last sentence implies that Arnold consciously determined to become president of the FUA in the first six months of his term as director for District 14. That was not the case; as Shirley (Platt) Deneka says, Arnold did not aspire to that office. Instead of pursuing the presidency, Arnold worked to make the locals in his district informed and effective. He organized sessions on the conduct of effective meetings. He urged locals to invite guest speakers who could stimulate discussion of problems pertinent to the organization, to become involved in community projects, and to participate in group activities such as organized agricultural tours. At board meetings, he would introduce perspectives based on his study of agricultural economics. Soon, word filtered to other districts and locals that Arnold understood the larger context. Alex McCalla, a president of the Junior FUA during Arnold's time as president, recalls the reaction of his father, a farmer at Bremner, towards Arnold. McCalla's father had great respect for Arnold, but thought he was an economist because he spoke so analytically and rationally about farmers' circumstances.

Sometime in 1955, when circumstances developed that made Henry Young's staying on as president very unlikely, several directors talked with Arnold about his willingness to stand for president at the annual convention in December 1955. They recognized his ability, they were aware that he had connections in Ottawa, and they emphasized that he was unencumbered by the baggage of previous affiliation with either the United Farmers of Alberta or the Alberta Farmers' Union. Donna was not happy about the prospect of Arnold once again assuming a position that would take him away from home much of the time, although of the children only twelve-year-old Margaret still lived at home. Because of his strong sense that one should contribute to the fullest extent of one's ability, he agreed to let his name stand; his supporters (including Dean Lien) started to campaign on his behalf.

The election was contested. A resolution to waive the five-year limit on the tenure of president was introduced in hopes that Henry Young could continue, but it was defeated. Other candidates for the presidency included Carl Stimpfle, former president of the FUA and AFU; Uri Powell from the Peace River District, another former AFU member; and Frank Maricle, a long-time AFU activist who had visited the Soviet Union and had been involved in the 1950/1951 "communist" controversy in the FUA.

For many of the delegates, the convention of December 1955 was their first opportunity to hear Arnold Platt speak. His years of participating in debating clubs and practicing public speaking ensured that his style reflected his character—dignified, logical, witty, — eloquent yet down-to-earth. The substance of what he had to say convinced his listeners that he understood the big picture. He knew what farming had been like, what it was like at the present, and, most importantly, he had a vision of where

it was going. Only through farmers cooperatively working together could the family-farm model survive the changes being wrought through the mechanization of agriculture and the urbanization of Canadian society.

The delegates agreed that Arnold represented the new kind of leader that the changing circumstances required, and they elected him president. In spite of her earlier hesitation about Arnold's taking on the responsibility, Margaret remembers that Donna was excited when she heard the news. The practice of the FUA was that the newly elected president would take office almost immediately, and Arnold took office in January 1956.

Leaving Lethbridge meant disrupting a well established life. The family owned a house on 7th Street South in Lethbridge, Donna was active in the United Church women's group and in a crafts group, the Lethbridge Handicraft Guild, of which she was a founding member. Margaret liked her school and did not want to leave it. Arnold had been an active member of the Kiwanis club since moving to Lethbridge in 1948. Each summer, the family rented a cottage in Waterton from their friends, the Beswicks, who farmed near Spring Coulee. Donna and Margaret lived there for a

8th Annual Convention, Farmers' Union of Alberta, 1956. [Eileen Nagel Collection, Woking]

good part of the summer, while Arnold commuted between the National Park and the farm near Standoff—about an hour's drive.

In January 1956, the family proceeded to make the change. They rented out their house in Lethbridge and were fortunate that an acquaintance at the University of Alberta had a house for rent in the Garneau area, a few blocks from the apartment that Donna and Arnold had lived in when Arnold attended the university. The move gave them an opportunity to live together as a family for the first time since 1948. Both Shirley and Wayne were attending the University of Alberta, Shirley in medicine and Wayne doing a Master's degree in engineering. But the family hardly had the house to themselves. A parade of visitors on farm-related business came from the FUA office just north across the river, on 98th Street.

Arnold immediately took on the responsibilities of leading the 31,000-member organization. The new year began with the presentation of the annual brief to the provincial cabinet. The following week, Arnold attended the annual meeting of the Alberta Federation of Agriculture (AFA), a coordinating body that represented fifty-four agricultural organizations, including agricultural commodity groups, agriculture co-

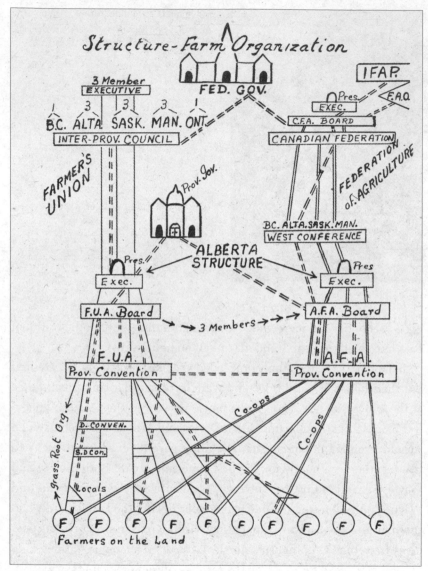

Organizational chart

ops, and the Farmers' Union. The chart and key, reproduced here from the *Organized Farmer* of September 1956,[20] illustrate the complexity of the relationships.

As president of the FUA, Arnold was also a member of the board of the AFA. In his often-quoted address to the AFA, Arnold set out his philoso-

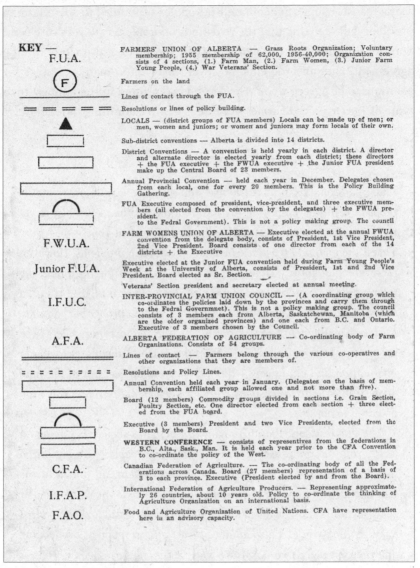

KEY —

F.U.A.

FARMERS' UNION OF ALBERTA — Grass Roots Organization; Voluntary membership; 1955 membership of 62,000, 1956-40,000; Organization consists of 4 sections, (1.) Farm Man, (2.) Farm Women, (3.) Junior Farm Young People, (4.) War Veterans' Section.

Farmers on the land

Lines of contact through the FUA.

Resolutions or lines of policy building.

LOCALS — (district groups of FUA members) Locals can be made up of men; or men, women and juniors; or women and juniors may form locals of their own.

Sub-district conventions — Alberta is divided into 14 districts.

District Conventions — A convention is held yearly in each district. A director and alternate director is elected yearly from each district; these directors + the FUA executive + the FWUA executive + the Junior FUA president make up the Central Board of 23 members.

Annual Provincial Convention — held each year in December. Delegates chosen from each local, one for every 20 members. This is the Policy Building Gathering.

FUA Executive composed of president, vice-president, and three executive members (all elected from the convention by the delegates) + the FWUA president.

to the Fedral Government). This is not a policy making group. The council

F.W.U.A.

FARM WOMENS UNION OF ALBERTA — Executive elected at the annual FWUA convention from the delegate body, consists of President, 1st Vice President, 2nd Vice President. Board consists of one director from each of the 14 districts + the Executive

Junior F.U.A.

Executive elected at the Junior FUA convention held during Farm Young People's Week at the University of Alberta, consists of President, 1st and 2nd Vice President. Board elected as Sr. Section.

Veterans' Section president and secretary elected at annual meeting.

I.F.U.C.

INTER-PROVINCIAL FARM UNION COUNCIL — (A coordinating group which co-ordinates the policies laid down by the provinces and carry them through to the Fedral Governmnet). This is not a policy making group. The council consists of 3 members each from Alberta, Saskatchewan, Manitoba (which are the older organized provinces) and one each from B.C. and Ontario. Executive of 3 members chosen by the Council.

A.F.A.

ALBERTA FEDERATION OF AGRICULTURE — Co-ordinating body of Farm Organizations. Consists of 54 groups.

Lines of contact — Farmers belong through the various co-operatives and other organizations that they are members of.

Resolutions and Policy Lines.

Annual Convention held each year in January. (Delegates on the basis of membership, each affiliated group allowed one and not more than five).

Board (12 members) Commodity groups divided in sections i.e. Grain Section, Poultry Section, etc. One director elected from each section + three elected from the FUA board.

Executive (3 members) President and two Vice Presidents, elected from the Board by the Board.

WESTERN CONFERENCE — consists of representives from the federations in B.C., Alta., Sask., Man. It is held each year prior to the CFA Convention to co-ordinate the policy of the West.

C.F.A.

Canadian Federation of Agriculture. — The co-ordinating body of all the Federations across Canada. Board (27 members) representation of a basis of 3 to each province. Executive (President elected by and from the Board).

I.F.A.P.

International Federation of Agriculture Producers. — Representing approximately 26 countries, about 10 years old. Policy to co-ordinate the thinking of Agriculture Organization on an international basis.

F.A.O.

Food and Agriculture Organization of United Nations. CFA have representation here in an advisory capacity.

Key to organizational chart

phy of agriculture, his way of working, and his views on cooperation and organization. He talked about the way that his background as a scientist informed his problem-solving processes. But science had not made him a materialist; he believed strongly in the supreme value of ideas in determining the nature of human existence. He showed himself to be a pragmatist, using science-based principles of inquiry to solve human problems but realizing that the two kinds of problems are very different. Solutions to scientific problems must be repeatable, ultimately forcing agreement. Human problems, however, involve too many variables for solutions to be agreed upon. His speech was printed in the January 1956 issue of *The Organized Farmer*. Its core is worth examining more closely:

Scientific Approach

I have had some training in science, and the approach to any scientific problem is to first obtain all the information possible; secondly, to get the best advice possible; and thirdly, to decide on a course of action. That is the method I try to use in dealing with farm problems. However, there are difficulties. Time does not always allow for accumulating information or for discussing these ideas with others and, as a result, a course of action must sometimes be charted without proper background. Mistakes in judgment can be made at any time, but are more likely to be made when background is lacking. For this reason I always try to obtain information and am always willing to listen to advice, but in the final analysis must take the responsibility for my own actions, and this I am prepared to do....

The greatest contribution a man can make to society is having an idea. From the mind of man have come the concepts of an organized society, of law and order, of systems of government, all aimed at the ultimate ideal of freedom of the individual from economic want and fear of aggression. I think you will all admit we are desperately short of ideas today. I think you will also admit, at least after a moment's reflection, that the best place to obtain such ideas is among farm people. Here is a proud, freedom loving people with a deep compassion for their fellow men, whose daily work is done in an atmosphere conducive to thought and meditation. Farming is more than raising wheat, cattle and hogs. It is also raising scientists, statesmen and humanitarians. Farm organization is more than floor prices and freight rates—it is a great forum of people uniquely endowed to give more than their share to humanity.

Broad Thinking

Now, if we are going to think, each of us will think differently. Our thoughts are a product of our inheritance, our environment and the information we have....

Since we all think differently, the job of any organization is to weld the thinking of its members into an overall program so that action can be taken. In our concept of organization we say that each member has an equal voice and that the majority rules. This is a practical sort of scheme which allows us to get along and take group action on our problems. There are two things we should keep in mind at all times. Firstly, you do not achieve unity by majority rule, but only by education and persuasion. You do not necessarily convince a man he is wrong by out-voting him. Secondly, we as individuals must realize that, if our organization is to succeed and make progress, we must accept the principle of majority rule, at least on most issues. We farm people are too prone to feel that if you won't do it my way then I'm getting out. Sound and lasting organizations will not be built on that basis.

We all want unity on the farm front. How many times have you heard farmers and farm leaders say, "If we could just get together we could get what we want." I believe that, and I am going to do what I can to advance the idea.

Arnold explained his reasons for thinking that unity would not be achieved by creating a single farm organization. Instead, the model exemplified by the Alberta Federation of Agriculture should be made to work more effectively:

So we have all these groups together in the Alberta Federation of Agriculture to emphasize, I hope, those things we can all agree on and minimize those things on which, as yet, we do not think alike.

I would be remiss if I did not offer some comments on how we might get closer together, to work together in an even more friendly atmosphere and in general, learn to live with our differences.

Tolerance Asked

I would ask you other members of the Federation, in the interests of
agriculture and of unity, to be tolerant of us in the Farmers' Union, to
keep your minds open and to encourage us to think boldly and imagi-
natively about the problems that face us. I would ask you to go along
with us whenever you can—stretch a point if possible—because we do
represent a large cross-section of farm opinion. If you can't agree with
us on some point, ignore it if you can. If you feel it is too important to
ignore let us disagree privately first, and if it must be public let it be with
as much good grace and understanding as possible.[21]

Arnold regarded agriculture and its people as central to the nation's
economic and social well-being. This may surprise us in the new millen-
nium, when the farm population constitutes only 5.6% of the total
population in Alberta (2001) and agricultural production only 2.4% of
the provincial gross domestic product. But, in 1956, Alberta's farm population was 332,191, or 29.6% of the total population; farm income was
between 25% and 30% of the total personal income in the province.[22] The
numbers alone warrant Arnold's claim that the economic well-being of
agriculture was important if the "freedom of…the nation from economic
want" is to be maintained.

Arnold promised to concern himself and his organization with "floor
prices and freight rates"—commodity prices and the costs of production—
but that was not all he would be concerned with. Farming is more than
that. When Arnold spoke of "raising scientists, statesmen and humanitarians" he was referring to the "family" half of the expression "family
farm" and acknowledging the impact of technology as revealed in farm
population trends. Not all those born and raised on family farms would
go into farming, and young people growing up on farms needed to have
the education and the opportunity to serve humanity in various ways.
Similarly, the focus of farm organizations extends well beyond economic
matters. As a "forum of people," such organizations provide a model for
democratic leadership and participation for people everywhere.

In his speech, then, Arnold identified three interdependent areas of emphasis: ensuring that farmers were free from economic want; improving government and organizational relations; and preparing for the future of agriculture and its people through leadership development and education. As a consequence of his success in making the FUA a credible organization, he was able to exercise considerable influence on federal government policies that improved the economic well-being of farmers, not only during his term as president but throughout the 1960s. He also put in place two enduring institutions dedicated to leadership development and education: the Goldeye Camp, and the Farmers' Union and Cooperative Development Association (now the Rural Education and Development Association or REDA).

Organizational credibility was of immediate importance, because the FUA continued to house two factions: one that favoured fiery rhetoric and "direct action," such as striking, dumping milk, and forming tractor blockades, to influence government policy; and one that believed facts and reason were more likely to be effective. Arnold had won the election because the majority believed in the latter approach, but Henry Young had been elected vice-president and Uri Powell was on the board of directors. Arnold had to avoid alienating the constituency these men represented while uniting the board and the membership in developing and supporting sound policies that governments would have to accept because they were so logically compelling. Alex McCalla, who was elected to the executive of the District 6 Junior Farmers' Union in 1955 and became president of the Junior Farmers' Union in 1957, remembers Arnold's effectiveness in building consensus:

He was very clear at the outset of a discussion in framing what he thought the issues in the debate were. So they were not nebulous discussions such as let's talk about rail policy today. He was very clear in laying out the parameters of the issue and was also very good at summarizing where we'd been so far: "recall that at the last meeting we discussed this and this seemed to be the consensus we came out with. Subsequent to that, these are the developments that have occurred and here's what we have to decide today." Then he was an attentive listener. I don't remember Arnold ever taking the lead shot—some leaders will start out and frame the debate by doing that—but he listened. And he would listen and he had the sense to listen long enough and the presence of mind or whatever it was to know when to break in and say something like—he'd pause and say "let me summarize where I think we are now," and then ask if there were more comments. And then he would bring it to a close. Quite frequently he would add to it—he'd put his own pieces in. He was so reasoned, so calm, so sincere, that he almost always carried the day. Occasionally he'd get caught short. If he lost a vote, that's the way it was and he moved on. He had some people he did not like but he never displayed that publicly that I can remember. Whether he thought you were smart or dumb he always listened to what you had to say.

My recollection is that he and Henry Young did not get along well at all. They came from different worlds. But I don't remember Arnold ever publicly demeaning Henry Young or running Henry Young down after he became president. He [Arnold] was a listener. He was rational, calm, collected. He made you feel that you had your say. That was the great part of it.[23]

Arnold gave Henry Young the opportunity to have his say in *The Organized Farmer*. When intensive lobbying in Ottawa required that FUA executives be there for considerable periods of time, Arnold encouraged Henry Young to go even if Arnold himself was not there.[24]

But Arnold, behind the scenes and through speeches and presentations, was working at changing what all members of the FUA had to say and how they said it. Research reports informed policy, links with agricultural researchers at the University of Alberta were strengthened, and new concepts of leadership were developed through intensive programs. Arnold also focused on developing future leaders by attracting young people to the Junior FUA and then ensuring that they had substantial work to do.

In public forums and on the convention floor, Arnold also built consensus through his unusual conduct. Harry Patching remarked that previous presidents had been up front at centre stage, talking on almost every subject and speaking to every resolution. Arnold did not do this. He sat back and listened, or he went onto the convention floor to hear what delegates were talking about. Photographs taken at the conventions show Arnold in the middle of the floor, not on the platform. He was also very effective in the hospitality suites and in the meetings after the meeting, staying until the early morning hours discussing policy. His emphasis on policy over personality attests to his genius as a leader. He had good ideas, he presented them clearly and, as his classmates at Vermillion had said many years before, he was a "good fellow."

Economic issues dominated the agenda of the FUA, and for good reason. Costs of production exceeded income from sales of agricultural commodities. Commodity prices were declining, while costs of production were growing, creating the "cost/price squeeze." On the farm, over coffee, and at the innumerable meetings of farm organizations, the solution was straightforward: the government should guarantee "parity prices" to producers, and control costs of production by regulating the costs of machinery, credit, and transportation.

Arnold's analytical mind told him that such apparent simplicity hid complexities that government ministers and senior officials would be delighted to probe. For example, parity could mean several things: farm parity, as defined by the Farmers' Union was "that gross income from agriculture which will provide the farm operator and his family with a standard of living equivalent to those afforded persons dependent upon other gainful occupation."[25] Or parity could be applied to prices, usually involving some form of indexing prices for agricultural commodities in relation to other prices, the relationship between the two being at parity in some base year that represented the ideal relationship.

Arnold would have an opportunity to gauge Ottawa's reaction within three months of being elected FUA president. Arnold's election as president opened the way for him to join the boards of other farm organizations: the Alberta Federation of Agriculture, the Canadian Federation of Agriculture, and the Interprovincial Farm Union Council (IFUC). It also gave him immediate entry to the offices of people in Ottawa with whom he was already well acquainted and who introduced him to many others.

He was not a "name dropper," and it is doubtful that many members of the FUA or its executive knew that Arnold's connections with the federal minister of agriculture, Jimmy Gardiner, and his deputy minister, Gordon Taggart, went back to the 1930s and Swift Current. Gordon Taggart had been the first superintendent of the research station there, having left to become minister of agriculture in the Saskatchewan government while Jimmy Gardiner was premier. During the war, Taggart had become head of the Food Prices Review Board, and he was therefore well-acquainted with the concepts of regulating costs and prices underlying parity schemes. As a Fellow of the Agricultural Institute of Canada (AIC), Arnold was also well acquainted with the senior agriculture officials in Ottawa, the researchers in the department, and the major agricultural- ists at the universities. They all belonged to the AIC, and participated in its activities.

After hearing the presentation of the IFUC brief to the federal cabinet in March 1956, Arnold observed that

> we farm people are not spending enough time in Ottawa acquainting those in authority with the thinking of farm people. In all such discus- sions I am also impressed with the necessity of being sure of our facts. One mis-statement can ruin a whole presentation.[26]

He then did what his connections allowed and made him so influen- tial. He stayed on in Ottawa for several days for private meetings with members of cabinet, members of parliament, and senators. In these discussions he learned what people in Ottawa were thinking. Without betraying any confidences, he then reported his impressions to the FUA members, noting where he thought progress was possible.

He concluded that they needed to create "better arguments through better research."[27] This he and his colleagues in the various farm organi- zations proceeded to do. By March 1957, when the IFUC delegation and its three rail cars full of supporters from Western Canada presented a brief to the federal government, they had distilled the concept of parity into three basic points: "effective price support, efficient marketing, and efficient production."[28]

Arnold believed that government and farmers shared responsibility for actions that would result in parity. The first point, effective price support, required direct federal government support. With regard to the second point, efficient marketing, producers had the responsibility to make use of legislation that enabled the establishment of producer-controlled marketing boards. Such boards would control production, and would also regulate prices to producers and consumers. Marketing boards would prove especially useful in creating efficient markets at "parity prices" domestically. For commodities such as wheat that depended on international trade, government should take a greater role in marketing while simultaneously using the national treasury to support prices when prices on world markets were below the costs of efficient production.

The third point, efficient production, was primarily the responsibility of farmers, but governments were responsible for ensuring that the credit needed to create farm units of viable and efficient size was available at reasonable rates of interest. Government was also responsible for supporting research that would inform more efficient production and better marketing.

The argument for subsidizing grain prices depended on an understanding of the international wheat market. Technology was improving yields, and surpluses were driving prices down. Some countries, particularly the United States, were not only subsidizing grain production at home but were also subsidizing its purchase by friendly countries, driving grain prices down even further.

Jimmy Gardiner was not prepared to subsidize grain prices at home, and the Minister of Trade and Commerce, C.D. Howe, seemed unwilling to deal with the external forces. By May 1957, Arnold was frustrated. In one of his most strongly worded editorials, Arnold lashed C.D. Howe and the Liberal government for its lack of response to the United States, "gift" of wheat to Poland as a "reserve store":

> *The truth of the matter is that the United States is waging economic warfare. They are using their agricultural surpluses for political and economic ends as national policy. In the process they are paying no attention to agreements or to accepted trading practices, nor are they*

very much concerned with who gets hurt in the process. They believe that what they are doing is in the national interests of their country and they will continue to do so for as long as they continue to think so. In all fairness, they are not the first major nation in history to attempt to use economic strength to gain political ends....

You bet it is a tough fight, but when are we going to start fighting?

We have been repeatedly told that we can't afford a price war with the United States. Of course we can't but we do have other weapons. We don't have to buy United States oranges, or dates, or lettuce, or even their steel or cement. We can get these from some other place or we can do without. We don't have to spend our vacations in the United States parks or taverns. We don't have to ask our citizens not to buy from the US. We can tell them not to buy. We did it in the other war we were in a few years ago. Perhaps a few years of such a policy would change some of the thinking south of the line.

There are some other countries that need to be reminded about a few things. We buy 25% of all the coffee produced in Colombo [Columbia]. The coffee crop in Colombo is just as important to them as wheat is to us. Colombo buys or is given all its wheat from the United States. This is only one example.

Insofar as the United States is concerned we have another weapon. Their defence against Russian air attacks depends on our radar screens.

Perhaps this sounds as though we were mad. We are mad. This whole business is a straight case of using economic strength to the detriment of smaller nations. We don't like being pushed around, and we don't see too much difference whether it is done by physical or economic means. Most of all we don't like people or nations who let themselves get pushed around. Come on, Mr. Howe, let's get on with this tough fight you were talking about.[29]

Jimmy Gardiner, C.D. Howe, and the Liberals did not have much time to fight. They were defeated in the election of June 10, 1957, and John G. Diefenbaker headed the new Conservative minority government. "The

Man from Prince Albert," John Diefenbaker understood the problems of prairie farmers, and so did his ministers from western Canada. Gordon Churchill, Minister of Trade and Commerce, was from Winnipeg; Alvin Hamilton, Minister of Northern Affairs and Natural Resources and Chair of the Cabinet Wheat Committee was from Saskatchewan; and Douglas Harkness, Minister of Agriculture, was from Calgary.

Arnold continued to speak out, and in July 1957 wrote:

> *It's my opinion that now is the time for the farm unions and other farm organizations to make a really determined effort to get those policies for agriculture that we have been talking about for so long. We are certainly going to make an all-out effort in the next few months.*[30]

The following month, in August 1957, he went to Ottawa with the Interprovincial Farm Union Council to meet with Diefenbaker, the cabinet, and senior civil servants and make the case for agriculture. Arnold did not report at the time that he had had a private meeting with Diefenbaker—he told that to Gerald Schuler and later to me—but he did report his impressions of Diefenbaker:

> *My impressions are that he is a man of boundless energy, has a real concern for the common man, a better-than-average knowledge of agriculture, and wants to help farm people. Unquestionably, Mr. Diefenbaker is the leader and runs the show.*[31]

As Arnold told the story, the private meeting occurred in mid-August, unscheduled and unannounced. Arnold simply showed up at the prime minister's office and walked in. The secretary, recognizing Arnold as someone from "the West" and with the understanding that Diefenbaker's door was always open to such visitors, showed him in.

By the end of their two-hour discussion, Arnold had laid out the issues and positions that would inform much of Diefenbaker's agriculture policy during his time as prime minister. The results were obvious almost immediately. On September 7, 1957, Diefenbaker made his first speech in the United States when he was at Dartmouth College to receive an honorary doctorate. As one reads Denis Smith's report of Diefenbaker's speech in his 1995 biography, one sees a clear similarity between Diefenbaker's stance and Arnold's editorial on the United States and the grain market:

The Prime Minister's first foray into the United States occurred on September 7, 1957, when he received an honorary degree from Dartmouth College and chose the occasion to talk about the "neighbourly problems" of the Anglo-Canadian-American community—the old North Atlantic Triangle in which Diefenbaker saw Canada's place. He had a message of both friendship and candour. The natural friendship of the two countries, he said, had grown out of their shared heritage of freedom, and was now deepened by their common defence of democracy against "the Red Menace." In face of that menace, "unity is the only certain hope for the survival of freedom everywhere in the world." The parallel interests of the two countries meant that they could trust one another and speak frankly about their differences. In that spirit he wished to "deal with one or two economic matters that are causing unrest within my country."

Canada, he [Diefenbaker] noted, was a major trading nation, yet 60% of its exports and 73% of its imports were accounted for in cross-border trade with the United States. Canadian exports to the United States were primarily raw or partially manufactured materials, because US tariffs blocked sales of most manufactured goods. This concentration of trade, and its nature, had "inherent dangers for Canada. It makes the Canadian economy altogether too vulnerable to sudden changes in trading policy at Washington." Canada also suffered a continuing and increasing deficit in commodity trade with the United States, amounting to $1.3 billion in 1956. Canadian grain exports were declining in the world because of unfair American surplus disposal programs. As a result, Canada had an unsold wheat surplus in 1957 of 700 million bushels. The overriding challenge of military and economic aggression by the Soviet Union, he argued, demanded economic as well as military cooperation in the west. He hoped that the joint US-Canadian cabinet commit-

tee on trade and economic questions—due to meet in Washington in October—would resolve the issue of surplus agricultural disposals.[32]

Whether Diefenbaker's linking of agricultural and defense policies contributed to his government's subsequent difficulties with the United States over defense in such cases as the Cuban crisis and the Bomarc missile debate cannot be assessed here, but it is evident that Arnold counselled such a linkage.

Dealing with the matter of surplus wheat in a way that would keep its price high enough to ensure profitability was fundamental to achieving the goal of "parity pricing." The domestic market for other agricultural commodities could be regulated through producer-controlled marketing boards. Because agricultural experts believed that food production in other parts of the world would increase at an even greater rate than in Canada, the export market was not likely to have a significant impact on the demand for agricultural commodities other than wheat. Arnold "did not think there was any possibility of developing large export markets outside of Canada for our food products except for wheat."[33]

Wheat was different. Hungry people in various countries needed wheat, and Canada produced much more than it could consume. Canada and the United States were the main exporters of wheat, providing about 80% of the wheat exported worldwide, with each country averaging about half of that market or 40%. The export market, however, was determined as much by politics as by economics. That market in all its complexity needed to be clearly understood, so that Canada could work together with the United States in developing sound policies.

Arnold had been studying wheat production, marketing, and consumption since the mid-1930s and the "World's Grain Exhibition and Conference" in Regina. He decided that the time had come for another international conference on wheat, one that would focus on marketing it, and he began to promote the idea. As *The Organized Farmer* reported in July 1958, "for the past two years the president, Arnold W. Platt, has been promoting a get-together of representatives of the interested nations as a first step."

The conference convened at Brookings, South Dakota, and ran from July 20 to August 9, 1958, with Arnold and Dr. S.C. Hodson, chief economist with the Department of Trade and Commerce representing Canada as well as "a group of official observers from the Canadian government and farm groups."[34] Arnold was in his element, first preparing for and then attending the conference. Not only was the work necessary to the economic well-being of Canadian farmers, it was part of that greater humanitarian service to which he was committed and which he believed to be the role of Canadian agriculture.

The tone of his November 1957 editorial on the issue of surpluses shows that he brought his head and his heart to the problem; he was utilitarian and compassionate at the same time. He outlined three options:

1.   *"starve enough people out of agriculture to reduce production." The problem with this solution is that it drags down the rest of the economy because farmers' purchasing power is reduced.*

2.   *"restrict production to the point that the price is right." This doesn't work well for grain but is possible in the rest of the agricultural economy.*

3.   *use our surplus production to help the underdeveloped people of the world to industrialize so that they can get some of the people off the land and have room to produce more....If we reject this idea then I think we can find plenty of work for our displaced farm people making tools of war. We will need them. The underprivileged, the hungry, the cold, will not forever stay away from our shores while we bicker what to do with abundance.[35]*

Arnold came away from the conference believing that Canada should use its surplus wheat to feed the hungry people of the world. In *The Organized Farmer* of September 1958, he wrote:

Essentially, what we have to do is to extend credit to underdeveloped countries in the form of both food and cash. This will cost each of us taxpayers some money. We should recognize that going into such a scheme we could lose all the money and food we have lent. That is all we can lose. Here is what we could win.

We could get our money back with interest. We could develop in time enormous commercial markets for food and industrial goods.

We could solve most of the price problems for our food products and help to get parity for agriculture.

We could bring a little nearer "Peace on earth and good will towards all men."

I think it is a good gamble.[36]

He also remarked on his impressions:

It was invigorating to talk to the men who are doing the planning for their countries. The[y] have so much to do and so little to do it with, and yet they are full of enthusiasm and hope that they can build a better life for their people. At the same time it was frightening to hear at first hand the terrific problems they face and how short of time they are. Illiterate and hungry people will not wait long for better conditions. They can turn with mob-savagery on their own leaders if they are incited to do so. Under such circumstances democracy has a hard time to exist. Because of the pressure of economic problems and the illiteracy of the people, dictatorship, in one form or another, has great advantages.

These problems are our problems, because we all have to live together on this little planet that can be circled in a matter of hours. If the problems are to be solved successfully it will require all our understanding, all our help and all our sympathy. We mustn't try to make people over in our image, or to extract political commitments for any help we can give. You can't buy friendship with dollars or with wheat, but you can obtain friendship by being a good neighbour.[37]

There was also time for some fun:

I had occasion to discuss the matter of farm unity with a number of farm leaders from the U.S. and other countries, one evening at Brookings. Our conclusion was that the great unsolved sociological problem of this age

was, while farmers are deeply suspicious of their neighbours and of their
own organizations they take, without question, everything that any two-
bit salesman or cattle buyer says as gospel truth.[38]

This work on the policies and politics of the wheat market was the highlight of Arnold's work on agricultural policy during his time as FUA president. It also prepared Arnold for his role in the development of the fourth
International Wheat Agreement in Geneva in 1959, after he had left the
FUA presidency. His view on the unfairness of United States wheat export
policies was confirmed by U.S. Assistant Secretary of Agriculture Don
Paarlberg's statement that in the last four years the United States had
moved 948 million bushels under various disposal schemes compared
with 545 million that it had moved for dollars. Paarlberg also stated that
"during the entire period not a bushel of U.S. wheat moved into export
without some form of government help."[39]

Other policy initiatives also met with some success. In February 1958,
Arnold summarized what he believed had been accomplished:

In our Price Support program we asked that prices be set at a parity
level. The new Bill says that cost of production will be taken into consid-
eration, in setting prices. We are not satisfied that this meets all our
requirements but it is a forward step.

We asked for forward prices. We have them.

We asked for deficiency payments—and they are provided for.

We asked for limitation on the amount of deficiency payments any
one farmer could receive. This has not been done but we have the prom-
ise of the Minister that it will be done if it is necessary to discourage
large corporation type farms.

We asked for cash advances. We have them.

We asked that grain be sold on credit for local currency when neces-
sary to help underdeveloped countries. Some 25,000,000 bushels has
been disposed of by this means so far this year.

We asked for a world food bank. The Prime Minister proposed at the
recent NATO meeting that NATO undertake such a proposal amongst
the countries concerned.

We asked for a realistic and complete farm credit scheme. Speaking at the C.F.A. annual meeting, the Minister of Agriculture said that this was the next major farm legislation that the government would introduce.

We asked for crop insurance. Three Provincial Governments have already set up a committee to study this, and the Federal Government has agreed to work with them in a joint effort between federal and provincial governments to make crop insurance a reality.

We asked for soil and water conservation policy. It has been promised by the Minister, and he has said that they will not wait until the Senate Committee completes its investigation before legislation is introduced.

Yes, it has been a year of solid accomplishments.[40]

Arnold did not take personal credit for these accomplishments. Diefenbaker's government believed that the success of the country's economy depended on agriculture. Even though writers such as Peter Newman and Ramsay Cook rejected such a view as myth,[41] the numbers previously cited indicate that, in the West, primary agricultural production was responsible for 30% of personal income and about the same percentage of the provincial GDP.

Because income from primary production does not include income derived from work in the sectors related to agriculture, 30% understates the impact of agriculture on the Western economy. Ontario and Quebec also were major agricultural producers, although the success of other industries there resulted in agricultural production constituting a smaller percentage of the whole than it did in Western Canada. Diefenbaker may have had many faults but his understanding of agriculture's place in the Canada of the 1950s was based on facts and he had an agricultural economist, Dr. Merril Menzies, as his chief economic advisor to confirm those facts.

Arnold was right in saying that events and people had come together to make 1957 and 1958 an opportune time for recognizing agriculture's rightful place, and he helped farm organizations to seize the opportunity. Dr. Menzies had just completed his doctoral dissertation on Canadian wheat policy.[42] As fellow academics, Menzies and Arnold spoke the same language. They also understood the role of vision in shaping politics, Dr.

Menzies being responsible for incorporating the older vision of "go West, young man" into the new vision of Canada as a northern country.

Through their thorough research and thoughtful presentations, the organizations representing agriculture were able to support the policy proposals they believed necessary to successful agriculture. Arnold's work behind the scenes, after meetings, and in off-the-record conversations, helped prepare decision-makers to be receptive and responsive. As Harry Patching said, "Arnold was very diplomatic; he wasn't forceful. The Members of Parliament respected his views because he was so knowledgeable and because he did not do a lot of talking. He had a quiet way of doing things."[43]

Arnold was very good at policy development, as his colleagues in agricultural organizations realized. He was also very good at making farm organizations effective in presenting such policies to governments; during his time as president of FUA, he made at least nine trips to Ottawa. But he also believed that farmers should do as much for themselves as they could. Establishing producer-controlled marketing boards was necessary if farmers were to be able to control production and prices for commodities other than wheat. Arnold agreed that marketing boards would require "the sacrifice of our independence of action for the common good" of enjoying "security in parity,"[44] but this sacrifice was necessary if farmers were to act responsibly. They could ask for and expect subsidies for producing commodities such as wheat, for which the export market determined the price, but they could not expect government subsidies to support prices for those products whose prices were determined by the domestic market. Not only was the establishment of marketing boards the principled course of action, practical considerations made it the necessary one. If farmers did not establish marketing boards, corporations following the model of vertical integration would take over the production of commodities such as eggs, poultry, milk, hogs, and cattle.

Arnold set out the case in his address at the University of Alberta's Feeders' Day on June 1, 1957:

Will we, or will we not, have vertical integration in Canada? The answer depends on the farmers. Agriculture will not remain static. Corporate

finance is prepared to gamble on vertical integration in the food indus-
try. If farmers do not take action vertical integration seems the most
likely change that will occur.

If farmers do not want this type of agriculture they have two courses
open to them.

First, they can attempt to have it made illegal by legislative action,
as the farmers of the United States are doing today. I do not think this
course of action will be effective. Governments will be loathe to kill a
scheme that gets agriculture out of their hair, and it will be difficult to
get the consumers concerned about it until it is too late.

The second course of action is relatively simple and wholly within the
farmers' hands. They have the legislation to seize control of their own
products and to market them as they see fit through their own market-
ing boards. By so doing they would effectively kill for all time the possi-
bility of vertical integration down to the producer level. Whether they
will or not time alone will tell, but the time might be much shorter than
many think.[45]

As Arnold foresaw, vertical integration is unusual where commodities
such as milk, eggs, and poultry are controlled through marketing boards,
whereas the production and price of cattle and hogs are increasingly
controlled by those corporations involved in making feed, feeding,
processing, and marketing them.

To keep their end of the bargain with government, farmers were also
responsible for producing goods as efficiently as possible. Arnold identified three areas in which farm organizations could increase farmers'
efficiency by reducing their costs of operation: farm accounting and farm
business management, insurance for vehicles and buildings, and farm
supplies. Under his leadership, the FUA set up a farm business management and accounting service in January 1957.

After several unsuccessful attempts to persuade the provincial government to implement mandatory motor vehicle insurance, in April 1957
the FUA created a pooled insurance plan through the Cooperative Fire
and Casualty Insurance Company. Local FUA officers became insurance agents and, for the price of their FUA membership, farmers could

The president among the delegates. Farmers' Union of Alberta Annual Convention, Edmonton, 1958. [Eileen Nagel Collection, Woking]

join the insurance pool and receive significantly lower insurance rates. Arnold's brother-in-law, Frank Oxford, an insurance agent and later the owner of Oxford Agencies in Edmonton, helped initiate and manage the program.

Other cooperative agencies involved in providing farm supplies or in storing and handling grain, including the United Farmers of Alberta Cooperative, Canadian Cooperative Implements Limited, the Alberta Wheat Pool, and United Grain Growers, provided their members with products and services at competitive prices while returning profits to members through re-invested dividends and cash. Through his personal relationships with George Church of the UFA, Gordon Herrold of the Wheat Pool, and John Brownlee of the UGG as well as through formal connections with the Alberta Federation of Agriculture, Arnold encouraged strong connections between the FUA and the co-ops.

All of these initiatives contributed to farmers' efficiency, but the long term sustainability of the family-type farm depended on changing the nature of farming. Not only was farming policy increasingly complex,

but the farmers also were faced with new crops, new fertilizers, herbicides and pesticides, bigger and better machinery, new processes in feeding animals and in operating packing plants, changing consumer expectations, and many other changes. Farm operation had never been so complex; farmers, who had learned on the job in the 1930s and 1940s, were overwhelmed.

Arnold identified the questions to be addressed in an editorial in August 1958: "What are the desirable feasible objectives? What are the feasible economic units? How can they be initiated? How can they be maintained to provide a reasonable standard of living?"[46] He did not have answers, but he believed that research and education were essential to finding them; the success of the next generation of farmers depended on it. Research and education were also essential for those young people who were growing up on farms but would not farm. This group was about twice the size of the group of young people going into farming, as the FUA discovered when it prepared its brief for the Cameron Commission on Education.[47] This meant that young farm people needed to know about

things other than farming. To address these issues, Arnold helped establish the Goldeye Lake Camp and the Farmers' Union and Cooperative
Development Association. He also served on the Board of Governors of
the University of Alberta from 1957 to 1962, where he helped create the
Department of Agricultural Economics. (Arnold's substantial contribution to education is discussed in more detail in Chapter 5).

In a letter to the delegates at the annual FUA convention in December
1956, Arnold wrote:

> It may seem harsh and heartless, but for the sake of the union, we must
> always bear in mind that we should take all that we can from a man and
> when we have taken what he can give discard him for another who has
> a contribution to make.[48]

Two years later, by late 1958, Arnold had been president of the FUA for
three years. He felt that he had accomplished the things he had set out to
do and, as he told Alex McCalla during a road trip to yet another district
convention, he'd been on that road several times.[49]

He had, quite literally, been on the road; he had visited all the locals at
least once and attended each of the fourteen districts' annual conventions.
Just before the FUA annual convention in December 1958, he announced
that he would not seek re-election as president, saying "I find that I must
have time to attend to my personal affairs which cannot be found while I
am holding the important and demanding office of president."[50]

Arnold did not provide details, but changes in his own farming operations needed attention. Arnold had no independent means, and the
section of land he owned he held in partnership with Herb Chester.
Frequently, meetings outside the province had required him to be away
for weeks at a time, sometimes during peak farming periods. Quite likely
as a consequence of his not being able to devote as much time to farming
as he needed to, the partnership, which had started out as Farstad and
Associates and then in 1954 become incorporated as Sundance Farms,
was being dissolved. For the 1959 crop year, Arnold and one of the
Sundance partners, Herb Chester, would continue to farm two sections
of land that had been part of the Sundance lease; they had also bought a
section of land on the Milk River Ridge.

Arnold had another reason for resigning from the FUA presidency. Although unable to disclose this at the time, he had been asked to serve as a commissioner on a Royal Commission on Transportation that was to be appointed in the spring of 1959. While such an appointment was not political and consequently the FUA constitutional prohibition on political appointments would not apply, Arnold believed that continuing as president while acting as commissioner would create a conflict of interest.

During his time as president, Arnold had resisted invitations to seek political office, but this invitation was different. Margaret (Platt) Oikawa remembers the federal liberal party asking him to run, either in the 1957 or 1958 election.[51] Arnold and Donna discussed the prospect; Donna did not want the life of a member of parliament's wife, and Arnold's private view was consistent with his public view. He believed that he could be more effective as an advisor unaffiliated with any political party. He also believed that an effective politician had to be interested in "personal aggrandizement"—not a bad thing if one had ability.[52]

Arnold definitely had ability, but he was not one to put himself forward. At about this time, the provincial Liberal Party also approached Arnold. When Harper Prowse resigned as leader of the Alberta Liberals in 1958, Arnold was asked to consider the job[53] but, in addition to his reservations about seeking political office and to Donna's objections, Arnold felt he did not have enough money to take on the position. Nonetheless, he attended the leadership convention, held October 31 and November 1 of that year, at the Macdonald Hotel in Edmonton. He may have been exaggerating when he told me that he had to hide in a broom closet to avoid being drafted from the floor,[54] but there's more than a kernel of truth to his story. R.H. MacDonald confirms that being drafted from the convention floor was a very real possibility. As he remarks in his biography of Grant MacEwan, "a group of enthusiastic supporters sought to draft the chief magistrate of Edmonton, but Mayor Hawrelak declined their invitation."[55] Instead of allowing his own name to stand for the leadership, Arnold supported Grant MacEwan, who subsequently won.

Arnold loved to delve into a subject fully and deeply, and the Royal Commission on Transportation would provide an opportunity to do so on a substantial, significant, and challenging issue. The issue had defeated all previous challengers. The work also required Arnold to work within a national rather than a provincial context. Arnold's experience had led him to believe that most agricultural issues needed to be addressed at that level or at the international level. Consequently, Arnold accepted the appointment. His work on the commission would not stop Arnold from influencing agricultural policy. Instead, it would allow him to focus on an element of it that had been a problem for farmers and railroads since the Crow's Nest Pass freight agreement of 1897–1898.

Arnold knew that he would be pressed to remain on the FUA executive, but he did not believe past presidents should continue as part of the executive. He addressed the subject in his statement of resignation:

> *I cannot however accept nomination for a place on the executive. In this case I cannot plead lack of time but I have strong feelings that it is not in the interest of the organization for senior officials to seek junior posts. One of the many things we must always do is develop a continuous supply of leaders. This I have tried to do and I think I have been successful. These people must be given the opportunity to accept senior positions. If you do not do this, you will lose them and you will end up with a few old timers and no one to replace them, when they eventually die. Our executive must be composed of mature, experienced and reliable people but don't, please, make it a senate.*[56]

The issue of *The Organized Farmer* that published Arnold's statement of resignation also re-published part of an assessment of Arnold's presidency that Tommy Primrose had given in the *Calgary Herald* on October 22, 1958:

> *Arnold Platt, president of the Farmers' Union of Alberta, is the man organized farmers have needed for many, many years. With all due respect to the farm leaders in Alberta who have gone before Mr. Platt, it is the sincere and humble opinion of the writer of this column that Arnold Platt is the great man of farm organization.*
>
> *There is no intent to proclaim Mr. Platt as a messiah of farmer organization. Rather, there is the simple observation that the president of*

the FUA is a man of great purpose and moral strength, a man with the courage, ability and vision to speak and work for farmers of Western Canada as no one has ever spoken or worked before.

In the original article, Primrose continued:

The FUA leader is a man who still believes in a farmer as an individual and [in] the near sacredness of free enterprise. He speaks of farmers not as an economic unit but as an important social part of our society.

Mr. Platt is not a man who coldly calculates his position and possibilities. He is clever and astute but he is also a warm human being with a kindly and humorous twinkle in his eyes and an admirable wit. While he wages an economic battle for the section of society he represents, I have the feeling Mr. Platt is giving as much time and consideration to the social and spiritual side of farming as to the economic department.

The next chapter will deal with Arnold's contribution to that social and spiritual side as it looks at his work in education and leadership development.

Shaping the Future

Arnold Platt and Education

"The future and planning for it has always interested me." That was how Arnold introduced his tape-recorded recollections.

For Arnold, the future was education. His mother had been a teacher; with her house closed and inaccessible after her death, her world and all that it represented was gone before Arnold was a year old. Perhaps that world's absence intensified Arnold's drive to get an education.

Arnold's need for education was never completely fulfilled. The short-cuts he took left him with what he considered major gaps, the never-completed doctorate having left his private dream of a professorship unfulfilled. His early curiosity and love of learning had been stalled by the era's conventional ideas about what a twelve-year-old farm boy should do:

> *I could see no value in schooling at the time. We were told work was a* *virtue—that nothing of value could be gained without work. There was* *work to do on the home farm at Innisfree…* [and] *the prospect of going* *to work was exciting.*[1]

While Arnold could joke that, when he heard the word "culture" he would reach for one of his early papers on the culture of micro-organisms and their differential sex ratios, Arnold was no instrumentalist regarding education. To him, education encompassed all that human-kind could imagine and do. After his interview on the development of Rescue wheat with Claire Taylor of the *Free Press Weekly Prairie Farmer* in 1946, he continued the conversation by talking about poetry. Wallace Stegner's *Wolf Willow* or Paul Hiebert's *Sarah Binks* contributed just as significantly to his love for and understanding of Saskatchewan and the prairies as had his own investigation of the culture of *Cephus cinctus*. He could quote Alexander Pope's *Essay on Man* ("Presume not God to scan/the proper study of mankind is man") or Francis Bacon's *Of Studies*: ("Reading maketh a full man, conference a ready man, and writing an exact man"). He appreciated the visual arts and music. He believed that, for young people to participate fully in the future by shaping it, they needed education not only to become farmers or managers, doctors or engineers. They needed education to become citizens of the world. Just as the economic problems of agriculture required an understanding of global changes in production and marketing, so the problems of people required an understanding of people everywhere.

The premises underlying Arnold's passionate commitment to education can be inferred from what he wrote and said about the subject.

He believed that without education it would not be possible to understand the fundamental principles of western democracy, live by them, and encourage our governments to put them into practice. He wrote an editorial in *The Organized Farmer* questioning U.S. foreign policy, which supported dictators, tyrants, and leaders of minorities, citing as examples the American support of Sigman Rhee in Korea, Ibn Saud in Arabia, and Chiang Kai Shek instead of Mao in China.

> *We who have so much to offer that these people want—the dignity and freedom of the individual, the right to decide by whom and how he shall be governed—offer instead support of their most reactionary leader, and charity under the guise of economic aid. When are we going to put moral principles above political expediency?*[2]

These opinions demonstrate Arnold's belief in fostering the ideals of citizenship. Similarly, he believed that education was necessary to rid us of our prejudices so that we can learn to get along with each other. In his editorial, "Making Friends," written in the context of the Cold War, he wonders why people in the uncommitted areas of Asia and Africa had difficulty aligning with the West. After referring to some of the atrocities perpetrated by Western whites against African-Americans, Chinese, or Indians living in the West, he says,

> *I suggest if you were a Negro, Chinese or an Indian, you might be just a little skeptical of the western world and its ideals when you had put your papers down.... If we are going to win the struggle for men's minds, then we had better insist that these moronic imbeciles who indulge in racial intolerance be confined like other dangerous animals that threaten the safety of us all. And we had better be thinking about what has to be done to see that all human beings have an opportunity to attain at least a decent standard of subsistence.*[3]

For Arnold, "thinking about what has to be done" so that all human beings could live free from want and oppression was part of getting an education. First, he offered help to all farm young people wanting to get an education beyond high school:

> If you want to go to University, or an agricultural school, or a techni-
> cal school, or business college, and money is holding you back, enquire
> about the help that is available. See your local high school principal.
> He has a lot of information. If you still cannot find something suitable
> write the farm union office. We will do our best to help. We see no reason
> why any farm boy or girl should not take advantage of our educational
> opportunities because of lack of money.
>
> To all farm boys and girls—if you really want to further your educa-
> tion, if you have a satisfactory record, if you promise to work hard, we
> will help you.[4]

The existing institutions were not doing all that was necessary to provide farm people with an education that combined the economic and social elements of agriculture with the big picture. Arnold had a vision and organizational ability, and put them towards the establishment of two new educational institutions to serve farm people's needs—the Goldeye Camp and the Farmers' Union and Cooperative Development Association. He also became a member of the Board of Governors of the University of Alberta so that he could influence the nature of higher education more generally.

Carrol Jaques in her thorough history of Unifarm includes a chapter on the Goldeye Camp that appropriately credits Arnold with recognizing the need for such a camp and providing the impetus for getting it built. I won't recapitulate her account but will add to it a few illustrations of the way in which Arnold's genius for working in the background helped bring the camp into existence.

From his first meeting with the FUA Board as president, Arnold showed his concern for education and the Junior FUA. That first meeting dealt with seven major issues, including three having to do with educa-tion: establishing an occupational council bringing together farmer, labour, and teacher representatives; setting up a reference library for the FUA; and preparing a brief for the Royal Commission on Television Broadcasting. The board also recognized that the work of the Junior FUA needed review.[5]

Arnold underscored the importance of the Junior FUA by devoting his February 1956 editorial in *The Organized Farmer* to the subject. Education and the Junior FUA came together in Arnold's mind when he went to Montana to call on the president of the Montana Farmers' Union, Leonard Kenfield, probably in the summer of 1956. Kenfield took Arnold to their camp, Arrowpeak, in the Highwood mountains. When Arnold came back, he said to Dean Lien, then vice-president of the Junior FUA, "we have to have a camp in Alberta." Both Arnold and Dean farmed near Lethbridge; Montana was close, and they arranged to visit the camp together.

The following summer, 1957, when Dean was elected president of the Junior FUA, Arnold encouraged him to attend the Montana Farmers' Union convention and the camp in Montana. Dean came back, ready to work with Arnold in realizing his dream. As Dean remembers, "it was his dream, nobody else's. I was the Junior President but Arnold really was the push on that. I pushed along with him." That summer, Arnold, through the Junior FUA board and the Alberta Wheat Pool, also arranged for Alex McCalla to represent the Junior FUA at the American Institute of Co-operation's sessions in Colorado. In *The Organized Farmer* of September, 1957, Alex McCalla reported on his visit, describing the American Institute's camp as "a university without a campus. It is incorporated as a college to provide an educational institution devoted to 'teaching the science of cooperation, with particular reference to the economic, socio-logical and legal phases thereof.'"[6]

The two needs had come together. The Junior FUA would have substantial work to do in establishing a camp that would provide an educational program in agriculture and leadership for the farm people of Alberta. As was Arnold's way, he retreated into the background once the idea was on its way to being implemented, and the junior leaders were given the opportunity to develop.

The camp became the main topic of Junior FUA meetings during the following year. The FUA executive and members were also involved in the discussion, although not formally until the annual FUA convention in 1958. The Junior FUA held its annual meeting during Farm Young People's Week at the University of Alberta in June 1958. The leadership team of the Junior FUA was strengthened, as Dean Lien was re-elected president, Alex McCalla was elected first vice-president, and Gerald Schuler was elected to the executive as director for District 13. The convention's keynote address by Dr. Walter Johns, then vice-president of the University and soon to be president, signalled the meeting's focus on education. Arnold was a member of the Board of Governors of the University of Alberta, serving to connect the university, its leader, and the leadership group of the Junior FUA.

Alex McCalla moved that the Junior Board take steps to establish a camp, past-president Walter Scheidt seconded, and the membership approved the motion. They elected Alex, Tom Nisbet (second vice-president), and Carl Culler (director for District 14) to a committee responsible for investigating the possibility of a junior camp. Even though Arnold wanted the camp built, he knew that the FUA members were loathe to commit to supporting something that would be costly to build and to operate. He insisted that the FUA Board consider the recommendation before allowing the motion to be presented to the annual convention in December 1958.

Accordingly, Arnold put the Junior FUA motion on the agenda for the summer FUA Board meeting in July. Alex McCalla remembers the board being skeptical at that summer meeting. George Loree spoke in favour, as did Laura Gibeau. At a crucial point in the discussion, Arnold spoke up:

> I think this is a good idea. If you're going to put together a camp committee, then this is going to be a Farmers' Union activity, and I think it should have more members than just Junior FUA people.[7]

The board decided to set up a new camp committee. Laura Gibeau, George Loree, and Arnold from the FUA executive joined the junior members, and the board authorized the new committee to find a potential site for the camp. The senior board also asked that the committee present the idea to the executive of the Farm Women's Union of Alberta, which they did. The FWUA supported the project enthusiastically.

On a late summer day in early September, as Alex McCalla recalls, Dick Schroter, District 6 Junior FUA director from Bremner, Alex McCalla, and Arnold set out from Edmonton on a one-day mission to find a site. Alex and Dick smoked cigars in the front seat while Arnold and his pipe kept the back seat full of smoke. The group wanted a place in central Alberta, preferably out on the prairies between Edmonton and Calgary. They first visited Pigeon Lake, but found that no public land was available. The situation was the same at Sylvan Lake. There was public land available at Pine Lake, but they were not impressed with the lake or the site. The group crossed Highway 2 again, and went west to Sundre, having heard that a small lake nearby might be suitable—it turned out to be more muskeg than lake. It was nearly three o'clock when Arnold remarked, "We need help. Obviously we're not doing very well. Let's go talk to an old classmate of mine, Bob Steele, who is head forester at Rocky Mountain House."[8]

They told Bob Steele what they were looking for and he took them over to the big map on the wall and said:

> You'll never find what you're looking for out there [pointing to the prairies] but have you ever thought about going to the mountains? Banff and Jasper are way too developed and right now there is no highway to this lake. It's off David Thompson trail. The road from here to Nordegg is gravel and pretty bad, but someday this is going to be a main thoroughfare through here. There is this beautiful little lake, pristine and clear, just west of Nordegg, Goldeye Lake. It's about a mile long with a stream outlet. On one side there's a high bluff where you could build your cabin. It's 75, maybe 100 miles out there. Just get in your car and you can get out there before dark.[9]

By five o'clock, the group was back on the road, driving on the worst washboard road imaginable into the late afternoon sun. It took two hours to drive the 60 miles to Nordegg. The lake was still six miles away, but no road actually went to it. A trail went to a campsite partway to the lake. With trees blocking the sinking sun from view, they managed to get the

car to within about 200 yards of the lake. Alex McCalla described what
they did:

> *So we set out to hike around the lake along the south shore. As we got*
> *around it we had to climb because there was quite a steep hill but we got*
> *up on top—I would guess a couple hundred feet up off the water. You*
> *stood up on that point and you looked out across the lake and the sun*
> *was just setting behind the mountains. It was an absolutely gorgeous*
> *view. I can see Arnold standing there, his hands on his hips, and saying,*
> *"By god, we'll build it here."*[10]

They drove back in the dust and the dark, arriving back in Edmonton at
about midnight. In the next few weeks, they managed to get a grant of
25 acres from the provincial government, giving them effective control
of the lake. Bob Steele had described the lake's small size as insurance
against any further development. The development of the camp would
take up all the lakefront that provincial regulations would allow to be
developed. The lake was effectively theirs.

In December 1958, both the Junior Board and the annual FUA convention approved the plan for developing the Goldeye Lake Camp. The
Junior FUA was responsible for implementing the plan. Immediately, and
before Arnold left the presidency, the camp committee—Alex McCalla
(chair), Arnold Platt, Laura Gibeau, George Loree, Dean Lien, and Tom
Nisbet—prepared a publicity and fundraising manual for the Junior FUA
locals to use. Arnold's concept of the camp's aim, purposes, and uses
come through clearly in the statement included in the manual:

> *Aim—The aim of the project is to provide an educational, recre-*
> *ational and leadership training ground for the farm people of*
> *Alberta.*

> *Purposes and Uses*
> To provide
> 1.   *An area for citizenship, education for the young people in this*
>   *Province, especially the farm youth in Alberta.*

2.   *To provide leadership training in such things as parliamentary procedure, the organization of clubs and meetings, debating, chairmanship, panel discussion etc.*

3.   *To provide training in safety measures—courses tentatively to be provided by the St. Johns Ambulance or the Alberta Safety Council or other organizations dealing with farm safety, general safety in the home and safety on the highway.*

4.   *For to provide* [this wording is one of Arnold's stylistic idiosyncrasies] *extension and educational courses—to be provided by such organizations as the Forestry Department, the University Department of Extension etc.*

5.   *To provide leadership courses of the nature of the Banff Leadership Course—to assist in the field of adult education in the field of citizenship—a field greatly lacking in Alberta at the present time.*

6.   *The camp will provide recreational facilities to be used in an integrated program with the overall balanced camp program. The camp is not specifically a recreational area but recreational facilities will be used in the overall program.*

7.   *The camp will provide fellowship and friendship between young people and older people whose walks in life and aims in life are similar. Fellowship and friendship are important components of a balanced community.*

8.   *The camp will provide a place for the Jr. F.U.A. to carry on its educational program for its members and the youth of Alberta. The use of the camp will not be restricted to the members of the farm organization. It will be open to the rural people of Alberta and any organization may utilize the camp for educational purposes. It must be impressed that primarily this camp is for the members of the Farm organizations, young and old, but that also its facilities are available to all the farm people of Alberta whether or not they are members.*[11]

Arnold left the FUA in January 1959, removing himself from any further direct or official involvement with Goldeye. In the background, though,

Goldeye, the pavilion, 1967. [Platt Family Collection]

he continued to influence its development, often becoming involved when a push was needed. The first main building, the pavilion, reflected Arnold's thinking. Just as Arnold believed the FUA should be known for the reasonableness of policies that reflected an understanding of international agriculture, so the camp should be seen as substantial and significant. The log pavilion, which would have a floor-to-cathedral-ceiling glass front on the central part of the lodge and wings extending to either side, should reflect that image. To complete such a building, the FUA would need to borrow money. Arnold convinced the new FUA president, Ed Nelson, to assume the debt; Nelson agreed, even though members criticized him—not Arnold—for that decision.

Gerald Schuler would become director of the camp in the summer of 1961, and supervise the first full season of courses. He was also there to see the pavilion started. Gerald notes that the project brought him close to Arnold for, even though Arnold was involved with the Royal Commission on Transportation by this time, he had a way of coming into the project when it was not moving forward.

The camp needed electricity. The main power line was four miles away, and the budget did not allow for an immediate connection to the grid. Gerald had located a diesel-powered generator that would get the camp through the summer program and construction, but the generator would cost $800. He talked to Arnold and Ed Nelson. Arnold was a good friend of George Church, President of the United Farmers of Alberta Coop, and, through the stock growers association and connections going back to his Saskatchewan days, Arnold was also well acquainted with the Cross family, owners of Calgary Brewing. According to Gerald, a member of the Cross family made a donation of $800 to Goldeye. Gerald credits George Church with initiating the request, but he "always had a feeling that somewhere behind the scenes, Arnold had moved it along a bit."

Two other buildings at Goldeye owe their existence to Arnold's creative fundraising: the Church-Hoppins Memorial Building and Blunden Manor. Early in 1964, when Arnold was corporate secretary for the UFA, Gerald met with Arnold to talk about his lack of success in raising money for another building at Goldeye. Arnold simply said, "I think UFA can cure that; leave it with me." A month or so later, Gerald received a phone call from Arnold, who told him, "UFA will build a staff building at Goldeye. Where do you want it?" Arnold's strategy had been to have UFA build a Church-Hoppins Memorial Building, because everyone had loved George Church and Wilf Hoppins. George Church, President of the United Farmers of Alberta from 1945 until his death in 1961, had been a friend and guide to Arnold for many years; and Wilf Hoppins had been general manager of the UFA Cooperative from 1951 until his untimely death of a heart attack in late 1963. The UFA head office and the UFA locals put up $35,000 for the building; Arnold had a strong hand in the design and engaged Dorothy Lien to do the decorating.

Arnold then advised Gerald on how to use the UFA donation for leverage with other agricultural organizations and with corporate groups. He suggested highlighting the $35,000 donation from UFA as a target for other donors to match, but added, "You're not going to get $30,000 from those groups. They're too damn tight. But don't let them talk you into anything less than $10,000."

When the Church-Hoppins Building was dedicated, on July 1, 1965, Senator Donald Cameron eulogized the contributions of the two men for whom the building was named. Arnold did not participate in the program nor was he recognized in the program notes, although he was on the platform. Gerald Schuler remarked that Arnold "did not want any acknowledgement other than that the result was effective. He was most unusual in this."

Blunden Manor at Goldeye also owes its existence to Arnold's opportune intervention. Charles Blunden, a long-time member of the UFA, had bequeathed his farm in the Granum district, near Fort MacLeod in southern Alberta, to the United Farmers. When Arnold joined UFA as corporate secretary in 1962, Wilf Hoppins asked him to look over the farm some time on his way to his own farm on the Milk River Ridge. Arnold reported that the Blunden farm

> did not resemble any farm that I had ever seen. It consisted mostly of alkali flats and on the upper slopes, the fox-tails grew reasonably well; in the lower slopes it was stunted, and in the center, there wasn't any at all. The higher ground was a mass of gravel. When we first took our soil samples off that, the soil lab thought we were kidding them and we were looking at foundation material rather than farm land.
>
> I went back to Wilf to say that there was nothing we could do with that. "Is there anybody that we could possibly give it to? Blunden gave it to us, maybe we could find somebody to give it to," but he said, "no, we are stuck with it and now you go farm it but you know the board of directors don't want any more losses on that thing. We are about $6,000 in debt now, so you know it's got to pay and we can't afford to spend any money on this deal."[12]

Arnold knew a bit about land reclamation, and he consulted a neighbour to the Blunden farm, George Lantinga, about the success he had had at his own farm. Arnold took the good advice Lantinga offered and proceeded to make the farm productive and prosperous.

The UFA did not really care to have its corporate secretary and board responsible for managing a farm, but the Blunden bequest stated that, if the farm was sold, the proceeds should be used to build a community hall in the Granum district. By the time the Blunden farm was in good enough shape to sell, farms in the area had been consolidated and the district population had no use, need, or desire for a community hall. Arnold consulted with the legal people administering the will and suggested that a "community hall" at Goldeye might satisfy the terms of the will. Thus the farm was sold, and the proceeds were used to build Blunden Manor at Goldeye.

Blunden Manor was intended to realize another part of Arnold's vision for Goldeye: it was to be used for adult groups. In his address at the dedication of Blunden Manor in August 1973, Arnold explained his reasons for wanting adults to spend time there:

> *I don't envisage this as a policy-making institution. I envisage this as an institution where people can come to gain information, to see visions, to dream dreams and most of all, to get those one-in-a-million good ideas that change the way of life of people everywhere. It is a place to develop leaders, a place where we can assess change and welcome change that is good instead of spending so much of our time opposing change because it is change....*
>
> *I would like to see this, as I say, [as] a center of excellence, a Banff School of Advanced Management, if you like, for agricultural people, where the things that we do here for people of all ages are the very best that can be done any place. Where we bring our best people and we expose them to the best minds that we can find. And out of that will come a vision of what the future of rural Alberta can become.* [13]

Arnold wanted Goldeye to draw the senior agricultural leaders of farm organizations, businesses, and the university together to develop policy and formulate strategies for influencing government. Having been responsible for establishing the Rural Leadership Conference for training senior leaders at the Banff School in 1957, he believed that those senior leaders needed a place to continue their education in a less formal setting. He thought that out there in the trees at night with no reporters present, maybe over a glass of scotch, such leaders might be able to break free of the views determined by the particular interests they represented. Just as importantly, Arnold envisaged leaders coming to Goldeye to continue their education by meeting with younger people, "to listen, above all to listen to what these young people have to say."[14] As Gerald Schuler noted, that part of Arnold's vision has not been realized; only once did such a group get together, and the result discouraged another attempt.

At least once more "things were not going forward" at Goldeye and Arnold helped to find a way to solve the problem. By 1977, Goldeye was very successful: "In total, 2,315 people took part in activities at Goldeye in 1977, a far cry from the twenty-three enthusiastic young people who had lived in tents and sat on piles of lumber at the first 'camp' in 1961."[15] However, by this time the centre needed substantial maintenance and renovation. Youth camps had never paid for themselves. Without investment in improvements, the centre would not be able to attract the conferences it needed to provide income to sustain its operations.

Unifarm and the cooperatives that now operated Goldeye did not have money to invest. The General Advisory Committee for Goldeye appointed a sub-committee on Goldeye Lake Centre Administration, with Arnold as chair to suggest solutions. The other members were Leda Jensen, Dr. Elsie McFarland, Ed Ness, Cornie Versluys, Bob Steele, Jack Muza, and Gerald Schuler—people well known in agricultural organizations in Alberta. Arnold appreciated the irony in the role:

> Despite the fact that this sub-committee is composed of quite distinguished citizens we sit rather low on the totem pole. Let me illustrate as best I can the route our recommendations will take.

1. Sub-committee on Goldeye Lake Centre Administration
2. General Advisory Committee
3. Policy Committee
4. Unifarm Executive
5. Unifarm Board of Directors
6. Annual Meeting of Unifarm.[16]

The sub-committee's job was to recommend improvements and new facilities that might be required in the future. Characteristically for Arnold, he and the sub-committee decided that the terms of reference had not properly defined the problem; any solution offered within those terms of reference would therefore fail. Only a complete re-thinking of the situation would lead to the appropriate solution. Arnold reported that the committee was unable to make any recommendation; the facility depended on programs, but the committee had no official role in designing those programs—there was no point in recommending facilities without knowing the plan for programs. Arnold then outlined the group's reasons for thinking that the existing administrative structure could not work. He left the outline of a solution with Gerald Schuler, who then presented a plan to establish the Goldeye Foundation Society.

The plan worked, and Goldeye continues to fulfill its purposes. The recommended plan was accepted at the annual meeting of Unifarm and, as Carrol Jaques writes,

> the Goldeye Foundation Society was created in 1978 as a charitable organization able to issue tax receipts for contributions to build and maintain the physical structure at Goldeye. Institutional members of the Goldeye Foundation were assessed a substantial annual membership fee while individual memberships were available for anyone interested in being involved in the Goldeye Centre. The board consisted of representatives of member co-operatives and representatives of individual members.[17]

Arnold visited Goldeye whenever he could, participating in the centre's twenty-fifth anniversary celebrations in 1983. He would be pleased that the centre now attracts groups of all kinds, including a group of monks from Europe that holds regular retreats at Goldeye.

No plaque at Goldeye memorializes Arnold's contribution but, if one knows where to look beside one of the paths to the west of the pavilion, one will see a post cut off at almost ground level beside a tree. The tree was planted by Dr. Alf Petersen, Arnold's long-time friend from the Department of Agricultural Economics at the University of Alberta. The post bears the simple inscription, "In Memory of A.W. Platt."

Goldeye is a wonderful place to develop citizens and leaders, but a place doesn't make a program. Realizing the complexity of the body of knowledge farm people needed to acquire and seeing no agency engaged in developing, consolidating, and communicating such knowledge, Arnold believed that the FUA should emulate the work of the American Institute of Cooperation by establishing a similar agency.

Carrol Jaques recognizes Arnold as the originator of the Farmers' Union and Co-operative Development Association.[18] Arnold believed that all the major farm organizations should be involved in supporting Goldeye and in sponsoring the development of a program in farm organization education, which would be offered through Goldeye and the locals. In September 1958, he convened a group of farm leaders—including Ellen Armstrong of the Farm Women's Union of Alberta, Russell Love of the Alberta Co-operative Wholesale Association, George Church and Wilf Hoppins of the United Farmers of Alberta Co-operative, Simon Roppel of the Alberta Poultry Producers, Allan Gibson of the Alberta Wheat Pool, and Frank Allison of the United Grain Growers—and presented them with a proposal.

Arnold had prepared and circulated a memorandum before the meeting to prepare them for that proposal. No doubt he had also talked to each of them before the meeting. When George Church moved that a planning committee be appointed and that it be chaired by Arnold, and that the committee prepare a report on proposed activities and a budget, everyone agreed. A month later, the group met and approved the committee's outline for an education program.

The outline was specific enough to constitute a plan, and comprehensive enough to justify its $30,000 budget. The organization should develop and deliver short courses at about 80 locals a year. It should also develop courses for the 15 district executives in addition to one annual course for leaders at the provincial level. That last course should focus on developing leadership ability at an advanced level, while also engaging those leaders in an advanced-level study of the "situations and conditions affecting the agricultural industry." The plan identified nine services that the organization should offer, including information and communications services, special event planning, and farm opinion surveying. Arnold and the planning group stressed that "continuous evaluation of the program was essential" and recommended that such evaluation be done by an outside agency so that it would be "searching and unbiased."[19] The farm organizations approved the plan at their annual meetings later in 1958 and in early 1959, and the Farmers' Union and Co-operative Development Association was created.

By this time, Arnold had left the FUA. Ed Nelson was equally committed to the project, and saw it through the stresses of becoming established. Arnold took no further official part in the organization, although he was never far away as one of his protégés, Kay Dowhaniuk, took on the position of director, and another, Gerald Schuler, became assistant director in 1962. During his time as corporate secretary of the United Farmers of Alberta, from 1962 to 1972, Arnold's calendar contains numerous entries for lunch with Kay or Gerald.[20] Others at UFA represented the organization on the association's board.

Arnold resigned from his position at UFA in 1972, and from about 1973 to 1977 he participated in the general advisory committee of what FU&CDA had become, the Rural Education and Development Association (REDA). His membership in that group illustrates how Arnold stayed connected with organizations and people involved in education, even though his work did not require it.

Shortly before Arnold left the FUA president's office, he wrote the agricultural education portion of the FUA brief to the Royal Commission on Education in Alberta, the commission chaired by Senator Donald Cameron. Having attended both the Olds and Vermillion Schools of Agriculture as well as the University of Alberta's Faculty of Agriculture, Arnold knew the history of agricultural education. Being aware of trends in the rural population, he could also see something of the future. Earlier, he had advocated that education that was not exclusively agricultural be available to farm young people, and he took the occasion of the commission's inquiry to develop the point more fully. Senator Cameron agreed with Arnold's point, and incorporated the FUA recommendation into his 1959 report:

Noting that the [agricultural] schools' programs "had not kept pace with modern needs," the Commission recommended a major reorganization of the schools which would include expansion and moderniza-

tion of the agricultural courses, and the introduction of non-agricultural
vocational programs which would increase their potential clientele. In
recognition of this expanded mandate, the schools would be transformed
into community colleges, which could be operated either by local school
authorities or by the Department of Education as part of the provincial
college system.[21]

Once again, Arnold had prepared the way for changes. Harry Strom as
Minister of Agriculture implemented the recommendations for trans-
forming agricultural education in 1963, long after Arnold had left the
FUA.

Arnold was involved in education in another way from 1956 to 1962.
As has been mentioned, he was a member of the Board of Governors
of the University of Alberta during that time, and he was very effective
in linking the university with the provincial government. Arnold's work
with Alberta's universities, particularly with the University of Alberta,
continued to demonstrate his commitment to the future of Alberta's
people. As a researcher, he had good reason to continue his associations
with the Faculty of Agriculture at Alberta. He had hired graduates of
the Faculty and had engaged faculty members and graduate students in
some of his field tests. He was one of the few Faculty alumni to have
developed a commercial wheat variety, and his work was well known and
respected.

It was the custom at the university that the Board of Governors include
at least one member of the rural and agricultural community served by the
university. When that position became vacant in the spring of 1956, the
premier of the province did not have to look very far for a new appointee.
Before Arnold became president of the FUA, Manning had little use for
farm organizations, but Arnold had changed that. Arnold, having taken
office as president of the FUA in January 1956, had impressed Manning
as a farm leader with good sense and good judgment, one worth listening to. Members of the Board of Governors were appointed by order-in-
council, so the appointment required the premier's support, but I have
been unable to determine who recommended Arnold for the appointment. Dr. Walter Johns, then the university's vice-president, was on the

board, but whether his friendship with Arnold pre-dated Arnold's time on the board is not known.

As with so much of what Arnold accomplished in agricultural research or policy development, most of his achievements while on the board were made behind the scenes and have not received public acknowl-edgement.[22] He helped revise the curriculum for agricultural engineer-ing, supported the university's efforts to establish a school of veterinary medicine at Alberta (there being no school in Western Canada at that time), and helped the Banff School expand its programming in courses that were profitable. He also advocated the strengthening of continuing education through university extension work.

The Survey Committee on the future of Higher Education in Alberta was an early attempt at rationalizing higher education in Alberta by iden-tifying particular roles for universities, junior colleges, technical schools, and adult continuing education. Arnold strongly supported the rational-ization of program offerings, and spoke on the subject at a board meeting in December 1960. In a letter to the Executive Committee, he outlined elements of higher education that warranted review by the Survey Committee on the Future of Higher Education in Alberta, and the board agreed that these proposals should be considered in the committee's deliberations.

During the time that Arnold was on the Board of Governors, it was responsible for the Banff School. Because he saw the Banff School as having a significant role in continuing education, he was one of its strong supporters while he was on the board:

> I remember well the early days of what is now the Banff Centre. Our aim was to give rural people cheap conference space and an opportunity to try a bit of the fine arts. To subsidize these activities we had to have profitable conferences. Who got priority? It all depended on how the accounts stood. As an aside, when those in charge gave up and said let the government do it, the original objectives were lost.[23]

Arnold was likely referring to the Conference and Short Course Division of the Banff School. In 1956, when Arnold joined the Board of Governors, the Banff School reported to the board through the university's Director of Extension, Donald Cameron, who was also Director of the Banff School. Cameron and Arnold were well acquainted, having been in undergraduate and graduate programs at the same time at the University of Alberta. Cameron received the M.Sc. in Agriculture in 1934, and Arnold in 1936. Helen Platt recalls Arnold saying that he had encouraged Donald Cameron to expand the Conference and Short Course Division to pay "for all that ballet, theatre, and painting."

In Cameron's own account of his work at the Banff School, he reports that the division began to expand at about the time that Arnold joined the Board of Governors:

> One of the most gratifying aspects of the School's growth and devel-
> opment was the rapid expansion of the Conference and Short Course
> Division. A total of 64 groups and 6,000 people participated in a series
> of schools, short courses, seminars and conferences for periods as short
> as two days to a maximum of 12 weeks. In all of 1957 there were only two
> weeks in which the School was not occupied by one group or another.[24]

Arnold contributed at least one new offering to the Short Course Division in 1957, the two-week Rural Leadership Conference. Two years before the FU&CDA was established, Arnold saw the need for senior leaders of farm and rural organizations "to discuss, study and more fully understand the economic, sociological and human relations factors and influences affecting farming, farm living and rural organizations."[25] He first persuaded the Faculty of Agriculture at the university to work with knowledgeable people in the major farm and cooperative organizations to develop the curriculum, and then he persuaded the farm and coopera- tive organizations to sponsor a number of their senior leaders' partici- pation in the course. In his role as president of the FUA, Arnold also encouraged people in rural communities to attend the two-week Rural Leadership Techniques course, also at the Banff School. This course was first offered in 1950 and formed the basis and the model for the new, more advanced course.

While Arnold was a member of the Board of Governors, the Banff School added new buildings to support its growing programs. Senator Cameron deserves credit for planning those buildings and for raising the necessary money, but Arnold supported the purchase of the Harmon House for the Banff Centre. The minutes record that some members questioned the need for "additional dormitory facilities." Arnold responded that

> *the Banff School of Fine Arts has done a great deal of good for the University as a whole, especially in the southern part of the Province and he felt that, in most cases, an expenditure of this sort might very well prove to be advantageous to the University, especially if it could be used during the off-season or winter months.*[26]

Arnold's contribution to the work of the Banff Centre was appreciated. He was always welcome at the Banff Centre and was assured that it was a place for him to stay whenever he visited Banff—though he seldom, if ever, took up the offer.

While on the board, Arnold was an effective advocate and supporter. He also demonstrated his ability to initiate change. He was responsible for two major changes at the university: he helped to limit the provincial government's direct involvement in the university's financial affairs; and he enhanced the academic program by persuading the university to establish a department of agricultural economics.

When Arnold joined the board, the provincial government directly controlled the university's budget. Arnold described the situation as he found it:

> *The Social Credit Party, when they formed the government, looked upon the University with some well-founded suspicion. As tensions deepened, the government kept a high degree of control by appointing trusted civil servants to the Board of Governors. In the early fifties, when the University was rapidly expanding, planning, particularly financial planning, became very difficult because the civil service appointees had veto power over the rest of the Board and Administration, even on minor*

John Proctor and Arnold reminiscing at the Faculty Club, University of Alberta.
[Platt Family Collection]

matters. It so happened that the President of the Farmers' Union and the manager of the Canadian Petroleum Association [John Proctor] were on the Board of Governors at the same time. They pointed out the problem to the Premier. He agreed that the Board appoint a finance committee with NO civil servants and that the committee deal directly with the Provincial Treasurer—Mr. Hinman. This action not only set a precedent but also resulted in the funds available being used to better advantage.[27]

In the self-effacing manner so characteristic of Arnold, he claims no personal responsibility for influencing then-Premier Manning; as Arnold describes it, Manning changed the powers of the civil service appointees because the Farmers' Union and the Canadian Petroleum Association asked for that change. The reality was slightly different. As Gerald Schuler observed, and as I have noted previously, before Arnold became president of the Farmers' Union, Manning had little time and less regard for the organization or its leaders. He met with them only for the Union's annual presentation of its brief.

Arnold changed that relationship. He and Manning were very different people—Arnold would have had no success in changing Manning's thinking by inviting him for drinks at the Faculty Club—but Manning respected people with integrity, and Arnold never gave anyone an occasion to question his. Arnold's solution to the difficulties brought about by the civil servants' veto power shows his ability to also understand government interests. He did not go to Manning demanding that the government stop its interference in the work of the university; instead, he offered a solution that provided ultimate control to the Provincial Treasurer. By shifting that control from the administrative to the political level, Arnold and John Proctor ensured that the university and its board effectively controlled the finances of the university's operation. The Provincial Treasurer could control the amount of the government's grant to the university but was unlikely to determine the university's priorities.

The minutes of the Board for December 20, 1961, record the establishment of the new Finance Committee:

> IT WAS MOVED by Mr. Kelly and Mr. Proctor that a Finance Committee of the board be set up, comprised of Mr. Platt, Mr. Manning [not the Premier] (with the power to name a substitute), Mr. Thomson, Mr. Stewart, and Dr. Stanley, with the Chairman, the President, and Dr. Taylor [the Vice-President] serving as ex officio members, and that this committee be empowered to examine both the current and capital estimates, and make recommendations thereon to the Board of Governors, in view of the information concerning the probable limit of the Provincial Grant. CARRIED.

Arnold's second major initiative led to the creation of a new department of agricultural economics. The department came into existence in January 1962, when Dr. Travis Manning came from Oklahoma to take the position as head. That Arnold had much to do with establishing the department is not recorded in Travis Manning's history of it in *The First Fifty Years: A History of the Faculty of Agriculture 1915–1965*,[28] and Dr. C.F.

Bentley, Dean of the Faculty at that time, does not know the extent to which Arnold was involved, as Dr. Bentley was not involved in the board discussions or those between Arnold and the president that resulted in the department being established.[29] The archival files related to the establishing of the department don't contain a proposal from the Faculty of Agriculture to establish it, a gap that suggests the impetus may have come from elsewhere.

In the notes for a speech he gave at the Newest Forum for the Arts, Goldeye Centre, in July 1988, Arnold credited the Farmers' Union with persuading the university to establish the department and with persuading the government to fund it. While it is true that the Farm Women's Union of Alberta (FWUA) had asked the Board of Governors to establish such a department in April of 1959 and the Farmers' Union reiterated that request in letters to the president in April 1961, it is very likely that Arnold encouraged Mrs. Hicks of the FWUA and Ed Nelson of the FUA to write those letters. From what Arnold told me, from Gerald Schuler's recollections, from Dr. Joseph Richter's observations,[30] from the fact that Arnold chaired the provincial advisory committee for the department from the time that it was established, and from the information in the archives of the University, it seems reasonable to conclude that Arnold played a critical role.

Dr. Joseph Richter says that the department owes its existence to Arnold. Arnold led an informal group of influential farm people in Alberta, who championed the cause of such a department. Arnold and Dr. Richter became acquainted while Arnold was on the Royal Commission on Transportation (1959–1962) and Dr. Richter, then a member of the Department of Economics at the University of British Columbia, was working on behalf of the Liberals and the Vancouver member of parliament, Arthur Laing, in trying to influence the work of the commission.

Dr. Richter recalls that, in 1961, Arnold came to visit him in Vancouver to find out what a department of agricultural economics should look like. He also suggested that Dr. Richter might be the right person to head the new department. Dr. Richter agreed to consider the possibility because, according to Dr. Richter, Arnold was one of the few people in Canada at that time who fully understood how important the area of agricultural economics was to the entire program of agricultural study and research. By this time, Arnold had gained an understanding of the global agricultural economy through his work at the international conference on wheat marketing at Brookings in 1958, his membership on the advisory committee to the Canadian Wheat Board, and his participation in the six-week talks in Geneva that led to the fourth International Wheat Agreement in the spring of 1959. This experience had convinced him that, contrary to the view dominant in most faculties and colleges of agriculture in Canada at the time, one couldn't solve all the problems of agriculture by looking through a microscope.

Dr. Richter agreed to meet with Dr. C.F. Bentley, Dean of the Faculty of Agriculture, to talk about coming to the University of Alberta. The meeting likely occurred sometime after March 27, 1961, at which time Dean Bentley had received an unsolicited letter from Dr. D.R. Campbell, Head of the Department of Agricultural Economics at the Ontario Agricultural College in Guelph, recommending Dr. Richter as a likely candidate for the position.[31] Dr. Richter learned that the Faculty of Agriculture did not yet have a department of agricultural economics, and there was no assurance that the Faculty actually wanted such a department.

Recent events had revealed the difficulties associated with establishing such a department. Only a few months earlier, in January 1961, Dr. Gordon Ball, a renowned Canadian agricultural economist with a doctorate from Iowa State, had resigned from the university. Dr. Ball had come to the University of Alberta from his professorial appointment at Iowa in the summer of 1959 to take an appointment as Professor of Farm Management in the Faculty of Agriculture. Dr. Allan Warrack expressed the belief that Dr. Ball, who had supervised Dr. Warrack's doctoral work, came to Alberta because he was promised that he would head a department of agricultural economics that was about to be established.[32] Archival records support this: in October 1960, Dr. Ball wrote to President Johns re-stating an earlier proposal for the establishment of a department of agricultural economics and attaching a letter of support from the Farmers' Union of Alberta; Dr. Ball was concerned that his proposal had not been acted upon.[33]

Other documents reveal that the Department of Economics in the Faculty of Arts resisted any expansion of teaching and research in agricultural economics in the Faculty of Agriculture. From the perspective of the Department of Economics, Agriculture could do farm management but agricultural economics belonged in the economics department. Dr. Ball met with the Head of the Department of Economics, as did Dean Bentley, but the conflict could not be resolved. Consequently, on January 20, 1961, the Executive Committee received Dr. Ball's letter of resignation.[34]

The province's agricultural community was outraged. They flooded Dr. Johns with letters questioning the goings-on at the University and wondering why the department of agricultural economics wasn't being established. Dr. Richter believes that the Faculty of Agriculture wanted jurisdiction over research and teaching in agricultural economics but did not want a department of agricultural economics. Establishing such a department would shift the balance of power in the faculty from applied natural sciences to applied social sciences, and the preponderance of power in the faculty favoured an emphasis on natural science.

Dr. Richter is probably correct in his assessment of the situation as there is no mention of establishing a department of agricultural economics in all the correspondence between Dean Bentley and President Johns subsequent to Dr. Ball's resignation. Dr. Johns supported the Faculty of Agriculture, hiring one or two specialists in agricultural economics, but his memo to Dean Bentley on July 3, 1961, acknowledges that Dr. Bentley is "having great difficulty in securing the appointment of a satisfactory senior man in the field of agricultural economics and farm management." His memo went on to say that

> the only solution to the problem of the needs of the rural communities of Alberta in agricultural economics and farm management lies in the appointment of one or two staff members in the Faculty of Agriculture who will work closely with the other departments in the Faculty and will give their attention primarily to the needs of the agricultural economy of the province.[35]

He did not advocate or suggest the establishment of a new department, and the archival files related to establishing the department of agricultural economics are silent on what happened in the six months between

Dr. Johns' memo to Dean Bentley and January 1962, when Dr. Travis Manning became head of the new department. It is possible that the gap in the records exists because the impetus for creating the department came from outside the Faculty—from Arnold—and that Arnold did his persuasion in person.

Through his network of connections with economists, established through the international bodies with which he worked and now extended through his work on the Royal Commission on Transportation, Arnold knew or knew of the leading people in the field. Whether he had met Travis Manning at one of the North American agricultural conferences that both attended is not known, but Arnold told several people, including Joseph Richter,[36] Gerald Schuler,[37] and me,[38] that he had persuaded Travis Manning to leave his position in the United States to take up the appointment at the University of Alberta. Arnold also led the informal group that subsequently became the Advisory Committee to the Department of Agricultural Economics in persuading Dr. Johns that the only way to attract the highly qualified senior people he wanted, and the university and province needed, would be to establish the new department. As has been noted, Arnold also persuaded the provincial government to provide funding for the new department.

With the establishment of the new department, the informal group became the Agricultural Economics Advisory Committee of the University of Alberta. For the first six years, Arnold chaired this group of seventeen "bona fide Alberta farmers who hold positions of leadership in agriculture."[39] The committee's constitution and its records of activities show that this was no passive group of farmers who met once a year to hear the dean and department head tell them what was going on at the university. Its constitution gave the committee the following four functions:

(a) *To ascertain, discuss, and assess the relative importance of the current economic problems of agriculture, with special emphasis on problems of economic growth and adjustment.*

(b) *To review and evaluate plans and progress reports on the agricultural economics research and teaching programs of the University.*

(c)   *To help the University obtain the moral and financial support necessary to develop agricultural economics research and teaching programs at the university*

(d)   *To consider and evaluate current and potential policies and programs affecting the well-being of agriculture.*[40]

The committee established the offices of chairman, vice-chairman, program director, and secretary. The program director was responsible for preparing "materials on research, teaching, financing, and other plans concerning the development of agricultural economics programs and shall present them, together with a progress report on the previous year's operations, for Committee to review at the Annual Meeting." The annual meeting usually lasted two days and included seminars, presentations by guest speakers, and reports prepared by the program director.

The committee did not just meet once a year and go home. It involved itself in the operation of the department by establishing a subcommittee on finance. The subcommittee established a budget for the committee, which included salaries for a research associate and a graduate assistant to help the committee with its work. The committee developed and implemented a province-wide fundraising plan, using the money it raised to support the department's research program, funding both capital and operating expenses. The committee raised money to support research, and it also decided which research proposals to support.

The committee embodied Arnold's vision of the interrelationship of academic leadership and agricultural leadership. Ideas flowed both ways, strengthening innovation. Had Arnold's style of leading not been so self-effacing, such a committee could well have been considered to be meddling in the academic program of the university. Instead, it was seen as a valuable resource, and Arnold was called on for advice. Dr. Richter recalls that, for the first ten years of the department's existence, no substantial decision was taken without the head of the department consulting Arnold.

Arnold's colleagues on the board recognized his abilities and, in early 1958, when Dr. E.P. Scarlett's term as chancellor was coming to an end, Arnold was asked if he would consider the appointment. Arnold's daughters Shirley and Margaret recall that this was a position that he wanted very much. As the titular head of the university, the chancellor presides over most of the ceremonial occasions, including convocation. The chancellor also chairs the University Senate, a body that through its diverse membership links the university with the community. At the University of Alberta in the 1950s, the chancellorship was not only a ceremonial office. The chancellor, as a member of the Executive Committee as well as of the Board of Governors, involved himself in the university's operation and governance.

Arnold was tempted. He believed strongly in the work of the university and through his connections he was confident that he would be able to obtain greater support for it. Donna had become accustomed to his public life, and accompanied him on many of his trips around Alberta; she'd learned to live with a houseful of guests by heeding his advice to "just send the laundry out." However, Arnold had no independent income. He had to earn a living by farming or by holding office, and the chancellor's office provided only an honorarium. The chancellor was expected to pay many of the costs of the office, especially entertainment costs, out of his own pocket. Arnold lacked the resources to do that, so was forced to decline the invitation.

Arnold finished his term as a member of the board in April 1962, but he kept close ties with the university. As already noted, he chaired the Advisory Committee to the Department of Agricultural Economics until the end of 1968. In the course of his work on agricultural policy through the 1960s and 1970s, he consulted with members of the Faculty of Agriculture, including Travis Manning, Alf Petersen, Joe Richter, and Michelle Veeman. He conducted occasional seminars, and assisted graduate students with their theses. When the Department of Agricultural Economics and Rural Sociology came up for review in 1975, Arnold was part of the review team. In 1992, when he was 82 years old, he participated in a review of the undergraduate curriculum in agriculture. He was an active member of the Faculty Club until the early 1990s.

But, after leaving the board, the highlight of his association with the University of Alberta came on June 2, 1965, when Chancellor Galbraith conferred the degree Doctor of Laws on him. While he was always careful

Chancellor Galbraith conferring the honorary degree Doctor of Laws, 1965.
[Platt Family Collection; University of Alberta Photographic Service, Accession # 65-692-10B]

to note that the honorary degree was not an earned degree, he was proud that the university had recognized his achievements and contributions, both as a researcher and an agricultural leader. The occasion, with its processions, pomp, and pageantry, gave Arnold much pleasure. Donna and Margaret shared in the celebration, as did some close friends, including Gerald Schuler and his wife.

Arnold took the occasion seriously, and that was reflected in his convocation address. He began by setting out what he considered to be the salient issue in higher education, the anti-intellectualism resulting from the rising conservative point of view. Demonstrating a characteristic boldness in expressing his opinion, he predicted that Alberta would lead the way in this movement. This was not the kind of leadership he wanted Alberta to demonstrate, and he provided an antidote:

> *To counter this force I would hope that we could accelerate three programmes now in existence and institute some reform of the governmental process.*
>
> *The existing programmes I have in mind are: firstly, formal education at our schools, colleges, and universities—we must continually increase both the quantity and the quality. Secondly, that we greatly increase research in the social sciences. We need to know a great deal more about this creature man in his present environment. Thirdly, that we start to put some real money and talent into continuing education for all who wish to participate. For too long we have failed to give this programme the status and the support that it warrants.*[41]

Arnold realized that in themselves these programs were not revolutionary and, even if they were implemented in schools and universities, they would likely not change the conservative ethos that he saw becoming dominant. He did not use terms such as "dominant ideology" or "marginalized people," but he understood those concepts ten or fifteen years before they had become part of academic discourse.

Demonstrating an appreciation of irony, he proceeded to turn a long-standing preoccupation with Senate reform held by certain Conservatives into a scheme for countering conservatism's influence:

> *The aim of* [Senate] *reform should be to give some official recognition to minority groups that have little chance of being elected to parliament or provincial legislatures. Those people I have in mind are young people, most business executives, many professional people and all those who express ideas that are new, different and ahead of their time.*

I would propose that on the national level we replace the Senate with such a group; that they have somewhat the same powers as at present in delaying Commons legislation and have greater powers to initiate legislation. At the provincial level I would suggest that such groups be formed.

Those appointed or elected should be between the ages of 25 and 45 at the time of their appointment or election and they should serve one 10 year term. I recognize that some older men could make perhaps even greater contributions but I think the danger of domination by older men who are out of touch with youth and the world they live in is too dangerous to allow. After all, they already dominate most of government and business now.

As to how they get there I would have some elected by university students, some by professional groups, some by business groups, some by certain national organizations, some by university faculties and a few appointed by governments at various levels.

Such a group could be expected to sponsor proper legislation to deal with the problems that beset us because of the technological revolution. It would provide a forum for new ideas and concepts of the new and greater society. It could, by information and legislation, help to relieve the fears of those whose livelihood and values appear threatened. It would help us from making the dangerous mistake [of thinking] that we can go back when, in fact, we must always go forward.

No such body was established.

Arnold knew that government would not reform unless it was under intense pressure. No single individual could provide such pressure, but the graduating students to whom he was speaking could begin to do so. Through his work in education, Arnold tried to inspire people, especially young people, to take the opportunities given them to improve the human condition. His accomplishments helped to create the conditions necessary "to make our opportunities realities"[42]. He provided the site—Goldeye—and the organization—UF&CDA (REDA). His emphasis on a broad curriculum was intended to expand the understanding of

UFA contributes to the 3AU Campaign. George Sayle, president of UFA, in the centre.
[Platt Family Collection]

students by combining the social and human elements with the scientific and technical.

In the mid-1960s, two new universities were established in Alberta: the University of Calgary and the University of Lethbridge. As a member of the University of Alberta Board of Governors, he was involved in planning the new campus in Calgary. He was also involved in discussions leading to the establishment of the University of Lethbridge, as a member of the board, as a resident of the City of Lethbridge, and as a farmer in the district; although he moved to Calgary in 1962 to take up the position of corporate secretary for the United Farmers of Alberta Cooperative, Arnold continued to farm near Lethbridge.

When the University of Calgary became an autonomous university in 1966, Arnold was appointed to its first Senate. The University of Lethbridge was created in January 1967. The rapid growth of universities in Alberta strained the capacity of the provincial government to pay for the necessary buildings, so late in 1968 the three universities decided to work together in a provincial and national fundraising drive. From 1968 to the end of 1972, Arnold was the provincial chair of the Three Alberta Universities Capital Campaign.

Arnold's connections with the three universities and with people throughout the rural areas made him a good head of the part of the campaign that was focused on the rural areas. James B. Cross of Calgary Brewing Company and the A7 Ranch near Nanton was honorary chair of the entire drive; Fred McKinnon of Triad Oil in Calgary and part of the McKinnon ranching family was local chair; and Francis Winspear of Edmonton chaired the out-of-province campaign.

As Donald Duff, the fund director, observed in his progress report a year later in October 1969, Arnold had "probably the toughest of all jobs in this campaign." Nevertheless, right from the start, Duff commended Arnold "for the fine job that is being done."[43] Arnold traveled the province, using all his abilities as an organizer as he persuaded people to chair regional committees and to work as canvassers. He explained what the universities were doing for rural Alberta.

Obstacles appeared almost immediately. Economic circumstances on the farms were once again depressed. The two new universities had no reputation and no alumni and, while the University of Alberta had both, its alumni records were completely inadequate. Arnold reported that

> the rural areas do not necessarily believe the government should pay for the full cost of education, but economic conditions have been depressing, and there has been no follow-up in the provincial AU Fund organization, with the result the organization has fallen apart.[44]

Consequently, as Duff said at that meeting, "in the rural areas the campaign is now concentrating on the prime prospects." Even the "prime prospects" encountered difficulties, as the case of the Alberta Wheat Pool shows. When the 3AU campaign leaders met with the executive of the Wheat Pool, they obtained a pledge of $500,000 over ten years, subject to delegates' approval at the annual meeting. However, at the annual meeting on December 10, 1969, the delegates defeated the resolution supporting that pledge.

Arnold's work was not limited to the rural part of the province. Pictures showing him accepting substantial cheques from Canada Brewing and the United Farmers of Alberta Cooperative confirm Helen's recollection of his having used his connections in the major cities as well as across the province to support the campaign.

In spite of the difficulties, by the time Arnold left at the end of 1972, the campaign had raised close to 60% of its targeted $25 million. Of the just under $15 million raised in the province, only $211,000 came from outside the cities of Edmonton, Calgary, and Lethbridge. That amount represented a large number of calls, though, many of which had been made by Arnold, as it took 609 donors to raise it.

Not only did Arnold help to create conditions that allowed people to get an education, he also helped to educate them. Through his deep and personal interest in so many of the young people with whom he worked, he proved himself to be a great teacher. It would be impossible to list all those for whom Arnold was a mentor.

Arnold seemed to believe in testing before teaching. As Dean Lien said, "he threw you in the deep end; it was either sink or swim." Was Paul Babey ready to take on the presidency of the FUA? Could Alex McCalla chair a session of the FUA annual meeting? Arnold may have pushed people to take on responsibilities for which they did not feel ready, but he did not do so irresponsibly. No one ever sank. He assessed people's abilities without seeming to do so, and was a good judge of their abilities.

Arnold did not tolerate failure, but he did understand and accept mistakes. And he supported those to whom he had given responsibility by publicly taking responsibility if they made mistakes. Sometimes he would suggest how a situation might have been more effectively handled, but as often as not he had already demonstrated it. His protégés did not make the same mistake twice. They seemed to resolve not to put him in such an awkward spot again and face the next challenge better prepared.

The betterment of society—that was education's purpose and Arnold's mission. Gerald Schuler summed up Arnold's commitment to his students, saying "he valued you if you were working for the betterment of society and not just for yourself. If you were one of these, then there never was a stronger mentor or a better friend."

Arnold in Geneva, 1959. [Platt Family Collection]

Not Made in Alberta

National and International

Agricultural Politics

and Policies

In January 1959, Arnold and his family moved back to Lethbridge, but that city wouldn't be Arnold's home for very long. He had agreed to go to Geneva at the end of January, as part of the Canadian delegation negotiating the Fourth International Wheat Agreement. Negotiations were expected to continue for six weeks. On his return, he would need to first spend time at the farm on the Milk River Ridge and then begin shuttling

At Geneva, 1959. Middle row: J. Wesson (Saskatchewan Wheat Pool), J. Brownlee (United Grain Growers), Arnold, and Alf Gleave (Saskatchewan Farmers' Union). [Platt Family Collection]

between Lethbridge and Ottawa as the work of the Royal Commission on Transportation began.

Hectic preparation took up what was left of the month after the move. Arnold had to acquaint himself with the background work already done and with the issues that required resolution. He did not yet have a passport. The inoculations required to enter Switzerland made him sick. On January 28, barely able to board the plane, Arnold thought about little except getting the trip over with so he could lie down. His strong constitution did not need much time to recover, though, and after a short rest he was ready for the first meeting of the Canadian delegation.

The room was full of familiar faces and good friends, the fifteen-member Canadian delegation consisting of senior federal government officials, representatives of the Canadian Wheat Board, and representatives of the producers' organizations. Jake Warren, Assistant Deputy Minister of the Department of Trade and Commerce, headed the delegation. Less than a month before the start of negotiations, he had been called on to replace Charles F. Wilson, a Canadian diplomat based in Copenhagen.

Wilson had headed the Canadian delegation that had negotiated the three previous agreements, but he had been made an alternate head of this delegation, probably because he disagreed with the Department of Trade and Commerce about whether importing countries should undertake to buy "guaranteed quantities" or a specified percentage of commercial purchases of wheat from exporting countries. The Department favoured the latter.[1]

The other Alternate Head was W. Riddel, Assistant Chief Commissioner of the Canadian Wheat Board, another person Arnold knew from his work as a member of the Wheat Board's advisory committee from 1957 on. The producer advisors included a number of Arnold's good friends from farm organizations: John E. Brownlee, President of United Grain Growers and former United Farmers of Alberta Premier of Alberta; Alf Gleave, President of the Saskatchewan Farmers' Union; and Gordon Harrold, President of the Alberta Wheat Pool. William Parker, President of Manitoba Pool Elevators, and John Wesson, President of the Saskatchewan Wheat Pool, were also there, and George Robertson of the Saskatchewan Wheat Pool was there as an observer.

Fifty-two countries were represented, forty-four with official delegations and eight as observers. The Canadian delegation, with fifteen members, was the largest, followed by the United States with eight; the United Kingdom with seven; Japan, France, and the Netherlands with six members each; and Australia and India with five each. The United States and Canada controlled the exporting group. In recognition that the United States and Canada were the main exporters of wheat, providing about 80% of worldwide wheat exports, each averaging about half of that market or 40%, 339 votes were allocated to each of the two countries. All other exporting countries—Argentina, Australia, France, Italy, Mexico, Spain, and Sweden—together had 322 votes, for a total of 1,000 votes.

Delegations from the nine countries were in Geneva to negotiate an agreement that would stabilize wheat marketing. In his report,

International Wheat Agreements, 1949–1964, A.S. Ivanov describes the conditions that resulted in the need for these agreements.[2] They can be summarized as follows. The first agreement (1949–1953) reflected an international shortage of wheat immediately after the war. Two subsequent agreements (1953–1956 and 1956–1959) were created in times of surplus, but did not fully recognize oversupply as a semi-permanent condition. As noted in Chapter 4, technology's effect on grain production was to increase supply. According to Ivanov, by 1959, the countries involved in the agreements understood the situation:

> *Supply and Demand position in the world wheat market for the last decade is characterized by continuous oversupply in exporting countries and steady demand by importing countries, considerably restricted by their purchasing power. Thus in the wheat market there exists a substantial gap between actual requirements and effective demand. The governments of some exporting countries support their internal production and sometimes subsidize maintenance of stocks and export of wheat.*[3]

The Canadian delegates' responsibilities were based on the role of the group to which they belonged. Federal officials were the chief negotiators; negotiating and accepting the agreement were the responsibilities of the federal government. The Wheat Board had to comply with whatever terms were negotiated, and its representatives were there to ensure that those terms would allow the Wheat Board to fulfill its obligations to producers. The farm leaders, who also represented the primary producers, had a central role equivalent to a veto. The producer advisors' unanimous approval was required before terms as negotiated could be cabled to the minister for approval.[4]

A briefing note for the minister, Gordon Churchill, set out Canada's objectives:

> *First, cover a major (75% or more) and expanding portion of the international commercial trade in wheat: in this context, importing member countries should undertake to obtain their import requirements under*

*the I.W.A., and the adherence of the United Kingdom to the Agreement
would be essential.*

*Second, discourage uneconomic production, particularly in tradi-
tional net importing countries, thereby allowing wheat from Canada
and other exporting member countries to compete on equal terms:
in this connection, the I.W.A. should provide for a periodic review of
national wheat policies; and*

*Thirdly, cover non-commercial and surplus disposal transactions
as a means of coordinating unilateral surplus disposal and allied
programmes: this should provide a safeguard against encroachments on
Canada's traditional commercial export outlets, while at the same time
helping to raise net consumption levels in low-income countries.*[5]

Wilson's description of the groups' responsibilities suggests that Alf
Gleave understates the role of the Canadian delegation in his remark
that they were only there to "look and listen."[6] Both Gleave and Charles
Wilson agree that much of the real work was done in private conversations. Arnold's accounts to his daughter Shirley, to Gerald Schuler, and
to me confirm that often these casual conversations were over coffee; he
also mentioned that the hospitality suites and bars played a significant
role.

The delegation was expected to host members of other delegations at
cocktail parties and dinners, but the expense allowance provided by the
government did not provide for such entertainment expenses. As Arnold
told Shirley, the Canadian delegates had to get money from the agencies
they represented or pay out of their own pockets. As Arnold no longer
represented the Farmers' Union of Alberta, he paid. For those occasions
when entertainment meant spending the evening in a nightclub, Arnold
discovered a way of saving money. He invited an older secretary with the
delegation to accompany the men. When she was with them, the bar girls
left the men alone—the girls did not come over to sit on laps or order
expensive drinks.

Arnold was always very effective in late-night socializing in people's
hotel rooms, talking until two or three in the morning over scotch. He
got to know people this way, engaging in sometimes profound and always

clear-headed discussions about issues and ideas. One big idea dominated Canadian thinking: the International Wheat Agreement should cover all trade in wheat, including non-commercial movement such as food aid. The United States—as Arnold had written in *The Organized Farmer*, as he had discussed with Diefenbaker, and as had been re-affirmed at the conference in Brookings—moved so much wheat outside of commercial trade that such shipments made up about one-third of global wheat trade.[7] Gleave's account confirms that this non-commercial trade was the main issue for Canadians:

> *The exporters' group was dominated by the United States, the rich man in the club. They were not too enthusiastic about the intervention in the market place that resulted from commodity agreements, such as the IWA, but they went along. They were at the height of their influence and power; they could afford to be generous, and they were, but the effect of their food-aid program under Public Law 480 was to cut into commercial markets as well as achieving the primary aim of feeding needy countries. J.E. Brownlee, in his 1955 statement, had condemned subsidized dumping of agricultural products in international markets; so had Henry Wise Wood in the twenties, and one of the principal objectives of the Canadians was to obtain through the wheat agreements a regular flow of product in the market place and fair prices through the negotiation.[8]*

It would be an exaggeration to suggest that those late-night discussions led to the compromise finally agreed to, but Gleave suggests that they had an effect:

> *While the hard-line bargaining went on in the endless meetings and working sessions of the professionals, there were informal discussions in casual encounters or over a cup of coffee between the Americans, Australians, and Canadians. The essential difference that emerged as between the United States and ourselves was that they had an internal price-support system that protected their producers from the instability of international market prices. The Canadians and Australians did*

not have similar guarantees from their governments, thus a satisfactory outcome of the negotiations was more important for them and for us than for the Americans.[9]

The United States and the other exporting countries finally compromised: while the Agreement would apply only to commercial transactions, they would report all transactions to the International Wheat Council. A press release at the conclusion of the negotiations, March 9, 1959, described the result:

> *The obligations of exporting countries and importing countries indi-cated above* [obligations for exporting countries to sell specified percentages of their crops within an agreed price range, and for importing countries to buy from members a specified percentage within that price range] *will relate only to transactions conducted on a commercial basis. Transactions which, as a result of govern-ment intervention, include features which did not conform with usual commercial practice will not be included. These "special transactions" are those which, although possibly falling within the price range of the Agreement, include features generally introduced by the government of the countries concerned relating, for example, to period of credit, rate of interest or convertibility of the currency payment. Whilst these "special transactions" will not be included, the Agreement provides that they shall be reported; and recorded by the International Wheat Council which will thus be able to maintain a survey of the whole international movement of wheat.*[10]

The Fourth International Wheat Agreement was stronger than previous ones because of this provision. It was also strengthened by "the abandon-ment of guaranteed quantities... and their replacement by undertakings of member importing countries to purchase a minimum percentage of their commercial requirements from member exporting countries."[11] As the Canadian briefing note indicated, the United Kingdom, whose re-entry into the Agreement was also essential to a strong agreement, was persuaded to come back in.

The United Kingdom's re-entry left only one major wheat exporter out of the Agreement: the USSR. (China did not become a significant importer until 1962.) The USSR had sent observers to the conference, and it was the conference's intention to persuade the USSR to join, so that it could become part of the next agreement.

Arnold told me that he played a part in realizing that intention. (I have been unable to verify Arnold's account, but it is consistent with his character.) According to Arnold, discussions intended to demonstrate to the USSR observers the advantages of membership in the International Wheat Council were not going well. Speeches dragged on, and heads were nodding but not in agreement, when Arnold slipped out of the afternoon session. He walked over to a nearby art gallery. One painting especially drew him into contemplation, and he sat down on a bench facing it. His reverie was interrupted by someone taking a seat beside him. At first, Arnold kept his eyes on the painting. So did the stranger beside him.

At one point, their side glances met, and they recognized each other. Sitting next to Arnold was one of the observers from the Soviet Union, probably Fedor Petrov, the Commercial Representative of the Union of Soviet Socialist Republics who was based in Switzerland. He too had decided that the afternoon could be better spent away from the session. The conversation rambled from the painting they both admired, to art, and then to farming. No doubt they noted similarities between the large collective grain farms in the USSR and the kind of farm Arnold operated on the Blood Reserve. They decided to have dinner together.

By the end of the evening, Petrov had come to realize that Canada was not the United States, that Canada's views on the international wheat trade were not those of the Americans, and that the United States did not control the International Wheat Council. Arnold would not have presented himself as anti-American or pro-socialist, for he was neither, but he would have noted some of the differences in politics and policies that distinguished the Canadian from the American interests. Arnold told me that, from that point, the attitude of the Soviet observers toward the Council changed and, when the Council convened to negotiate the Fifth International Wheat Agreement in 1962, the Soviet Union sent delegates and entered into the agreement.

The events in Geneva took only six weeks of Arnold's life, but they changed him. With his closest friends, he talked enough about having been there to suggest that the experience was a significant one for him, but I don't think that he ever fully articulated its effect. He had worked intensively with the leaders of the world's grain trade and, unlike some of the producers' representatives who were part of the group in Geneva, he discovered that he could consider himself one of them. As became obvious again in his work on the transportation commission, he grasped the technicalities and the politics of the issues.

This realization bolstered his self-confidence. The combination of demanding intellectual work and stimulating social activities invigorated his senses in ways that might not be matched even by the view of Big Chief Mountain from his farm on the Milk River Ridge. He needed both environments, and he realized that the house in Lethbridge provided neither. The irony of living a cosmopolitan professional life and a circumscribed domestic one came home to him. His experiences in Geneva predisposed him to find a way to resolve the irony, but he did not yet realize that his work on the Royal Commission on Transportation would do that.

Arnold had said that farm organization was more than feed prices and freight rates. He was about to realize too that freight rates were more than freight rates; they were the embodiment of "deep-seated regional discontents."[12] Freight rates were ostensibly the reason the Commission had been established. Almost since the construction of the railroads, controversy over freight rates had been perennial in Canada. Because railways were perceived to have a monopoly on transportation in many parts of Canada, their rates were subject to regulation, at first directly by the federal government and after 1903 by the government-appointed Board of Railway Commissioners.

Even though the Crowsnest Pass Agreement of 1897 and its modification in 1927 had enshrined in legislation Western Canadian farmers' costs of moving grain and unprocessed grain products by rail at the rates in effect in 1897, rates on moving other commodities and manufactured goods had increased periodically. Between 1946 and December 1957, thirteen rate increases had been granted. Every application for a rate increase triggered the presentation of briefs and petitions opposing such increases as inequitable or unjustified. As Darling says, "from the first post-war railway rate increase application in October 1946, rate applications and hearings were almost continuous."[13] If the federal government was not intervening in the setting of rates, it was intervening in the settlement of railway labour disputes. Freight rates and transportation policy had become a source of political conflict.

When he became prime minister in June 1957, Diefenbaker found himself in an awkward position in relation to freight rates. As a member of the opposition, he had argued that freight rates were inequitable and discriminatory and that across-the-board or "horizontal increases" exacerbated the inequity,[14] yet "in December 1957, the Board [of Transport Commissioners] authorized a final increase of 15 per cent."[15] Diefenbaker knew, and Western Canada reminded him, that his government could not allow such an increase without openly contradicting the policy that had won it support in the West. Diefenbaker twice postponed the date the increase was to come into effect.

After winning a huge majority in the election of March 1958, Diefenbaker's government rescinded the increase four days before it was to come into effect on May 3, 1958. While he may have temporarily stopped the flow of letters from the West, the issue was certain to come back. The railway workers' collective agreement had expired on January 1, 1958 and negotiations had not been concluded. The conciliation board averted a strike by recommending wage increases of 17% for the two-year agreement, and the workers accepted the recommendation; the railways said the settlement would cost them $67.8 million, and that they would need a 19% increase in freight rates to cover that cost.[16] If the railways couldn't increase rates, then they would not accept the conciliation board report and the workers would strike in November 1958.

Even with its huge majority, the Diefenbaker government realized it was vulnerable. Diefenbaker was away, and Cabinet discussed the issue for a day and a half before agreeing to the Board of Transport Commissioner's decision to allow railways to increase rates by 17%. The leader of the opposition, Lester Pearson, let it be known that he opposed the increase, and proposed a direct federal government subsidy to the railways instead.[17] Delay was essential—the government could not be seen to be taking direction from the opposition and it could not accept the recommendation of the Board. Another royal commission might be necessary even though the Turgeon Commission (1948–1950) had investigated the issues. In November 1958, Arnold received a call, asking if he would consider accepting appointment as a commissioner.

Arnold was a likely choice. He had demonstrated leadership on farm issues in the many presentations he had made in Ottawa, he was highly regarded as president of the Farmers' Union of Alberta, and he was known to be a rational pragmatist. On the subject of freight rates, he had written to Diefenbaker, asking that he postpone indefinitely the increases approved by the Board of Transport Commissioners on December 27, 1957 and opposing the increase of November 1958,[18] but without using the over-heated rhetoric often part of such presentations.

Arnold was seen to be representing the views of the FUA members, and those views were not all that different from Diefenbaker's. Furthermore, Arnold clearly was a person of integrity; he would resign as president and would not hold any other office in the Farmers' Union, so that he could be seen to be disinterested. He would resign effective January 1, 1959, even though the commission would not be officially appointed until May 1959.

Arnold was not known to be an expert on transportation, which meant he would bring a fresh perspective to the discussion. On a commission of seven members, only René Gobeil, a forestry engineer in Quebec, and Arnold had had no former involvement in freight rate hearings. The chair, Charles McTague, was a former Justice of the Ontario Supreme Court; Herbert Anscombe had been British Columbia's Minister of Finance; Howard Mann of the Maritimes was secretary of the Maritime Transport Commission; Murdoch MacPherson of Regina had frequently represented the Province of Saskatchewan at freight rate hearings; Archibald Balch was "chief agent and legislative representative of the Brotherhood of Railway Trainmen and member of the Canadian Labour Relations Board."[19]

Arnold was also unaffiliated politically, unlike four of the other Commissioners, who were Conservatives, and his appointment could be used to counter the charge that the commission would recommend whatever the prime minister wanted. Don Thomson of the *Lethbridge Herald* spoke for many in Western Canada when he wrote that this "farmer's farmer, ...this well-respected farm leader will be an able, understanding representative of the farming community of Canada on this new commission."[20]

The commission's terms of reference reflected the view that the freight rate structure was inequitable and discriminatory, and that the rate structure prevented the development of industries appropriate to local resources outside of central Canada. The terms acknowledged that railways operated under obligations and limitations "imposed upon railways by law for reasons of public policy,"[21] and that these might place a burden upon railways that could be more equitably distributed. The commission was to look at ways in which the railways might operate more economically and efficiently; in examining the issue of determining costs and revenues, it was to consider what assets and earnings the railway companies had in businesses and investments other than railways and how these should be taken into account in establishing freight rates.

During the May parliamentary debate, when the commission was appointed, Diefenbaker made it clear that the statutory rates for moving Western Canadian grain to export (the Crow rates established by the Crowsnest Pass Agreement) were to be left unchanged.[22] Arnold was rational and logical in economic matters and agnostic in religion, but he understood people's need for the comfort of belief. As he prepared for the first meeting of the commission in Ottawa on July 23, 1959, he read the Turgeon Commission report and reviewed the various provincial briefs on transportation that had come his way during his time as president of the FUA. The main points making up conventional wisdom in the West were:

(1)   *Railway freight rates reflect monopoly conditions such that the West must pay the freight both ways.*

(2)   *The Central Provinces benefit from competitive conditions that enable them to escape from the burden of increases in freight rates.*

(3)   *There are still basic differences in rate levels that are accentuated by the application of horizontal percentage increases.*

(4)   *As a result the burden of increases in freight rates falls entirely on the outer regions of the country.*

(5)   *Horizontal percentage increases, even on equitable base rates, are discriminatory to the regions because they widen the actual differences in rates with distance.*

(6)   *Finally, increases are bad in themselves since regional producers and consumers cannot afford to pay higher rates.*[23]

For Arnold, the question was whether these points were articles of faith, facts, or politically motivated fabrications. Whatever the commission's work would uncover, Arnold was clear about one thing: he would see to it that farmers got the best possible deal.

The issue of the Crow rates tested that resolve almost immediately. Western Canadians had been relieved that Diefenbaker had excluded those rates from the commission's consideration, but that relief did not last long after the first meeting of the commission. At its pre-hearing conference, the commission announced that it would consider the Crow rates in its investigation. According to Darling, this decision was taken in spite of the protests of "Western representatives."[24]

Joseph Richter's account supports the claim that Arnold did not want the commission to open up the issue.[25] This was not because Arnold thought the Crow rates were good for agriculture or the general economy—he did not. Nor did he think that freight rates in Canada could be considered without considering the Crow rates. He believed that, if the commission opened up the Crow rates issue, it would be forced into an either/or position. Given his own and the other commissioners' predilection for a market-driven economy, he feared that in a choice between keeping or abolishing the Crow rate, they would have no alternative but to recommend abolishment.

Abolishment without some guarantee of compensation would create a major disruption in Western agriculture. Because he could not obtain assurance of adequate compensation from government—for reasons that will come clear—Arnold argued for keeping the Crow rates. By the time the commission wrote its report, Arnold would find a subtly nuanced way of preparing the way for the abolishment of the Crow rates—but in July 1959 this was not foreseeable.

The commission planned an extensive program of research and public hearings. The chair, Charles McTague, took seriously the injunction in the Order-in-Council "that the Commissioners report to the Governor in Council with all reasonable dispatch" and directed staff to schedule public hearings beginning in September 1959. Those hearings were to invite representations from those interested in all transportation issues, not just in railway transportation issues, the commissioners having engaged in several exchanges with the prime minister about whether the commission was the Royal Commission on Transportation or on Railway Transportation. The prime minister favoured the more restrictive name but the commissioners prevailed.

Consequently, the commission heard 141 submissions in its 134 days of hearings, resulting in 22,666 pages of evidence.[26] Shortly after the hearings began in the fall of 1959, Chairman McTague became ill and was forced to resign. Murdoch MacPherson was appointed chair in December 1959. As no commissioner was appointed to replace McTague, and with one of the Western Canadian members taking on the responsibilities of chair, Arnold was left as the main voice of the West outside of British Columbia. The added duties required him to take an apartment at the Savoy on Slater Street in Ottawa late that fall, an unusual move for a member of a royal commission other than the chair.

Arnold made the move partly because he was doing what he had always done: immersing himself in his work. The commission's research program involved the country's leading economists as well as some in the United States and Great Britain. Arnold was in contact with the who's who of Canadian business, government, and academe. He met with academics and university leaders across the country; he met with leaders of the entire range of industries and organizations across the country, with premiers and political leaders from almost all the provinces, both in formal hearings and in more private lunches, dinners, and hotel-room discussion sessions. He gained the most current knowledge available in transportation economics and in the location of economic activity, usually from the people who were creating it.

This was the life Arnold loved, being challenged, learning on the run, and proving himself up to it. But he was not simply indulging his passion for issues and ideas; he had been asked to take on more responsibility. Unbeknownst to all but the inner group associated with the commission, the commission's second chair, Murdoch MacPherson, was beginning to suffer from a mysterious ailment, which interfered with his balance and caused him to have slight difficulty "with articulation of speech." As he wrote to Diefenbaker in July 1960, MacPherson had been suffering from this condition for several months.[27] The administrative secretary to the commission, Helen Roney (later Helen Platt)[28] recalls that Arnold was asked to come to Ottawa to take on some of MacPherson's responsibilities and that MacPherson's ailment was not to become public knowledge. Major Norman LaFrance, administrative head of the commission, made an office available to him. Arnold became a regular visitor to the commission's administrative offices and a significant presence in meetings across the country.

Helen recalls her first encounter with the "Commissioner from the West." She returned to the office from lunch to find the clerk who had stayed in the office almost in tears. A sandpaper-voiced, somewhat rotund little man was turning the air blue with pipe smoke and chastisements, as he berated her for her incompetence in taking dictation. Arnold hated to write in longhand, his writing being almost indecipherable and his confusion over the finer points of punctuation often blocking the flow of his thoughts. But he was a good orator and could speak in fully formed paragraphs. Feeling the pressures of the commission's voluminous correspondence, he had asked for a dictating machine, but none was available. Such devices were not then common in the public service.

Perhaps Arnold assumed that the machine was not available because of some make-work plot in which the union of public employees and the public service commission were co-conspirators and now the inefficiency was being compounded by the shortcomings of his secretary who could not take dictation. What he did not know was that the kind-hearted Helen had just hired the young woman to help her get back on her feet after she had fallen into poor circumstances in Montreal. Helen had not met Arnold, but she knew who he was. That did not stop her from setting him straight about how he was to treat staff! Arnold would later say that he fell in love with Helen at that moment—although he did not broach the subject with her until the commission's concluding celebration almost two years later.

"Nobody with a good car needs to be justified" as Flannery O'Connor has Hazel Motes say in *Wise Blood*.[29] That winter (1960) in Ottawa, Arnold decided that, as a commissioner on transportation, he needed either justification or a good car. While in Geneva, he'd come to appreciate Mercedes-Benz cars, the connoisseur of engineering and design in him liking their understated luxury while the farmer appreciated the practicality, longevity, and economy of the diesel engine. He bought a Mercedes 180D. While the Mercedes was a modern diesel car, Canada was not quite ready for it. One needed a long extension cord for the block heater and had to make sure it was plugged in before settling down for a winter evening's socializing. Arnold also appreciated the economy of tax-free fuel, and relished the irony of a commissioner of transportation using it. It reminded him of his experience in the 1930s, when he had bought lower-taxed liquor in Hull and sold it in Ottawa. As diesel fuel stations were not common in downtown Ottawa, on at least one occasion, Arnold filled the Mercedes' fuel tank with untaxed home heating fuel borrowed from nearby tanks.

The fall of 1959 and the winter of 1960 did not give Arnold much time for such diversions, however. In spite of McTague's ill health, the commission held hearings in Montreal and Quebec City, the four Maritime provinces, and Ottawa before Christmas. Under MacPherson's chairmanship in February and March, the commission then heard presentations throughout Western Canada. Two big issues dominated: Crow rates and branch lines. On the Crow rates, "more than half of the participants took advantage of this first formal opportunity to air their views."[30]

Not surprisingly, opinion divided along regional and occupational lines. On the Prairies both provincial governments and agricultural organizations were opposed to any interference with the grain rates, and there was often bitter resentment that the Commission was even listening to arguments of the subject. Had not the Prime Minister promised that their "charter" would remain? Two threads pervaded much of the Western arguments. First there was a genuine opinion that the Crow's Nest rates were remunerative, and did not place any additional burden on other shippers. Second, there was a general opposition to subsidies, in particular any subsidy that might be construed as a subsidy to the Western grain farmer.

In British Columbia, Ontario, and Quebec, on the other hand, much of the blame for the whole freight problem was laid at the doorstep of the grain rates.[31]

On the matter of branch lines, opinion was even more divided, as not even the Western Canadian provinces could come to an agreement. Manitoba took the position that "passenger deficits, uneconomical branch lines and commuter revenues" were just as responsible as the Crow rates in creating freight-rate inequity."[32]

To assess these competing claims, the commission needed to conduct independent research, especially on the subject of costs. The railways had started to use multiple regression analysis to show costs associated with the movement of grain, and "day after day of hearings were devoted to detailed examination and cross-examination of a parade of costing experts."[33] Arnold was one of the few commissioners who could and would involve himself on such a technical level as he drew on his work in mathematics and statistics to probe the methods behind the assertions. He encouraged the commission to employ experts who understood the costing methods, with the result that the commission published, in the third volume of its report, four studies of costing that provided the mathematical basis for implementing the changes in policy that they recommended. In Darling's view, this work constitutes one of the commission's most significant contributions: "The Commission's most important contribution to the Crow's Nest debate lay not in airing the rhetoric, but in examining the costs of the export grain traffic."[34]

Arnold would need to deal directly with Diefenbaker before the grain transportation study was complete but, before returning to Ottawa in the spring of 1960, he had to tend to his farm. Herb Chester and Arnold had given up the lease on 1,280 acres of land on the Blood Reserve at the end of the 1959 crop year, concentrating their energy on the 640 acres of land they owned and on other land they rented on the Milk River Ridge, southwest of Lethbridge. There they grew "High Quality Cereal and Forage Seeds." The Platt Farms Limited letterhead declared

We Specialize in
Thatcher Wheat, Cumino Sweet Clover,
Pubescent Wheat Grass, Nordan crested wheat, Merion Blue grass,
Climax Timothy, Creeping red fescue, Frontier Reed Canary.

The letterhead concluded with the Biblical injunction, "As you sow so shall you reap." Arnold had a great sense of irony; he'd been around farming for too many years to actually believe in such direct causality. But he did the seeding and then went back to Ottawa.

There he discovered that the consultants who had been engaged to do the study on the costs of transporting grain had run up against the most formidable political problem in the country: the prime minister. Diefenbaker would not allow the commission to hire the Economic Research Corporation of Montreal to do the study. Diefenbaker was likely displeased that the commission was examining the Crow rate against his directive that they not do so. Consequently, he was paying close attention to the commission's activities, including the details of who it hired to conduct studies and prepare technical reports.

Ever on the alert for the Opposition Liberal's plots, Diefenbaker suspected that the Economic Research Corporation was a front for the machinations of his political enemies.[35] The Economic Research Corporation had been engaged in November 1959 to conduct the study on costs, but, in late March or early April, Diefenbaker had forbidden the Treasury Board to pay any invoices it submitted—even though payment was to come out of funds that the commission had been authorized to use. Memos between Fred Anderson, Research Director of the Commission, and R.B. Bryce, Clerk of the Privy Council, and two letters from MacPherson to Diefenbaker, one on April 29, 1960, and another on

June 16, 1960, had failed to persuade Diefenbaker to authorize payment. He would authorize payment only to Dr. D.E. Armstrong, one of the principals of the Economic Research Corporation, but the commission also needed the work of the other three partners, Beach, Beckett, and Hay. D.E. Hay was the specialist on the costs of moving grain. As MacPherson pointed out in his June 16 letter to Diefenbaker, it had been necessary "to secure quickly the help of an expert group in this complicated field of costing that would have an independent, unbiased outlook and which had not been retained by any other party appearing before us."[36] The letter received no response.

MacPherson had to go into the hospital for tests, and Arnold decided to call on Diefenbaker. As Arnold told me the story, he walked into Diefenbaker's office unannounced, much as he had just after Diefenbaker had become prime minister in the summer of 1957. When Arnold asked what could be done about paying the consultants, Diefenbaker somewhat gleefully showed Arnold the cheque that had stopped at his desk. He was not about to pay any Liberals, he declared. Aside from assuring Diefenbaker that the consultants were not members of the Liberal party and reiterating that they were the people best qualified to do the work, Arnold did not tell me exactly how he persuaded Diefenbaker to release the cheque. It's quite possible that he argued that the Liberals wanted the Crow rate abolished, and that the only way to deal with the Liberals was to have the facts about the costs of moving grain and that was what the study would determine.

Arnold would have been correct in stating that the Liberals were arguing in favour of abolishing the Crow rate. Dr. Joseph Richter of the University of British Columbia had been hired by Arthur Laing, former Liberal cabinet minister and Member of Parliament for Vancouver, to go to Ottawa to try to persuade the commissioners to apply free market principles in assessing the issues. Dr. Richter told me that he had spent many hours in conversation with Arnold, trying unsuccessfully to persuade him to support the abolishment of the Crow rate.

Arnold knew that for the Conservative government to even think about abolishing the Crow rate would mean its defeat in Western Canada; for the commission to suggest that the Conservative government recommend its abolishment would discredit the commission with the government; and for him to be seen to support a study that favoured abolishment would discredit him with Diefenbaker. So, while Arnold argued that he supported the Crow rates, he did so because it was strategically necessary at the time. In fact, he believed that the Crow rates eventually would have to go—and he argued persuasively and successfully in support of the research that would ultimately lead to their abolishment in 1995.

This meeting of Arnold's with Diefenbaker was a precursor to a series of meetings in the fall of 1960 and the winter of 1961, as Arnold assumed more of the responsibilities of the commission chair. The government and Diefenbaker were anxious to receive the commission's report. Howard Darling explains the reasons for urgency:

After a year of hearings, events conspired to put the Commission in a position where it had to act boldly. The existing situation of the rate freeze could not continue indefinitely. Yet the scale of subsidization was such that it could be substantially reduced within a short time without requiring massive freight rate increases, which, given the freeze, would have then been economically and politically infeasible. The pressure on rates and subsidies was building as the Commission deliberated. The non-operating workers' contract was due to terminate in December 1960. The union demanded an increase of 25 cents per hour, which the railways said would cost $60 million. A conciliation board recommended a 14 cent increase, but the railways said a rate increase would be necessary. The union announced its intention to strike. The strike was prohibited until after May, 1961.[37]

The government wanted a report before May 1961, and it did not seem that MacPherson's health would allow him to fulfill his role as the chair. Arnold was asked to take over the writing of the report, but to do so unofficially. MacPherson's illness was not to be disclosed, as it was believed that MacPherson's experience with the issues and his record of representing the Province of Saskatchewan at hearings about freight rates was needed to ensure the report's credibility. These arrangements followed from a confidential memorandum from Robert Bryce, Clerk of the Privy

Council, to Diefenbaker on January 17, 1961. The memo is worth quoting
in full, because it sums up the direction that the commission's report was
likely to take, it identifies Arnold as the person with whom the prime
minister should speak about the commission's work, and it notes the
need for the commission to report in time for the spring session of parliament to deal with the rates and the impending strike:

> *Memorandum for the Prime Minister*
> *Re: Royal Commission on Transportation*
>> *In view of Manning's [Ernest Manning, Premier of Alberta] letter
>> to you urging that you give this Royal Commission more time to
>> report, I thought I had better find out where things stood. Therefore I
>> arranged to lunch today with the Secretary, Mr. Anderson of Regina.
>> He spoke to me very frankly about the problems and prospects of the
>> Commission.*
>>
>> *Anderson says that he thinks the Commissioners intend to put
>> in some kind of interim report by March 31st as you requested. This
>> would be followed later, possibly in the fall, with a final report that
>> would give the arguments, the details and analysis on which their
>> main conclusion was based, as well as a great deal of useful subsid-
>> iary information and recommendations. He is assuming that the
>> interim report will meet your requirements in regard to dealing with
>> the strike, as well as deciding about the subsidy which is to terminate
>> in April under the present legislation.*
>>
>> *In regard to substance, I did not ask Anderson point-blank what
>> they were going to recommend, but he told me enough that I got some
>> sort of picture which I thought it would be well that you have now but
>> I would not wish you to attribute it to him.*
>>
>> *The Commission are not likely to find any magic formula for equi-
>> table freight rates. They have not found one yet and their staff does
>> not see where it is going to come from. On the other hand, Anderson
>> feels that the railways could increase all their freight rates by an
>> average of about 5%, including the competitive rates and agreed
>> charges, without losing more traffic to the trucks. They have done a
>> lot of study of the costs of trucking and the nature of the competition*

between the railways and trucks and this will be a highlight of their main report. They seem to have concluded that the main problems of the railways are an over-expansion of their plant, both in total and in its distribution, plus a lack of modern competitive thinking in the setting of rates.

I got the impression that the main recommendation of the Commission would be that the whole railway system of Canada will have to be rationalized, streamlined and reduced over the next ten, fifteen or twenty years. In the course of doing this, its costs should be substantially reduced. Its freight rates (quite apart from the Crow rates) can and should be made more competitive, particularly when it concentrates on those services which it can provide economi-cally—i.e. the carrying of full-train loads of freight between centres where there is a good deal of freight to move, and from which it can then be distributed by truck. Pending this long-term streamlining of the railways, the Commission will probably recommend a substantial interim subsidy on a gradually reducing scale to meet operating costs until such time as the streamlining is completed and to be paid on condition that the streamlining goes forward.

The interim report would probably convey this main conclusion of the Commission and recommend that the interim subsidy be commenced this year and the basic principle behind the programme be accepted by the Government.

In regard to specifically Prairie problems, I got the impression that the Commission are apt to recommend that the streamlining in plant take place out there as well as elsewhere and that it will involve having a great deal less by way of elevator points in the long run than there are now. This will involve more hauling of grain by truck to elevators but Anderson claims that is now economic and sensible up to as much as forty miles. He says that this concentration of elevator points will also fit in with the current ideas of the Wheat Pools and the various elevator companies.

In regard to the Maritimes, he is urging on the Commission that they should not try to advise the Government as to the proper rate for the Maritime freight rates subsidy, as this is not designed to meet the *railway problem but rather to meet the Maritime problem with which they have not been concerned. On the other hand, the Commissioners feel that some recommendations concerning the Maritime Freight Rates Act will be expected, even though they recognize the logic of the situation. Anderson feels that logically the subsidy should be extended to trucking if it is really going to benefit the Maritimes now in the way it was intended.*

Anderson spoke very highly of Platt, the Commissioner from Lethbridge. He feels that Platt is much better aware now of the problem and the possible solutions and where the Commission really stands than is the Chairman, who is of course not well, or the other commissioners who do not have the background to understand many of the highly technical arguments that have been thrown at them from all sides. It might be useful to find some occasion to have a talk with Platt, perhaps inviting the Chairman to bring him along next week when he will be the only Commissioner there in the office with MacPherson.

I am not quite sure what kind of reply should be made to Manning in the light of what is set forth above. Anderson said that he would expect that a letter from Douglas [T.C. Douglas, Premier of Saskatchewan] would arrive at any moment and possibly one from Roblin [Duff Roblin, Premier of Manitoba] as well.

I would be inclined to write saying that you are aware of the problem confronting the Commission and the importance of their task but think it should be feasible for them to make at least an interim report by April that would enable Parliament to deal at this session with those things which will have to be dealt with at this session.
R.B.B.[38]

So began a series of meetings between Arnold and Diefenbaker, during which they discussed the substance of the interim report that was to be published by the end of March. They disagreed about two main points: the matter of "inequity" in freight rates, and the matter of branch lines in Western Canada. For years Diefenbaker had been declaring, in Parliament and in speeches across the country, that railway freight rates were inequitable and that this inequity was responsible for regional disparities and the country's lack of unity.[39] He recognized the political value of a report that would confirm that view.

What Bryce had suggested, Arnold confirmed. The commission could find no evidence of such inequity. Shutting down branch lines and elevators in Western Canada would cause serious political difficulties for the Conservatives. If the case for their retention could not be made on economic grounds, then surely the commission could recommend that they be retained for reasons of social and national policy. Arnold did not think that it was within the commission's terms of reference to make recommendations about social policy. Moreover, he was not as much concerned with short-term political requirements—although he was realistic about needing to consider them—as he was about addressing the fundamental problems of transportation. As he wrote in the *Report*, "we wished, in other words, to look for long-term solutions rather than for palliatives which would simply gloss over the problem on a short-term basis."[40]

That the meetings did not go well can be attributed almost as much to the differences in the characters of the two men as to their differences on the main issues. Diefenbaker was a morning person, usually arranging to meet with Arnold around 8:00 a.m. Arnold did not like meetings at such "ungodly" hours. Diefenbaker drank milk at those meetings while Arnold wanted strong black coffee. Shirley (Platt) Deneka also remembers Arnold talking about Diefenbaker's deafness. Diefenbaker did not want to acknowledge the problem, but often misunderstood what Arnold was trying to say. Maybe it was Diefenbaker's deafness that made those conversations sound like shouting matches, but that is not likely. Howard Darling relates that "the Prime Minister is reported to have stormed privately with the Commissioners" about the Crow rates[41] and, according to Shirley's and Helen's recollections, he "stormed privately" with Arnold over these and other politically sensitive matters.

Arnold's unwillingness to write the report that the prime minister wanted probably cost him an appointment to the Senate. Helen Platt recalls that it was understood that, when the commission's work was done, Arnold would be appointed to the Senate. Unlike the other commissioners, Arnold did not have a position at home to return to. His years as president of the Farmers' Union, and now his responsibilities as unofficial acting chair of the commission, had prevented him from putting his full attention to farming and his farm income had thus been restricted. A Senate appointment would allow him to continue in public service and would provide sufficient income. Helen and Arnold talked about where in Ottawa they would rent an apartment.[42] However, when the final volume of the commission's report was published, Arnold was not appointed to the Senate. Helen believes that Diefenbaker had blocked it.

Arnold likely came to consider the report's ultimate significance to be an even better reward than the Senate, but the realization of its significance was slow in coming. Darling writes:

> *Fortunately, the Commission was equal to the task, and thus has come to occupy a permanent and conspicuous place in Canadian transportation policy. It came at a point in time when the long dominant ideology had become bankrupt. In a few short pages of the first volume of its report, it swept them away and forever shifted emphasis to what would be a new ideology—competition. Railway deficits were found to be due to the collective burdens of uneconomic services and unremunerative rates, which could no longer be covered by all shippers in a competitive transportation environment.[43]*

The commission changed the framework for policy from a regulatory one, which was suitable when railways had a monopoly on transportation, to one that stimulated competition. In Jerry Fast's assessment, this change resulted in greater economic efficiency in transportation. It was the first Canadian report on transportation to argue that "economic efficiency in the national transportation system should be the sole objective of national transportation policy."[44] The commission separated national policy from national transportation policy, arguing that its job was to recommend policies that would result in goods and people being moved as efficiently as possible.[45] If such efficiency resulted in unwanted social changes that neither the government nor the people liked, then the government and people could address those changes through other means such as direct subsidy. On the matter of keeping branch lines and elevators going so that communities could survive, for example, the commission thought that keeping the lines and elevators open would not have the intended effect, saying:

> *Sober realism suggests, however, that it would be more correct to say that in most instances where the railway finds it necessary to reduce service or abandon a line, the communities have deserted the railway—making use of it only as a standby service when it is temporarily inconvenient to move goods and people by alternate methods.*[46]

Consistent with Arnold's view that, when technology driven change resulted in greater efficiency, it was better to accommodate the change than to resist it, the commission urged the government to ameliorate the consequences of such change by helping communities and people adapt.[47] Regarding the Crow rates, the commission decided that, with the information on the costs of moving grain to export that it had provided, the government now had a factual basis for deciding how much more than the money provided by those rates the railway companies needed. Said the commission's report:

> *We will recommend that losses associated with the obligation to carry grain and grain products to export positions at a rate set by statute, which must of necessity now be recovered from other shippers, should in future be borne by the Parliament of Canada, who in its wisdom sets the statutory rate. In this way Parliament remains the sole judge of whether or not the grain industry can bear rates higher than it presently bears for its movement to export positions.*[48]

Arnold had no doubt that governments would quickly tire of such a politicized process and would find a way out of the statutory obligation. They did tire quickly, but they would not find their way out of the obligation until 1995, a year before Arnold's death.

Not surprisingly, Diefenbaker's government tried to ignore the commission's reports. When the last volume was tabled in the House of Commons, "in the spring of 1962, just before the general elections returned a minority Conservative government, the Minister of Transport again warned the House not to expect early action."[49] In 1967, however, the Liberal government of Lester Pearson made the commission's work the basis for the new National Transportation Act. Several further studies, by the Hall Commission (1977), by the Snavely Commission (1977), and by Clay Gilson (1982), were undertaken before recommendations on branch lines were fully implemented and the Crow rate finally abolished.

Arnold's experiences in Geneva and on the royal commission gave him the opportunity to extend his influence, and they also extended his education. Because issues related to export markets and transportation affect almost all issues of public policy and politics in Canada, Arnold's understanding of the Canadian character grew broader and deeper during this time. Perhaps even more significantly, Arnold came to know many people in positions of power and influence and, because the nature of his influence depended so much on his personal relationships, these connections set the course for much of what he subsequently achieved.

These experiences also educated Arnold's heart. Of the relationships he established during this time, none was more important in changing the course of his life than the one with Helen Roney. It led to his decision to divorce Donna, a decision made difficult by their long years together and complicated by a law that made divorce a judicial process. Although those who knew Arnold and Donna well realized that the marriage had long been troubled, Arnold having told Jim Lore on one occasion in the 1950s that some men, himself included, owed their accomplishments to unhappy marriages, its dissolution in late 1966 surprised Donna and resulted in considerable bitterness. But Arnold's marriage to Helen in 1967 demonstrated that a joy-filled personal life was no bar to further achievement in public life.

The Freedom to
Serve Agriculture

Arnold Platt and the

United Farmers of

Alberta

It was August 1961, and George Church, President of the United Farmers of Alberta Cooperative, was dying. Farming, farmers, and farm organization had been his life. He was a man of vision who got things done. Seeing that farming was becoming as much about business as it was about politics, he led the transformation of the United Farmers of Alberta from a farm organization to a farm supply cooperative.

UFA Co-op Meeting, Edmonton, 1957. George Church, centre, with Arnold to his right.
[UFA Collection, Lethbridge]

Arnold described him as a leader who could get people to behave sensibly and decently. Church had demonstrated that ability at its self-effacing best when, in 1948, as president of the United Farmers of Alberta, he led the annual convention to adopt a resolution initiating amalgamation with the Alberta Farmers' Union. Realizing that the amalgamation's success required a leader from the Farmers' Union, he supported Carl Stimpfle as the first president of the new Farmers' Union of Alberta.

Arnold and George Church had become very close, Church having been a mentor to Arnold from the time that Arnold became involved in farm organization in 1951. When Arnold had an occasion to be in Calgary that August, he called on George Church in the hospital. When Arnold left that hospital room, he was more distraught than Helen recalls seeing him before or since.

But he also left that room with a new job. George Church wanted Arnold to come back to Alberta to help farmers and farm organizations work through the changes that were revolutionizing agriculture. If Arnold wasn't going to be made a senator in Ottawa, then maybe Arnold could become a one-person agricultural senate in Alberta. UFA would give him a seat.

George Church would create a new position at UFA: Executive Secretary. This position would require Arnold to take on responsibilities similar to those of the corporate secretary in a business established under the Companies Act. He would be responsible for ensuring that UFA fulfilled its obligations to members and to government as set out in its governing legislation, the *United Farmers of Alberta Co-operative Limited Act*, also known as the U.F.A. Act. He would organize the annual meeting, produce the annual report, oversee the election of delegates and directors, revise bylaws, and adjust district boundaries as necessary. So that Arnold could influence agricultural policy, he would also be put in charge of public relations. Most importantly, Arnold would be at UFA to advise the next president and he would be in Alberta as agriculture's *eminence grise*.

The prospect appealed to Arnold for a number of reasons—he had decided to separate from Donna, who would stay in Lethbridge. UFA's head office was in Calgary, and he would be able to get to his farm on the Milk River Ridge on weekends. He could continue his involvement with Goldeye, with the Farmers' Union and Cooperative Development Association, and the work in agricultural economics at the University of Alberta. Finally, this arrangement would give him a base from which he could work for the benefit of farmers and agriculture. It gave Arnold the right environment to work out some of his emerging hypotheses about farming as a business. Just as his going into large-scale agriculture in 1951 had been an experiment in applying an industrial model to farming, so would this be an experiment in applying a business model. He agreed to take the job for six months, starting in September 1961. He would stay for more than eleven years.

"Arnold did not really like cooperatives," Gerald Schuler remarked as he reflected on Arnold's time at UFA. Arnold saw UFA as a farm supply business, not as an ideologically driven model of operation that should replace private industry. As a business, it should provide products of good quality at good value and with good service. Being a member of UFA

UFA Board of Directors and board officers, 1962. [UFA Collection, Lethbridge]

meant being a shareholder as well as a patron. Dividends reflected the company's profitability.

The profitability of the farm supply business depended on careful market analysis. Arnold knew that, as farms were consolidated, the location of economic activity would also be consolidated. His studies in transportation had shown that highways and trucks were changing the nature of grain transportation. The village grain elevators at eight-mile intervals along a labyrinth of railway branch lines were not going to survive, and neither were the farm supply businesses clustered around those elevators. Arnold advocated that the UFA move away from local agencies and establish large farm supply centres in major towns throughout Alberta. There would be conflict with those who saw the UFA local as part of the social structure necessary for maintaining the values of the family farm; it was unavoidable.

In November 1972 as Arnold was preparing to leave UFA, he would allude to that conflict in a memo to UFA's general manager, Bill McCartney:

I want to enlarge on what I do in, what can loosely be called economic analysis, market research, etc. Not to make excuses, but in the hope that it may be helpful to you in assessing this field and what might be done.

Historically, I started playing around with sales figures the first week I was here, because I have an inherent interest in such matters and my work on transportation had taught me the value of sound management. However, I did not do anything seriously about this field until you became General Manager. Quite frankly, it was my intention to leave the Company because I knew that Wilf [Hoppins] and I would sooner or later come to the parting of the ways. [Wilf Hoppins died on December 30, 1963; Bill McCartney was appointed general manager in January 1964.]

With your appointment as Manager, my attitude changed and I decided to try and make a serious effort to see if I could be helpful in this field. In all honesty, I have reservations as to whether or not my employment in this area has paid off. I do feel, that with the background we now have, that it could pay off in the future. Some of the difficulties, or excuses were and are:

1. *I was not experienced in merchandising or marketing research and my statistical training was in a different field. I had and have a lot of learning to do.*

2. *It took time to build up a library of published material.*

3. *It took a lot of time to find doors and get them opened to obtain unpublished and other data that proved useful to us.*

4. *I suppose any part time job is frustrating, but it is particularly so in this type of work. What you are really doing is examining masses of data to see if you can find trends, relationships, etc. that will be useful to operating managers. By necessity, you are carrying a lot of things in your head. When you are interrupted to tend to other parts of your duties, it takes time when you get back to reorient yourself and proceed with what you had to leave.*

5. *Some of the work I have done could have been more useful. For example, one study showed areas where sales were below potential and the farmers there could be served from existing*

outlets. Here is what happened. Smith [Ward Smith, Manager of the Farm Supply Division] *was interested, and asked me to talk to his managers. I did, and they were interested, and in fact I spent the greater part of an evening with some of them and that was that. What should have happened—was that Smith should have said, here is one area that looks like something could be done. You go and talk to the manager concerned, convince him, and you two bring me a plan of action, and if I approve, I want you to evaluate what happens. If we had done this, these things would have happened—*

a.   *We could have increased sales, and I and others would have known that it was a good project.*

or

b.   *We couldn't have increased sales, and I and others would have known that somehow a mistake had been made, either in the original study or in our plan of action.*

      A study is not complete until it has been tried out and evaluated. Part of this is hind-sight on my part, and part is, that you can't do all the things you should do, when you have a number of other responsibilities.[1]

Arnold understated the impact that his market analysis had on UFA after Bill McCartney became general manager. Dean Lien, whom Arnold hired in 1965 to work in Information Services at UFA, credits Arnold with identifying the locations for the new farm supply centres. In 1964, centres opened in Vermillion, Camrose, and Grimshaw, followed by more in Hanna and Stettler in 1965 and in Westlock and Provost in 1966. Sales figures reflected the wisdom of those decisions. Sales almost doubled between 1961 and 1967, rising from $14.5 million to over $25 million.[2]

People at the UFA office in Calgary often wondered where Arnold was and what he might be doing. Arnold's market research included driving around the main streets and the back roads of the province, observing what was happening. It also included using the latest data and the newest tools for analysing them. Arnold spent considerable time acquainting himself with new computer technology as it was installed at UFA.[3] Perhaps most importantly, when he took action on his market research findings, he became involved in shaping the very trends that he was identifying.

The tide of change in agriculture during the 1950s and 1960s seemed unstoppable. Papers and speeches on the subject reiterated the familiar themes. Technology was changing farming. Farms were generally becoming larger and more specialized, although some more specialized seed or livestock operations operated on a smaller land base than did mixed farms. Supply management of dairy and poultry products was introduced. When associated quotas required a larger-scale operation than was feasible in mixed farming, chemical fertilizers replaced animal manure. Effective herbicides and pesticides were developed, increasing productivity—but also increasing the amount of capital required to produce a crop. Capital was also substituted for labour, as machines did more and more of the work of farming.

Smaller farms were consolidated into single holdings, resulting in rural depopulation. Some tried to turn back the tide, while others tried to ride it to good fortune. Three moments during his UFA years illustrate how Arnold tried to harness the tide and turn it to good fortune for farm organizations, for the farm supply business, and for farmers themselves through a new national farm policy. In 1963, as chair of a three-person committee to study farm organization, he recommended the amalgamation of farm organizations into one body. In 1966, recognizing that the western Canadian farm supply business could serve farmers most efficiently if it were consolidated, he brought UFA and the United Grain Growers together in establishing United Feeds, a precursor to what Arnold intended to be a single, large farm supply organization. Also in 1966, he accepted an invitation to present a new agricultural policy to the national meeting of the Liberal Federation of Canada, one in which he outlined the federal government's role in ameliorating the social and economic effects of agricultural change.

The Alberta Federation of Agriculture initiated the process of amalgamating Alberta's farm organizations by asking Arnold to chair a three-person committee charged with examining "the needs of Alberta farmers for organization to advance their cultural, social and economic welfare and to make recommendations for changes in existing organizations to better achieve these objectives."[4] Senator Donald Cameron and Leonard Nesbitt of the Alberta Wheat Pool were the other committee members. The reasons for bringing together the various farm organizations reflected the changes in the rural environment. In his characteristically direct way, Arnold summed up the effects of these changes:

> In the future, farmers will be a smaller percentage of the total popu-
> lation than at present. This is an inevitable result of technological
> advance, largely the mechanization of the industry. There is every
> reason to suppose the technological change will continue and that the
> labor content per unit of food will continue to decline. Associated with
> this will be an increase in capital investment. From the point of view of
> farm organization, this means a constant decline of political power. The
> farm organization of the future will have to depend on its arguments, its
> public relations and persuasive powers in getting the ear of government
> rather than on sheer political power....
>
> In addition to declining percentage wise, even in growing Alberta,
> farmers are likely to decrease in actual numbers.[5]

The effects of the declining numbers were evident to anyone who attended the various organizations' meetings, as Arnold did—one saw the same people again and again. The committee believed that farmers in the future would not have the leisure to go to the meetings of many organizations:

> The age of automation has resulted in a shorter work week for urban
> labor, but the farmer finds that as his operation becomes more complex,
> his hours of leisure become less and less. In the future, farm organizations
> will find it difficult to persuade the individual farmer to devote time
> to his organization. If they are to be successful in this attempt, their
> programmes must appeal to the real needs of the members. The day is
> here when farmers will not meet just for the sake of meeting. They will

only get together to accomplish something of importance to them in a reasonable length of time.[6]

Because of increasing specialization, the fragmentation of farm organization into commodity groups with narrow interests posed a further threat to the organizations' political effectiveness. Long-standing differences about the effectiveness of direct action—strikes, blockades, boycotts, and the like—posed another threat, one left unstated in the committee's report. Jim Lore, who had been associated with Arnold since Arnold first became a director of the Farmers' Union, observes that this disagreement is as old as farm organization in Alberta. Arnold's leadership of the Farmers' Union had been able to minimize differences over tactics, primarily by demonstrating the effectiveness of a moderate, reasoned approach.

But the effects of the changes in agriculture were too great for all farmers to be able to adapt. Many who were struggling to survive had lost patience with talk. They wanted action, and the National Farmers' Union (NFU) promised to instigate it. As Arnold later explained,[7] farm organizations were divided along the lines of those who were "making it" and those who were not, the NFU comprising the latter group. The Farmers' Union of Alberta, which was a grassroots, direct-membership organization, was the most vulnerable to losing members to the NFU. In Arnold's view, the NFU's tactics were not the only problem; its concept of farming was stuck in the past. A new, amalgamated farm organization that recognized the inevitability of change and worked with it to foster farmers' success was what was needed.

It is hardly surprising that Arnold felt the new organization should emphasize education, research, and information, especially given his role in establishing the Farmers' Union and Cooperative Development Association and the Department of Agricultural Economics at the University of Alberta, as well as his reputation for being able to make agricultural issues understandable to a wide variety of audiences. He envisioned an agency of networks that included adult education agencies, university departments, government departments, professional associations such as the Agricultural Institute of Alberta and the Agricultural Institute of Canada, and agricultural producers. Each of these three major departments—education, research, and information—should have an advisory committee modeled on the advisory committee for the Department of Agricultural Economics, which Arnold had helped to create and which he continued to chair.

Reflecting Arnold's understanding of organizational structures, the committee recommended that the county or municipal district be the unit of local organization, rather than the existing locals, which were based on old, and generally defunct, school districts. The committee made a compelling case for this change:

1. *the boundaries of counties are understood and used, unlike the old boundaries*

2. *the number of locals would be about 55, small enough to allow for good service from the head office*

3. *the unit has a population large enough to ensure adequate leadership.*[8]

But this recommendation created controversy and resistance, and was not implemented when Unifarm was finally created in 1970. It is doubtful that direct farmer membership in Unifarm could have been maintained at levels that would have made the organization viable beyond its twenty-five-year life. Arnold did not expect Unifarm as it was constituted in 1970 to last more than five or ten years;[9] agriculture was changing too quickly. By the mid-1970s, when Unifarm recognized that the old model of locals was not working and made the district the basis of local organization, farm population had declined even faster than the committee had anticipated, weakening the base for direct membership. As Carrol Jaques notes, "the farm population had been decreasing by about 1,000 farm families per year since the mid-1950s,"[10] and Unifarm was forced to rely on organizational memberships for its base of support.

Arnold also believed that the structure of the board of the amalgamated organization would limit its usefulness; it was too large. The report recommended that the board consist of twenty-four members:

The provincial board of the new Farmers Union would consist of a president and vice-president elected at the annual convention of the Association plus the 14 members elected from the present 14 Farmers Union districts plus 8 members from the present Federation Board.[11]

An earlier draft of the report, which Gerald Schuler remembered reading, had recommended that the board have no more than seventeen members. Arnold believed very strongly that a group of seventeen was the largest number of people that could work together as individuals who trusted one another. In a larger group, he felt, people would see themselves as representing interests and positions, thus limiting their ability to use their independent judgement in assessing issues and solving problems.

The report recognized the problem inherent in the recommended board structure and suggested that, once the new organization had been established, it should reduce the size of its board:

Essentially what we suggest is that the provincial board be composed of a combination of the present boards of both the Federation and the Farmers Union.

We realize that such a board is larger than desirable for the efficient transaction of business. As a result we would suggest that this new provincial board give consideration at some future date to reducing both the number of directors elected at large and the members representing farmer-owned co-operatives and commodity groups. In this way it should be possible to get the board down to more manageable proportions in the reasonably near future.[12]

When the new organization, Unifarm, was established in 1970, the board was even larger, with thirty-three members, than had been recommended as its initial maximum:

The board of directors consisted of the president, two vice-presidents, two representatives from the Women of Unifarm, and twenty-eight directors. In addition to the fourteen directors from the direct member side

elected at regional meetings, there were fourteen directors representing
commodity groups elected at their own annual meetings.[13]

While Arnold believed that farmers needed a single organization to
represent their interests, he also believed that Unifarm's structure inhib-
ited its ability to present innovative and creative solutions to agriculture's
difficulties. He continued to be a mentor to Paul Babey, Unifarm's first
president, and attended annual meetings, but he did not involve himself
in Unifarm's operations.

He began to give greater emphasis to finding business solutions to
farmers' problems. The business equation for farming consisted of the
same elements as any other business: when the value of sales exceeded
the costs required to produce the goods sold, there was profit. Farm
organizations spent most of their time trying to affect the prices of sold
commodities but, as Arnold had observed, the cost of inputs for capital and for supplies had been rising dramatically as technology changed
agriculture. The biggest increase in costs resulted from the increase in
the cost of land, this increase being driven by an increase in the amount
of land an individual farmer needed to make optimum use of the bigger
machinery as well as by the increase in the price of land itself. That farmers were willing to pay increasing prices for land, even as commodity
prices were declining, was an irony that Arnold addressed on a number
of occasions.

Individual farmers were assessing the optimum size of their farms;
many were deciding that larger machinery, the availability of fertilizers,
herbicides, and pesticides, and associated changes in cultivation practices would allow them to farm increasingly larger units. Land cost more
because those farmers who were able to raise the necessary capital were
competing with each other to buy additional land close to their existing
holdings. The farmers calculated that, even if the margin of profit per
unit was very small, the increase in production from the larger land base
increased the total profit enough to warrant paying the higher land cost.

During his time at UFA, Arnold thought seriously about the cost of
land as part of the farm business equation, but he did not develop these
ideas fully until the mid-1970s, when he wrote a report for the Alberta
Land Use Forum. His work at UFA focussed, not on land costs, but on the

input costs of managing the farm supply business: the costs of machinery and supplies. In both areas, Arnold looked for ways to increase efficiency "so that the economic position of the farmer can be improved."[14] For the farm machinery business, Arnold believed that a clear delineation of roles for manufacturers and suppliers together with consolidation of services would result in greater efficiency; for the general supply business, he considered the amalgamation of cooperatives to be desirable.

Arnold articulated his and UFA's views on farm machinery costs in a brief he wrote and presented to the Royal Commission on Farm Machinery, the Barber Commission, in March 1967. He described UFA's limited role in machinery sales:

> *We are primarily engaged in selling materials handling equipment and other items used largely in livestock enterprises. A partial list includes grain augers, truck hoists, bunk line feeders, self unloading wagons, feed mixers, grinders, rollers, gasoline motors, cattle chutes, scales, manure spreaders, fencing equipment and others. We do not handle tractors, combines or large tillage equipment.*[15]

Arnold did not advocate UFA becoming involved in the sale of such large equipment, nor did he think any of the cooperatives, including Cooperative Implements Limited (CIL), should enter that field. Manufacturers and distributors of large equipment should continue to own that part of the market. CIL should expand its manufacturing, and so should other local manufacturers.

Government could assist farmers by establishing a farm machinery testing laboratory that would test new machines "on a fee basis for individual designers and manufacturers who do not have facilities for such work."[16] He advocated local production because he believed that local innovations in equipment could better address local needs and because "many local manufacturers have successfully reduced costs by local production and passed at least some of these savings on to the farmer."[17]

Manufacturers of large equipment should adopt the model of large distribution centres pioneered by UFA, so that distribution costs could be reduced and supplies of parts be more readily available:

We are convinced that the only practical way to reduce distribution costs is to remove as far as possible, the wholesale function. In the distribution of other farm supplies we have pioneered this method in Alberta and have demonstrated that it can be made to work for many products. We see no reason why it cannot work for many farm machines. This does not mean that there are not many problems, some of which we have not yet solved, nor does it mean that you save all the costs involved in a whole-sale operation. Some of these must be passed on to the retail operation. Despite this, real savings are possible. For example, we purchase a small gasoline motor in truckloads from a manufacturer in Wisconsin and move them directly to our Farm Supply outlets. A farmer may purchase this unit currently for $53.00. Another retailer using exactly the same retail mark-up as ourselves and buying in small quantities from a distributor, must charge $69.12 for the same motor. We are quite sure that the distributor in this case is not profiteering. He is providing an expensive service that must be paid for if he is to remain in business.

The only way that progress can be made in reducing the wholesale function is to have retail outlets with a high sales volume. Otherwise, inventory and other problems make it impossible to operate efficiently. To achieve this when serving farmers, would mean drawing from a large area. This in turn means that some farmers have to travel a considerable distance for service. It is becoming more and more practical to do this because of highways and market roads. Whether the farmer travels this extra distance willingly or not, depends on whether or not he can save money by doing it.[18]

As already noted, Arnold had done the market studies that helped UFA decide on its locations for large supply centres. He had also been responsible for changing the administrative role of the UFA locals. Just as locals based on largely defunct school districts were no longer a suitable base for farm organization, so their usefulness in the management of local UFA agencies had diminished. In March 1964, Arnold proposed to the board that the locals' administrative responsibility for UFA farm supply outlets be eliminated, and that all members of UFA be direct members of the provincial organization.

What the farm organizations were unable to do as they amalgamated, Arnold was able to accomplish in the UFA cooperative. His message, delivered in meetings large and small across the province, was that the old model of organization developed in the horse and buggy era did not meet the business needs of the farmers who belonged to UFA. Efficiency of operation meant lower prices for farm supplies and efficiency required change. Two years later, in April 1966, Arnold presented the recommendation for change to the board, confident that the delegates at the June meeting would approve:

> Mr. Platt presented the recommendations of the Executive (1) that the administrative functions of Locals be abolished as of August 1st, 1966, and (2) that farm supply members be placed on a direct basis as of August 1st, 1966. He emphasized there was no suggestion that the locals be disbanded but no doubt many will disband if these two recommendations are put into force. If the Board approves these two changes, they should be discussed at the delegates' meeting in June and the directors can report back to the June board meeting. The directors will also be asked to attend summer meetings of secretaries by sub-districts to inform them of these changes. It is suggested they be set up as temporary advisory committees.[19]

The board approved, as did the delegates, and the management structure of UFA was changed to serve the needs of members through consolidated supply centres.

UFA was not the only company in the farm supply business, nor was it the only cooperative involved in it. Federated Cooperatives were involved, as were the Wheat Pool and United Grain Growers. Arnold began to think that consolidation might work even more effectively if all the cooperatives selling farm supplies cooperated with each other. He began to explore models that would allow such cooperation, initially in the fertilizer business, then more generally, and finally in the feed business. In 1965, he proposed that the cooperatives consider a new model for the supply of fertilizer:

A.W. Platt reported many farmers are concerned with the fact there is going to be duplication of facilities and effort in connection with fertilizer in Alberta. Private competition will be very strong. Development in the fertilizer industry means we will have to have some technical staff to keep up with our competitors. Service will be the key in securing farmers' business. One possible solution would be to establish a separate co-operative to be jointly owned by the Wheat Pool, Federated and U.F.A. Co-op., to distribute fertilizer in Alberta. This would eliminate duplication of facilities and would provide a highly efficient, low cost comprehensive distribution system that would be of great benefit to farm people and highly competitive with any private marketer. Such a scheme would also show that co-operatives can work together for the benefit of their members. Mr. Platt advised he had discussed this matter with Mr. Harrold and Mr. Malm of the Alberta Wheat Pool and had had a second short discussion with Mr. Harrold. They recognized the problem and showed interest in our proposal.[20]

When it became apparent that these talks were not going to result in action, Arnold drew on his lessons from experience and decided that the amalgamation of the cooperatives would have a greater chance of success if the idea were seen to be coming from a senior executive of another organization. Because several of the cooperatives operated inter-provincially, the amalgamation would need to include cooperatives operating in Saskatchewan and Manitoba as well as those in Alberta. Arnold decided to call on Charles Gibbings, President of the Saskatchewan Wheat Pool, to discuss the idea. The only extant record of those meetings, a letter from Gibbings' secretary to Arnold dated November 19th, 1965, suggests times at which it would be possible for Gibbings and Arnold to get together.[21]

At the UFA board meeting on December 3 and 4, 1965, Arnold drew the board's attention to a statement published by Gibbings, in which Gibbings advocated amalgamation of all large cooperatives in Western Canada. Such a big idea would take time to come to fruition. A conference in Banff was organized to look into the subject, but did not take place until September 1968.

In the interim, the idea needed a pilot project or a test case. If fertilizer sales would not provide the case, maybe the feed business would.

Arnold thought that the Winnipeg-based United Grain Growers (UGG) might be a good partner. He had had an excellent relationship with its former president, John Brownlee, one-time UFA premier of Alberta, the two of them having been in Geneva together in 1959. Arnold also was good friends with A.M. (Mac) Runciman, UGG's current president.

Arnold prepared a detailed study of the feed business in Western Canada and Bill McCartney, Chief Executive Officer of UFA, agreed that Arnold should talk with Mac Runciman. It was likely over lunch at the Ranchmens' Club in Calgary that Arnold and Runciman decided to proceed. Runciman suggested that Arnold get together with Jack Candlish to draft a model for the new enterprise and to draw up an agreement. On April 25, 1966, Bill McCartney and Arnold reported to the members of the UFA executive:

> *Messrs McCartney and Platt reported on meetings they had with representatives of United Grain Growers re setting up feed mills, etc. Members have been asking the Organization to go into the feed business for many years and it was felt this was the time to take action.*
>
> *It was suggested that the two organizations set up a wholly owned subsidiary to operate the feed business. The subsidiary would take over mills presently owned by the U.G.G., with the exception of the main mill in Edmonton which would be rented as present plans are for its removal within the next two or three years. It would be necessary to build several more plants during the first two years of operation to properly take care of requirements. Approximate cost was outlined by Mr. McCartney. Later a limited variety of farm supplies could be handled through the mills. Mr. McCartney felt it would not be too difficult to secure competent staff.*
>
> *Agreed to recommend to the Board that U.F.A. Co-op. enter into the feed business jointly with United Grain Growers Limited.*[22]

At its meeting on June 28th, 1966, the UFA board accepted the recommendation of the executive to ratify the agreement with UGG, and United Feeds was established.

The reasons for the limited success of United Feeds are not entirely clear. Reports on its operations in its first years were positive. The initial losses were expected and were not owing to sales being lower than projected; they were attributable to interest payments from United Feeds to its two parent companies. However, in January 1971, UFA decided to sell its shares in United Feed back to UGG. The board also decided to reject UGG's proposal that UFA and UGG amalgamate into one company.[23]

Attempts to amalgamate all the larger Western Canadian cooperatives had also come to nothing. The Banff conference in September 1968 recommended that a study be undertaken, and Professor Rogers of the University of Alberta prepared a report. Two other meetings, one in Edmonton in December 1967 and one in Regina in April 1969, led to the conclusion that nothing was likely to happen. Getting farmers to combine their purchasing power to buy supplies at the best possible prices was no easier than getting them to speak with a unified voice through a single farm organization. Arnold was enough of an informed realist to know that attempts at unity were likely to be futile.

Even as he initiated those attempts at amalgamation, Arnold was aware, from the Doscher Report commissioned by the Farmers' Union and Co-operative Development Association in 1965, that only 35% of Alberta's farmers bought all their farm supplies at a co-op; 52% of the farmers in the province didn't used co-ops at all in purchasing farm supplies.[24] And McCartney had reported to the UFA Board on June 22, 1967, that Federated Co-operatives based in Saskatoon was going into direct competition with UFA in Alberta by establishing its own farm supply centres.

One wonders whether the efforts at amalgamating farm organizations or farm cooperatives might have been more successful had Arnold led either of them as an organization president or farm co-op chief executive officer. He had demonstrated his abilities as president of FUA and had the capacity to be an effective CEO. However, Arnold was a man of ideas. Once he had explored an idea to its full extent, he preferred to move on to the next idea and leave implementation and day-to-day operations to others.

A similar question arises in considering Arnold's involvement in politics at this time. Once again, the Liberal Party, this time the federal party, asked Arnold to stand for election in a rural riding in Alberta. Helen recalls that she had to help break up a good party. It was 1963 or early 1964, and L.B. (Mike) Pearson was prime minister in a minority government. Pearson and Arnold knew each other quite well, and Arnold held him in high regard.

Arnold was staying at the Chateau Laurier, likely on business related to the Canadian Federation of Agriculture. Some of the staff members in Helen's office knew him from his time on the commission on transportation and, hearing that he was in town, thought this would be a good time for a party. They went with Helen to his suite. Arnold was delighted, but a bit anxious as well. He'd have to find a way to shut down the party before 10:00 pm—and that was almost contrary to nature.

But it would have to be done, as the prime minister and Mitchell Sharp were scheduled to call on him at that time. Arnold was also well acquainted with Sharp, most recently having been involved, as a member of the Board of Governors at the University of Alberta, in trying to recruit him as dean of the Faculty of Management. Helen stayed for the meeting, and Pearson and Sharp exercised all their arguments in trying to persuade Arnold to accept the nomination.

Whether it was the knowledge that he was about to enter divorce court and that the publicized details— adultery being the only permitted grounds for divorce—would make him more of a liability than an asset in the upcoming election campaign that deterred him from accepting, whether it was the fear that he might end up as an obscure backbencher that prevented him, or whether it was his recollection of Jimmy Gardiner's treatment of L.B. Thomson's potential candidacy that gave him pause, Arnold never said. He simply demurred.

He agreed instead to help the National Liberal Association develop agriculture policies to address the major transformation occurring in the industry, and to work with the Liberal Association of Alberta, but without actually joining the parties. He subsequently presented papers at the Liberal Association of Alberta's policy conference in Banff on December 3rd and 4th, 1965, and at the National Meeting and Liberal Party Conference in Ottawa on October 10, 11, and 12, 1966. The paper he presented to the latter group, *Agriculture and Rural Development*, was so well received that the National Association published it. Copies are still available in the Parliamentary Library and the library of the University of Toronto.

That paper distilled what Arnold had learned about agriculture policy in his thirty years of working in research, policy, and agri-business. As he had seen the impact of technological change on agriculture and analyzed its effects, he noted that "more significant changes have occurred in the last thirty years than the aggregate of all changes before that time."[25] The paper demonstrates Arnold's genius for explaining complex problems to lay people and for offering solutions that recognized the nuances of issues.

Technological change had created what Arnold described as the "farm income problem" in the developed, industrialized part of the world.[26] Advances in scientific knowledge, "new chemicals, new fertilizer practices, new machines" and new varieties of high-yielding seed stocks and high-performance livestock, combined with the "national interest in abundant food supplies,"[27] had created a "chronic oversupply with resultant low prices to the producer."[28] Arnold did not foresee any significant change to these "hard economic facts."[29] Successful farmers were responsible for doing everything they could to produce agricultural commodities as efficiently as they could, and government was responsible for developing and implementing policies that would encourage such efficiency. Arnold outlined five areas of policy and practice that government should follow in order to ensure the success of "commercial farms": fiscal policy, trade policy, research and extension, education, and farm finance.

Fiscal policy should discourage inflation, the paper recommended. "Policies of government that keep wages, prices and profits at reasonable levels are good for farmers."[30] He believed that current labour and management practices contributed to inflation, and argued that

> *strikes and lockouts are not a private matter but concern all of us and should not be needed in a so-called civilized society. Surely guidelines can be established, procedures developed and laws passed, if necessary, that will make these senseless tests of strength unnecessary before*

not only agriculture but our whole economy is pushed into another depression.[31]

Arnold also favoured a devalued currency, a Canadian dollar valued significantly lower than the American dollar because "it enables them [farmers] to be more competitive in world markets and makes it easier to move surplus production off the domestic market."[32]

Such a fiscal policy would provide the basis for effective trade policy, and trade was the main solution to the farm income problem. The country's population simply could not consume everything farmers could produce and, without trade, prices would be reduced even further. Unless trade policy expanded markets for agricultural goods, even efficient farmers would go out of business:

> *To the extent that we can expand trade in agricultural products we will help solve the farm income problem, facilitate necessary adjustments of the industry, improve our balance of payment position and keep food costs to our people low.*[33]

And freer trade would benefit Canadian agriculture. Arnold had participated in a conference on international trade and Canadian agriculture in Banff the previous January, and the consensus there had been that Canadian agriculture had enough competitive advantages for it to do well in a freer international market. Consequently, government should make freer trade "a major objective of government economic policy."[34]

Much of Canadian agriculture's competitive advantage depended on research and extension. "The importance of agricultural research to the Canadian consumer and to the farmer fighting for world markets cannot be overemphasized."[35] Arnold was not about to get into a debate about the appropriateness of economic research; if government funded the research, then government had an interest in the results. Arnold suggested that those concerned with the results "have a right to demand that such research whether short or long term, practical or basic, be oriented to problems that are inhibiting the full development of the industry."[36] Yet he emphasized that "only those engaged in research can determine the priorities dictated by the resources at their disposal."[37]

Arnold did not argue that the federal government should change its level of support for agricultural research; he knew from experience that the demand for research money was infinite. Instead, government should put significant resources into encouraging the practical application of research findings through extension:

> Research is of no practical value until the farmer puts it into practice. Allegedly because this is education and because education is a provincial responsibility extension activities have been left to the provinces. This artificial distinction between research and extension does not work and never has worked. Our persistent efforts to try to make it work has held back the efficiency of agriculture to a marked degree. It is of vital importance that this man-made difficulty be overcome and research and extension properly integrated. There are no fundamental difficulties except people who are geared to the existing situation and reluctant to make important changes.[38]

Extension was linked to farmers' need for education to upgrade their skills. Arnold cited the 1965 Doscher report in noting that

> Canadian farmers for the most part have a low level of formal education. In Alberta for example, only 6% have completed high school and only 1% have had some university training.... Most urban people have available a wide range of adult education programs with excellent instructors and adequate facilities. Most rural people who need it worst have little or nothing available.[39]

Arnold also recognized that rural depopulation was making the education of farm children and young people increasingly difficult. At that time, Arnold could only suggest that governments pay the higher costs of operating small schools with low class sizes. In the early 1970s, he would begin to think about encouraging people to stay on farms by linking transportation corridors with ways of holding land. Those ideas would find expression in his work with the Alberta Land Use Forum.

The financing of agriculture required considerable attention, because successful commercial agriculture now depended on significant capital investments—long-term, intermediate, and short-term. Farmers who needed to buy more land to develop an "economic unit" would require long-term credit because of the increasing cost of farm land. While government should be involved in providing such long-term financing, its policies should support the financing of land purchases at prices related to the land's productivity. Arnold suggested that current policy was encouraging increases in land prices to an extent that exceeded any increase in productivity, and recommended that such policy be amended.

He also believed that farmers did not always have to buy more land to create an economic unit. Instead, they could specialize: "Through educational programs many farmers could develop economic units through specialization and more intense cultivation rather than through buying more land."[40]

In addressing the needs of highly qualified people who lacked land but wanted to go into farming, Arnold realized he was attacking an article of free enterprise faith when he advocated that government corporations or private corporations should buy farms and "lease them out under proper arrangements to protect both parties."[41] But no other means of entry made sense. "Even if 100% credit were available the returns are not great enough to pay the costs that would be involved."[42]

In Arnold's view, while government should act to ensure the success of commercial farms, it should not act to prop up farms that had little chance of success in the changed environment. This meant that more people would have to leave their farms. His paper ended with a powerful plea for the government to take action to deal with the problems of these displaced and dispossessed people:

So far in this paper we have talked about the commercial farmer, his problems and the policies that would help him. Now let's talk about the farmer who isn't a commercial farmer, those who live in poverty and those who are being forced out of the industry with the hope of making a living elsewhere.

Let us be clear about three things.

1. *Many farmers have left; others continue to leave at the rate of 900 a month. This painful adjustment is not yet complete and will continue for some years to come. I am unaware of any plan whereby all these people can be retained in agriculture on economic farm units. Such devices as acreage payment or high support prices merely prolong the agony.*

2. *These people are the victims of technological change (automation, if you will) and deserve the same consideration as any other Canadian citizen facing the same problem.*

3. *It will cost Canada a great deal of money to deal realistically with this problem. It will cost a great deal more not to deal with it.*

There are useful things that can be done. Help could be particularly valuable in three areas:

1. *To establish on economic farm units some of the better trained young men who are being forced out of agriculture. Only a few could be accommodated in this way.*

2. *To train those willing to move out of farming, and to assist them in getting established in a new way of life.*

To provide the handicapped, the old, the sick and the illiterate with monthly cheques which would enable them to live out their lives with some comfort and dignity....

Despite the problems and difficulties, it is most important that this program proceed as rapidly as possible. This is an urgent matter. Those of us who live and work among the people concerned are well aware that rural poverty is not an interesting academic phenomenon; rather it is people with souls seared by grinding poverty and lack of hope who desperately need our help.[43]

This was Arnold's call to action: create the conditions that make commercial agriculture profitable and ameliorate the effects of change on the people who must be displaced. As we saw in Chapter 5, much of Arnold's work in education during this time was focused on agricultural economics, because he believed that research in that field was most likely to answer questions about what conditions were necessary for agriculture to prosper. But, as he said, rural poverty was not an academic issue and, in his view, no academic discipline would be likely to solve that problem.

Arnold encouraged farm organizations to be forthright in talking about the problem. He believed in acknowledging that not all "family farms" could survive. He believed that he could contribute to solving the problem by making it the focus of public and government attention. To focus this attention on the problem, he organized and chaired two conferences, one on rural poverty in 1968 and another on farm income in 1969. His many speeches reiterated the theme.

His voice was respected. Dean Lien, whom Arnold had hired to work as head of information services at UFA in 1965, recalls that government ministers and senior officials telephoned Arnold constantly to ask his opinion and seek his advice. As he was approaching retirement from UFA in 1972, Arnold's role as advisor became more formalized. The new premier of Alberta asked him to sit on a three-person committee, whose role was to review the salaries of members of the legislative assembly. When Lougheed's new government encountered hostility in rural Alberta for its plan to abolish the discriminatory Communal Property Act, the law that had restricted members of the Hutterite Brethren in buying farm land, it was Arnold with his reputation for integrity and fairness who was asked to deal with the issue. When Lougheed and Minister of Agriculture Dr. Hugh Horner asked Arnold to work with the government as chair of special committee on communal property and land use, Arnold accepted.

He wrote the president of UFA, his good friend George Sayle, saying that he intended to resign effective February 28, 1973. UFA had given Arnold the opportunity to develop his knowledge of business and management; he had helped the company grow and its people develop. UFA had given him the freedom to serve the community as he thought best. For this, UFA deserves much credit. UFA also provided Arnold with the stability of a second home for the twelve years that Arnold worked there—years that saw the break-up of his home with Donna, and the establishment of a new home with Helen.

Breaking up a marriage of thirty years was difficult. When Arnold had taken the job with UFA in the fall of 1961, he had rented a house for himself on Cornell Road in northwest Calgary, making it clear to Donna that he intended to live there by himself. Until the Royal Commission finished its work in early 1962, he shuttled between the apartment in Ottawa and the house in Calgary. Donna was taken by surprise and did not believe that Arnold really intended to leave her.

When their daughter Margaret came to Calgary to attend the University of Alberta at Calgary in the fall of 1962, she moved into her father's house. Donna sold the house in Lethbridge—it was hers, bought with money from her parents—and stayed with Margaret in the house that Arnold was renting. Arnold seldom talked of his deepest feelings, even with his nearest friends, but those who were close to him at the time observed that he often appeared unhappy and was often short-tempered. He spent as little time at home as possible, saw Helen when he could, and tried to think of how to extricate himself.

The farm on the Milk River Ridge near Jefferson became his retreat. Arnold and his son Wayne had built a three-room cabin there a few years earlier. He worked long days and evenings, and spent most weekends at the farm. He decided to raise cattle as well as the specialty crops of grass and clover seed. Because cattle needed more attention than a weekend farmer could provide, he hired Tom Fletcher to manage the farm. Arnold and Fletcher became good friends, and for many years worked together like partners. The relationship would become the model for Arnold's subsequent views on separating farm ownership from farm operation.

In Calgary, Margaret finished her first year of university. The offerings at the University of Alberta in Calgary were limited, and the recently constructed two buildings did not make much of a campus. She decided to continue her studies at the Edmonton campus. With Margaret gone, Arnold no longer needed a three-bedroom house and he began to look for an apartment. He was at last able to persuade Donna that he really did intend to leave her. She took an extended trip to visit Wayne, who had moved to Australia.

Until his divorce was final and he and Helen were married in 1967, the Ranchmen's Club in Calgary had been almost another home to Arnold. He had been introduced to the club, had applied for membership, and in September 1964 had been accepted. In those days, the Ranchmen's was *the* club and was exclusively for men. It was a place for Scotch and conversation, and Arnold often stayed until late into the night, talking about ideas. Many of the personal relationships that would become the basis for Arnold's influence were developed and maintained through the club.

He enjoyed the company, but the club could not be not a real home. For Arnold, only love between himself and a woman could create that. Helen was that woman; her vivacity and gregariousness uncorked those qualities in Arnold. Together they established themselves in a spacious apartment on the "twenty-fifth bend of the Elbow." It was a home in which Arnold was able to laugh again.

The Servant of the People Finds His Home

"Whatever possessed you to take on the job of Hutterite Liaison Officer?" It was a question asked of Arnold by several of his closest friends when Lougheed announced that Arnold would officially take the job on March 1, 1973. Arnold had been informally involved on weekends since January of that year.

In rural southern Alberta at the time, the distinction of being regarded as a "friend of Hutterites" was not the ideal capstone for a career. Arnold answered the question in various self-effacing ways: "The premier had been refused by two or three better-qualified people and was getting desperate; he could be very persuasive," or "I was terrified by the prospect of retirement at the Ranchmen's Club, reduced to discussing the day's headlines with the usual assembly of once very important people," or "I had started sheep farming as a retirement project and realized pretty quickly that I'd better find some way of financing the operation." These answers did not explain his decision to take on a job that alienated him from many rural Albertans who had been his friends for years. Even Dean Lien, who had been very close to Arnold, suggested that their friendship cooled when Arnold took the job.

Arnold's reasons for accepting the challenge were much deeper than his flippant remarks suggest. The controversy about Hutterites and their rights resonated with his interest in the practical political application of philosophical principles. He felt strongly that the principles of equality and of the protection of the rights of minorities needed the support of laws to make them fundamental to public policy. In 1971, when Lougheed's newly elected Conservative government proposed an Alberta Bill of Rights, Arnold recognized the significance of the bill.

After the repeal of the Communal Property Act and the government's suspension of the Communal Property Board in December 1971, protests swept rural Alberta and dominated the debates in the Legislative Assembly during the spring of 1972. Arnold agreed that the Communal Property Act, which had restricted the rights of Hutterites since its passage in 1947, was in violation of the proposed Bill of Rights, but he realized that passing one law and repealing another would not be sufficient to change public attitudes. Some process of public education would be necessary. If he was called upon to lead that process, his commitment to acting in the interest of the public good made it almost impossible for him to refuse—even though he knew that there would be no glory in becoming the government's "lightning rod."

Arnold also had a personal interest in the "Hutterite issue"; he wanted to address what he regarded as an earlier instance of poor judgement. In 1958, as president of the Farmers' Union of Alberta, Arnold had presented a brief on the subject to the Frame Commission, a brief he now believed he had written out of ignorance and misinformation. In his unpublished monograph *The Role of Government in Group Conflicts: A Case Study*, he wrote:

> *I arrived back from Ottawa the day before I was to appear before the Hutterite Investigation Committee. My secretary informed me that our Executive felt we were obliged to appear as our members in the south and east would be most annoyed if we did not. The annual meeting was coming up soon, at which time I would be up for re-election. She said press reports indicated that education was a popular subject and that the Committee seemed very interested in that topic. That evening I prepared a brief on education of Hutterite children. At that time I had not read one single serious book or article on Hutterites. I knew absolutely nothing of their beliefs or their views on education. I believed that what I presented was innocuous as I really did not want to offend the very few Hutterites that I knew and through ignorance failed to realize I could not have been more insulting or patronizing. Despite my ignorance and without consulting my Board of Directors or Executive I spoke for 30,000 Alberta farmers. I make this confession because it illustrates how easy it is to spread ignorance and how difficult it is for Government to know what people are really thinking.*[1]

By the early 1970s, Arnold's personal experience had made him more aware of issues involving minorities. His daughter Margaret's husband, Hy Oikawa, was from a family of second-generation Canadians of Japanese origin who had been forcibly relocated to southern Alberta during World War II.

A third reason for his acceptance of the position, which Arnold did not articulate, likely because he did not see the pattern at the time, had to do with his series of experiments in the evolution of twentieth century agriculture. He had studied and contributed to "scientific agriculture," had tested and applied that science to the model of industrial agriculture in his Sundance Farms, had helped to influence the politics of agriculture, and had shaped agri-business at UFA. But, while the family farm as traditionally perceived seemed threatened by the combination of science, industry, and business, the Hutterites' communal model of the family farm appeared to be thriving. This model was worth studying more closely, but not by itself. It needed study within the context of all the issues related to the use of land.

Arnold's appointment as Liaison Officer and Chair of the Special Advisory Committee on Communal Property and Land Use would give him the opportunity to engage in that study if the government accepted his argument to that effect. Arnold told me at the time that he would not have accepted the appointment if the government had not agreed to broaden the context of the inquiry. The government did agree, and simultaneous with the repeal of the Communal Property Act on March 1, 1973, and Arnold's appointment as Liaison Officer, the Government of Alberta announced the establishment of the Alberta Land Use Forum. While Arnold would not be one of the three members of the Forum, he was part of its work from the beginning. The Forum's broad terms of reference, combined with the Hutterites' unusual mixture of expressions of belief through traditional dress and dwellings with ultra-modern agricultural practices, provided Arnold the opportunity to carry out a study that would sum up all he had learned about agriculture and life.

February's anti-Hutterite protest march on the legislature was followed by rumours of impending land sales to voracious—and now unregulated and unrestricted—Hutterite "colonies" who, it was said, would buy up all the available land. To do his job, Arnold had to face protesters at meetings throughout southern and central Alberta.

From January 1973 to March 1, when he officially took on the role, Arnold and the committee of cabinet to which he reported[2] developed a strategy for addressing the issues. The first principle was that the Communal Property Act would be repealed and that no new form of restrictive legislation or regulation would be introduced. Premier Lougheed reaffirmed that commitment in his address to the protesters at the Legislative Building on February 23, 1973.[3] Believing that accurate information was the best basis for addressing the issue and thinking that a representative body with links to communities throughout Alberta would be able to establish guidelines for the expansion of Hutterite colonies and keep those communities informed, the government appointed a Special Advisory Committee on Communal Property and Land Use. Arnold was the chair; members represented the Alberta Association of Municipal Districts and Counties, the National Farmers Union, Unifarm, the Alberta School Trustees Association, and the two groups of Hutterites in the province, the Dariusleut and the Lehrerleut. The third element in the strategy was the establishment of an unofficial committee of Hutterite elders representing the two groups. This joint committee of elders would advise individual colonies on the appropriateness of buying particular parcels of land. Arnold would be its neutral chair. The strategy in place, the office was established just before the seeding-time spring rush of land transactions.

Arnold thought he was ready. Following his usual approach, as articulated in his first presidential address to the Farmers' Union in 1956, he gathered as much information as he could, developed guidelines for the operation of the two committees, and made himself available to discuss issues. He immersed himself in the story of the relationship between Hutterites and other Albertans, from the time of the Hutterites' arrival in 1918 to the repeal of the Communal Property Act in 1973, as it was told in scholarly and popular books and articles as well as in the succinct but comprehensive *Report on Communal Property 1972* prepared by the Alberta Select Committee of the Assembly (Communal Property).

He distilled the causes of the conflict to two: economics and values.[4] The first he understood as well as anyone could. The economic conflict between Hutterites and non-Hutterite farmers was but a small subset of the conflict resulting from the changing nature of twentieth century agriculture. In his words, the

> *perceived economic threat was not logical. The fears and economic insecurity of individual farmers were the result of rapid technological and social change, that all North American farmers faced. The Hutterites were too few in number to have any significant influence on these events.*[5]

Presenting the facts would help most people understand that. Hutterites farmed less than 1% of Alberta's farm land, and could not be responsible for the economic state of farming. The second area of conflict—over values—could be addressed by providing information and "improving communication between groups."[6]

Events in the County of Vulcan provided an almost immediate test of Arnold's ability to help individuals and groups resolve conflicts, and he learned that he was never too old to learn. He started by seeking to establish open communication. "Everything was to be above the table."[7]

> Everyone [in the County of Vulcan] expected that, with the repeal of the Act, Hutterites would attempt to acquire land for new colonies in this area.... The Elders and myself were aware that only two new colonies were being proposed for the County. Rumour, in the area, had it that anywhere from four to ten were likely. We reasoned that they had had their say to the Government and that the issue had been settled [on the steps of the Legislature on February 23 and subsequently with the repeal on March 1]. Also, if we kept them fully informed about what was going on, they would gradually realize they were not being threatened.[8]

Arnold met with the Vulcan Chamber of Commerce, and from that meeting followed two public meetings—one in Vulcan on March 16, the other in Lethbridge a week later. At both meetings, community leaders and Hutterite leaders shared the platform and discussed their differences. At first, the approach seemed to be working. The Calgary Herald reported:

> Cliff Wright, president of the sponsoring Chamber of Commerce, said he hopes similar meetings can be held in the near future. "I think it's a step in the right direction," he told The Herald. "It has obviously opened up a discussion which we did not have before, and I think it gave both sides some new information and understanding."[9]

The second meeting brought a similar response.[10] But then the economic reality of an actual acquisition came to the fore. Arnold set out the events:

The real estate agent for the Queenstown Colony was assembling land for a daughter colony in the Mossleigh area. Before all the options had been obtained the manager of the Queenstown Colony [David Decker] appeared before County Council to announce plans and to see if there would be any problems that needed to be straightened out. They received a very hostile reception. Immediately, the whole area from Barons to Mossleigh was up in arms. What followed was sad. Communication broke down entirely. Conduct became silly. A vigilante group was organized to follow the manager of the Colony wherever he went. Realizing this, he led them on—ostensibly to look at various farms. Intimidation of vendors, both real and potential, had some success with two results. First, the Hutterites were not able to obtain all the land they needed or where they wanted it. Second, the resentment between those opposing the new colony and those wishing to dispose of their land was bitter.[11]

I began working with Arnold as his research officer on May 1, 1973, just as the issues in Vulcan were reaching their most explosive state. The public meeting at the Mossleigh community hall on May 9 introduced me to the reality of the conflict that we were trying to resolve. The *Calgary Herald* report the following day did not mention the emotionally charged and threatening nature of many of the speeches, nor did it reflect the mood of the crowd as I gauged it from the back of the hall.

Speakers from the floor repeatedly stated that, unless the government reinstituted controls on land, buying by Hutterites, the community would resort to its own means of protection. "We'll burn them out" or worse was a common threat. The night before the meeting, Arnold received anonymous phone calls threatening him with harm unless he took action to limit Hutterites' buying of land. During the meeting itself, Arnold kept his composure as speaker after speaker berated him for his inability or unwillingness to prevent Hutterites from buying land in the area, "for letting Hutterites onto sacred ground."[12]

He responded by saying, "I am not a dictator in this.... I have no legal authority. If anything I'm a negotiator and adviser."[13] As he made his way out through the hostile crowd at the end of the three-hour meeting, he was afraid. He'd been given a note reiterating the threat of personal attack that he'd received by telephone, and the mood of the crowd made him take it seriously. In his subsequent self-deprecating account of the incident, he said it was a good thing that he had travelled all those back roads so many times over the past twenty-five years—because he had to drive them that night with the car lights off as he made his escape to Lethbridge.

Arnold realized that his commitment to openness had been too idealistic.

> *The blame for the whole fiasco rested on the Elders and my decision to make public the plans for a new colony prematurely. If we had waited until all the land had been bought and the vendors had had a chance to get out before making the announcement there would have been a great outcry—but conflict—particularly between non-Hutterites would have been much less.*[14]

He also said, "I am sure the Elders knew better but yielded to my wishes.... The Elders only tried it once as I had to learn, the hard way, to keep my mouth shut."[15] Consequently, he developed a different strategy for dealing with the conflict:

> *First, some conflicts cannot be resolved by discussion or negotiation and under such circumstances the best course is to proceed quickly and decisively with what is allowed by law. Second, yielding to threats only results in further threats.*[16]

From that point on, when a transaction was first proposed, Arnold used his extensive network of acquaintances throughout Alberta to inform him before he invited public discussion. "When new colonies were proposed for other areas, local, responsible people were asked to assess community reaction and any special problems that they could foresee—on a strictly confidential basis."[17] If special problems were identified, Arnold would pore over county and municipal district land ownership maps to see if possibilities for trades or other arrangements might be possible. As was his way when he needed to influence a course of action, he worked in the back rooms, or in these instances in the farmhouse kitchens. If he knew a little about the owners of quarter sections in the region, Arnold would get in his car and call on the people who had a direct interest in the proposed transaction. As he modestly reported "often it was possible to accommodate individuals who would be personally affected by the proposal. This is not to say that new colonies were welcomed, but usually they were tolerated."[18]

Arnold kept the interested public informed about land transactions that had been completed. We discussed the question of whether it was right to publish information about the land holdings of a particular religious group. We decided that in what was essentially a period of transition between the closely regulated time under the Communal Property Act and the relatively near future when the Special Advisory Committee would be abolished, accurate information would help allay fears of a "Hutterite takeover."

Arnold published an interim report in October 1973, in which he updated the information on each Hutterite colony's land holdings that had been reported in the Select Committee's 1972 *Report on Communal Property*. Annual reports were published in 1974 and 1975. The 1975 report prepared the way for the abolition of the Special Advisory Committee. The *Calgary Herald* reported:

> *Rural fears and protests that ending limits against Hutterite land buying would allow the sect to grab vast tracts of Alberta property are turning out to be baseless and mistaken.*
>
> *The sect has not boosted the speed with which it spawns new colonies and expands holdings since the Communal Property Act was repealed, says a report tabled in the legislature Wednesday.*
>
> *The finding comes from the special advisory committee on Communal Property and Land Use which was set up after the old restrictive legislation was repealed in March 1973.*
>
> *Municipal Affairs Minister Dick Johnston, who tabled the document, underlined what he called its "classic conclusion." The decades-old restrictions were repealed amid bitter legislature debates, demonstrations and fears that Alberta farmers were being undermined.*
>
> *There was a brief rush of Hutterite land buying immediately after the repeal. But the flurry of expansion now appears to have been only catching up for the sect, which had not been able to buy any new property*

between December 1971 and March 1973 while the government studied their rights.[19]

The transformation had required more than just a few annual reports listing land transactions. Arnold had told a meeting of the Dariusleut Hutterite Brethren at Stahlville Colony late in the fall of 1973 that what he wanted was "to have you accepted and for me to get out of business."[20] He acknowledged that he had not succeeded fully on the first object, but he had initiated several activities that were increasing the level of that acceptance. He wrote:

> *I must admit to personal values about which I feel strongly. It is that knowledge leads to tolerance and personal satisfaction. It brings peace of mind because we do not fear what we understand nor do we fear the values held by others even though they conflict with our own.*[21]

Under Arnold's leadership, the office of the Special Advisory Committee undertook a program of public education intended to provide accurate and unbiased information about Hutterite beliefs and values, and their social and economic practices. Arnold drew on his years of experience with the media, and used his many connections with print and broadcast journalists to ensure that they had good information about events that involved Hutterites. Helen worked with McVean Communications, and her contacts through that agency extended Arnold's network.

Because the news stories had national and international appeal, Arnold met with reporters from all parts of Canada and the United States. Writers and filmmakers from England, France, and Germany visited, and Arnold saw that they were given ready access to community leaders. In addition, we arranged for reporters and writers to visit Hutterite communities. Some of them stayed for a week or more, so that their experience could inform a more complete representation of Hutterite life than was usually published or broadcast. That many media people asked Arnold to review their stories before they were published indicates something of the respect these people had for his commitment to accuracy and fairness.

Arnold understood the strengths and limitations of the broadcast media. He was always available for interviews, but when issues were particularly controversial, he would insist that the interviews be broadcast live, unedited. Sometimes he had to be in a studio before six in the morning—no small sacrifice for someone who disliked early morning work as much as Arnold did.

Arnold realized that the creation of the multicultural society in which he believed needed more knowledge and public education than could be provided through journalistic media. It would require a long-term strategy, one that involved the education of young people. The liaison office compiled, edited, produced, and distributed a multimedia Hutterite studies kit for use in schools. It was sold at cost and almost every school district in the province bought one or more. Through his work with the Hutterites' committee of elders, Arnold also established a list of colonies that would accommodate visitors and tours. The Calgary Board of Education made such a visit part of its outdoor education program, and many other school districts followed suit.

Using his connections at the three Alberta Universities, Arnold initially participated in seminars. Eventually, he delegated that responsibility to me as part of a larger strategy of delegating responsibility for all issues involving Hutterites to me. Arnold wanted to avoid being associated exclusively with the Hutterites' buying of land, so that he would be able to make an effective contribution to his work with the Land Use Forum.

That delegation was part of his strategy of drawing the focus to the much broader issues of land use. As has been mentioned, the Land Use Forum was established on March 1, 1973, at the same time that Arnold became chair of the Special Advisory Committee on Communal Property and Land Use. The three commissioners of the land Use Forum were V. Wood, formerly Deputy Minister of Lands and Forests; Jack Davis from Calgary, an engineer who most recently had established the company providing cable television to south Calgary; and Ralph Brown of Acme, Reeve of the Municipality of Kneehill, and a farmer.

That Arnold was not appointed as one of the commissioners of the Forum had to do with political strategy. The Hutterite issue needed immediate attention, and Arnold had the status and credibility in rural areas to be able to deal with it. He agreed to work on land use in the background, forgoing the credit that would accrue to those in the more public role. His contribution to the Forum is acknowledged in a single line in the Forum's report: "Dr. A.W. Platt, P.Ag., Chairman of the Special Advisory Committee on Communal Property and Land Use, and his assistant, Diana Wetzel worked with the Forum on a fairly continuous basis from its beginning."[22] As had been the case with his work on the Royal Commission on Transportation, behind the scenes Arnold took a leading role, and the final report, much of which he wrote, reflects the perspectives, wisdom and judgement that his extensive experience had given him.

The Forum's terms of reference required the knowledge of many specialists to address the diverse topics, but it needed Arnold's general knowledge and his genius for organizing to frame the process of inquiry. I witnessed the way in which he made his contribution. The Forum's chair, V. Wood, was based in Edmonton, Jack Davis lived in Calgary, and Ralph Brown lived near Acme, about sixty kilometres from Calgary. Arnold's office suite in the Bowlen building in Calgary provided a convenient meeting place for the Forum to meet. As the only staff member for the special advisory committee and because of my responsibilities as its research officer, I was present at several of the Forum's meetings there. I was also Arnold's sounding board. From the outset, Arnold's leadership was evident.

Arnold had discussed the terms of reference with Dr. Horner and other cabinet ministers when he met with them on January 12, 1973. The topics to be investigated had been identified in the February 27, 1973 government motion to establish the land use forum, and the bill was passed in March, but the terms of reference and the membership of the Forum were not established until Order in Council No. 1447/73 was passed on October 1. By then, the initial land-buying rush of the Hutterites that followed the repeal of the Communal Property Act was over, and the idea that the Forum was not just a political attempt to divert attention from the controversy over Hutterites had a reasonable chance of success.

The scope of the Forum's inquiry encompassed the main issues with which Arnold had been concerned throughout his professional life:

1.   *the family farm;*
2.   *multi-use of agricultural land;*

3.   *the use of agricultural land for recreational purposes;*

4.   *land use in and adjacent to urban areas as it affects the cost of housing;*

5.   *future land needs of Alberta agriculture;*

6.   *corporate farms, foreign ownership of land, absentee ownership and communal farming;*

7.   *the common ownership of land, agricultural processing and marketing facilities;*

8.   *land use as it influences population distribution in Alberta;*

9.   *the extent, if any, to which the historical right of a landowner to determine the use and disposition of agricultural property ought to be restricted.*[23]

These issues were also part of the public's concern. By the 1970s, issues were expressed as much from an urban as from a rural, agricultural perspective. Books such as Donella Meadows' *The Limits to Growth, Small is Beautiful* by E.F. Schumacher, and *Diet for a Small Planet* by Frances Moore Lappé were having an influence on the public consciousness. Professional bodies such as the Agricultural Institute of Canada advocated the preservation of agricultural land for agricultural purposes.

In 1972, Saskatchewan established a provincial land bank program to help people who wanted to start farming. In February 1973, British Columbia introduced legislation establishing a provincial land commission with powers to control all land use by designating land for one of four purposes: agricultural, greenbelt, recreational, or urban land bank; as the *Western Producer* reported, "one of the key provisions of the legislation is that there is no automatic right to compensation for land designated under any of the four categories.[24]

In Alberta, land prices, both rural and urban, were increasing rapidly. From 1971 to 1974, agricultural land prices increased by 86%.[25] The 1972 oil crisis in the Middle East and the consequent surge in oil prices started an economic boom in Alberta. Urban populations grew. As the Forum reported, net in-migration to Alberta was estimated at 15,000 to 18,000 for 1975.[26] Between 1961 and 1971, lot prices had increased by 105% in Calgary and 118% in Edmonton;[27] in the following four years, average house prices in Calgary doubled again. Canada's public was ready to participate in land use planning.

In a speech to the annual meeting of the Alberta Institute of Agrologists in Edmonton on June 9, 1973, Arnold said that "most people would conclude that up to this point our system of land ownership and land use has served the agricultural needs of the Province well." He went on to say:

> The time has come to take a detailed look at land ownership and land use. I think such a study could do a number of things:
>
> 1.   It could set to rest many of the fears expressed by both rural people who fear for their economic survival and urban people who fear that they will be denied access to land.
> 2.   It could provide a better framework and hopefully some imaginative ideas to deal with such diverse problems as urban sprawl and very sparsely settled areas.
> 3.   It could determine to what extent we need new rules to protect the environment and at the same time make a judgement as to where existing rules and regulations on land use are unduly restrictive or unduly permissive.
> 4.   It would provide a forum for those who feel that society would be better served by socializing agriculture, by limiting farm size, by denying certain citizens the right to buy land, or whatever else they feel would improve conditions.[28]

Arnold's commitment to public participation had its roots in the ideals of agrarian democracy, influenced in part by the populism of the Progressives in the 1920s, and he brought his considerable experience in the processes of public participation to the work of the Forum. Helen's years of experience in organizing federal royal commissions also supported the Forum's work. At the Forum's first two meetings in Edmonton, in October 1973, Arnold presented an outline of what needed to be done and a model for a public participation process that would ensure that consultation included all who wanted to participate. "The Land Use Forum was instructed by the Government that one of the main purposes of the Forum, in addition to formal public hearings, was to hold meaningful discussions with the public on matters of land use."[29]

Public participation had to be informed by accurate and complete information, dispassionately presented. Lacking that, as Arnold's current experience with Hutterite issues was demonstrating, partial information or misinformation could fuel demagoguery and mass hysteria. To ensure that participants in public discussions had access to current information on the issues identified in the terms of reference, Arnold guided the Forum to commission nineteen technical reports.

Lougheed's government wanted to be seen as a government of action, and those studies and reports were completed and published by the end of August 1974—a considerable feat, given the range of subjects and the complexity of the issues. Arnold knew people in the Department of Agriculture, in the Faculty of Agriculture at the University of Alberta, and all the agricultural consultants in the province; Wood knew people connected with lands, forests, and recreation. The two quickly identified the people whom they knew to be best qualified to work on each of the topics and set up a liaison committee to supervise the work. Twelve of the reports were prepared by senior members of the civil service, and seven by consulting firms.

While the first phase was underway, planning for the second phase, the public participation phase, proceeded. Again, Arnold's contacts eased the process: the Forum called on Gerald Schuler and his Rural Education and Development Association to lead this phase:

> To meet the responsibility of giving the public the opportunity of studying and discussing the land-use issues, the Forum embarked on a public participation program during the second half of 1974. A private organization, the Rural Education and Development Association, was employed to arrange meetings in eighty rural and urban communities throughout the province. At these meetings, copies of the summaries and technical reports were made available and study sessions were organized. The

participants were encouraged and assisted in preparing briefs to the Forum giving their recommendations and views on the problems of land use which were of most concern to them.

The response to this program was satisfactory in the rural and small urban areas, but the response in the larger urban areas was minimal. There were just over 225 briefs received from this program.

While this public participation was going on, the Forum contacted and held meetings with private and public organizations interested in land-use issues. Meetings were also held with the planning commissions, officials of several urban and rural municipalities and with the senior officials of the departments of the government, who have responsibilities in land use.[30]

The Forum also conducted public hearings:

During the first part of 1975, public hearings were held by the Forum in fifteen centres throughout the province. One day was scheduled for the hearings in all of the centres except Edmonton and Calgary where two days were scheduled. It was necessary to extend to three days, the hearings in both Edmonton and Calgary, and to hold two final days of hearings a month later in these two areas to assure [sic] that everybody who wished to present briefs was given the opportunity.

The hearings were held in an informal manner to allow discussion from the Forum members and the public on the various briefs presented. Just over 280 briefs were received through the public participation program and the briefs received at the public hearings, together with the discussion at the hearings are included in the published Submissions, which amount to approximately 3,250 pages in eight volumes.[31]

Arnold wrote most of the final report during the last half of 1975, although he is not credited with having done so. I saw how he did the job so quickly. As he had done with the Royal Commission on Transportation, he commandeered a dictating machine (although this time he did not have to rile up an office administrator in the process). For each section of the report and following an organizational structure that the Forum

Writing the report of
the Land Use Forum,
c. 1976.
[Platt Family Collection]

members had agreed upon, Arnold made a concise, hand-written set of notes in point form. Using these notes, he then dictated each section. From the office next to his, I could hear him speaking into the machine, somewhat slowly and with an occasional break to erase and re-state.

When he had completed a section, he would give the tape to Diana Wetzel to transcribe. She was an expert, and Arnold let her know how much he appreciated her speed and accuracy. He would then make his revisions on the typescript. In that era, word processing was done only on mainframe computers with monitors, and government offices outside of Edmonton did not have such equipment. Mrs. Wetzel would have to retype the whole revised section. Sometimes Arnold's speed of writing and revising was too much for her to keep up with, and a draft would be couriered to the Edmonton office for retyping. While the content of the final report reflects the views of the Forum's members, the expression and the style of the report is Arnold's.

Sometimes Arnold's droll wit found its way into this august report. I recall a conversation we had about problems that young people faced in getting together money to start farming. In that drawl that characterized his most profound expression of what some had dubbed "platitudes from Platt," Arnold remarked that the best way to get into the game was for a young man to marry the only daughter of a rich farmer. Only those who knew him intimately could know the irony of that remark, given his own experience with Donna and Silas Oxford's offer of a farm. The remark found its way into the final report in the section on "problems of entry":

> The various ways that entry into agriculture is accomplished at the present time can be outlined as follows, but no estimates of their relative importance are possible.
>
> The first is by inheritance. This probably involves the greatest numbers and benefits young women as well as young men. Some of our most successful farmers have married the only daughter of a rich farmer.[32]

Not everyone appreciated the humour, as this letter from Myron Johnson shows:

> I would like to nominate the Land Use Forum report as the most profoundly reactionary document of the decade, and the Journal editorial in support of the report ("Myths challenged," Jan. 27) as the most naïve editorial of the decade.
>
> I note on page 129 of the report the suggestion that one of the best ways for a young man to get into farming, despite the high costs involved, is to marry the only daughter of a rich farmer. Is this another travelling salesman joke?
>
> If the authors of the report are serious, perhaps they could get together with The Journal editorial writers and draw up an inventory of eligible daughters of rich Alberta farmers.

Since the report is roughly 150 years behind the times, it is not surprising that the authors should favour the dowry system over land banking or low-interest loans.

Pardon me for laughing at the report but it hurts too much to cry.[33]

Given Arnold's previously expressed views on the issues related to land use, the report's recommendations should not have surprised many people. The Forum recommended that no new regulations be established to govern the use of land for agriculture. It regarded foreign ownership of land, corporate farming, communal farming, and vertical integration in farming and agricultural processing to be insignificant exceptions to the dominant model of the family farm:

We consider family farms to be individual owners, partnerships and family corporations. They comprise 99.3% of all farms, farm 93% of the total acreage, contribute 96% of total farm capital, and produce 95% of the agricultural products sold. Clearly they completely dominate the farming business in Alberta.[34]

The report's recommendation that no new processes or regulations be established to apply to the agricultural use of land meant that any attempt to regulate communal farms—or Hutterite farms—was a dead issue. Consequently, it recommended that the Special Advisory Committee on Communal Property be disbanded and that the office of Liaison Officer be abolished. Arnold left that position in March 1976, although the government continued the operation of the Advisory Committee and the office for another year.

The Forum realized that most issues associated with the use of land resulted from changes in use, and it focused its attention on laws, regulations, and processes associated with enabling or controlling such changes. Government's role was the provision of a framework for growth, development, and change. The Forum's first recommendation was that:

The legislature consider putting the following objective into legislation: The objective of the government is to enable individual human beings,

singularly or in association with each other, to have land to grow food
and trees, build shelters and factories, establish recreational areas and
such other useful activities as the ingenuity of man may design, according
to their individual desires and resources, within law that prohibits gross
misuse of the land itself as well as uses which affect adversely the welfare
of others or which lessen unduly the options of future generations.[35]

Most of those changes in the use of land were the consequence of urbanization and industrialization. The Forum deviated from what had been
expected of it when it gave substantial attention to such matters as the
planning process, urban land use, and housing, recreational use of land,
the use of land for transportation, and taxation. One of its most interesting recommendations addressed urban land use and housing through
taxation: it recommended a tax on the profits generated by a change in
the use of land.

Actions by government can and do affect the value and management of
land. The most are land-use changes such as agricultural to urban, and
by zoning regulations. We recognize that government must have such
rights to ensure orderly growth and development. It is our view that the
right to develop is not an ownership right, but a privilege accorded by
government for the public interest. It follows that windfall gains made by
a landowner belong to the government who created the increased value,
and not the landowner. Conversely, those who fail to gain approval to
develop, suffered no loss and are entitled to no compensation.

We recommend that the provincial government seek a change in the
federal-provincial-provincial tax sharing agreement that would allow
the province to establish a capital gains and unearned increment tax
on all land. The proceeds would be distributed to the municipality that
created the increased values for its use in providing infrastructure such
as utilities and transportation facilities. If such an agreement cannot
be reached, we recommend that the province consider the practicality
of levying an unearned increment tax, in addition to the federal capital
gains tax, to be distributed in the way we have outlined. [36]

The Forum did not believe that the conversion of agricultural land to urban use should proceed as fast as possible, provided that the municipality gained the benefit of the unearned increment tax; proper stewardship of land required that such conversion occurred only if it was really needed. The Forum believed that urban designs then current, which inscribed the sacred right of all to own a single-family house, were not in keeping with good stewardship. It recommended that subdivision design regulations be changed to allow a much greater variety and higher density of housing, and that governments stop subsidizing the financing of single-family housing:

> *The Forum suggests the only realistic approach to providing quality housing within the consumer's ability to pay is to increase overall densities within the total urban area. It is recommended that government recognize that the single-family detached housing unit is not a realistic goal for all Canadians and no subsidized mortgage money should be made available for this purpose.*[37]

These two recommendations attracted most of the extensive news coverage given to the Forum's report, not an entirely unintended consequence of the Forum's shift in emphasis from what seemed to be suggested in the terms of reference. The tax recommendation remained an interesting idea; market forces resulted in higher density urban designs becoming the accepted norm.

The Forum had done its job. With the publication of the Forum's report in January 1976, Arnold believed that he had made his contribution and that it was time to move on. He had agreed to do one more study for the provincial government, one that would examine the role of government in group conflict by looking at the history of its relationship with Hutterites, but that was a study he could do from his office at home.

He expected to start that study while living in Calgary, and then to complete it when he and Helen moved to the farm on the Milk River Ridge. That move occurred almost a year before they expected to make it; the market forces driving urban densities higher were affecting Arnold and Helen personally. Their apartment on 25th Avenue in Calgary was being converted to condominium ownership, and Arnold and Helen were not interested in buying. In late 1974, they rented a house on 14th Avenue South West near 11th Street, intending to stay there until some time in 1977, when they anticipated they would have completed an addition to the two-room cabin that Arnold and Wayne had built more than twenty years earlier.

However, the owner of the house on 14th Avenue sold the property to a developer, who also acquired the two adjacent houses. The house was to be torn down to make way for an apartment complex, and Arnold and Helen had to vacate. They decided to speed up their plan to move to the farm. They did not have time to build, but they had come across a vacant Christian Reformed Church at Seven Persons, near Medicine Hat, which was for sale at a very low price. As Helen and Arnold were not moving to Seven Persons, the church would have to come to their farm if it was to become their home. Building movers considered it a routine job and undertook the move. Arnold organized a work crew consisting of Margaret's husband Hy Oikawa, Eric Lughtiheid, who was Helen's daughter Carol Ann's husband, several neighbours, and himself to construct the footings and foundation. The church came to the farm in the summer of 1975. Along the way, the building movers encountered only one difficulty: the roof was too high or a power line was too low for the building to pass underneath. They had to cut the peak off the roof. In the spring of 1976, they made the farm their home.

There was another reason that Arnold and Helen had had to make the move, and it illustrated another of the observations about farming that Arnold had put into the Land Use Forum report: few farms owned by non-residents and managed by an employee succeeded. Arnold and Helen had decided to raise sheep to supplement their income during retirement, and had hired a new manager to replace Tom Fletcher when he left. The new manager had claimed to know the business but, under his management, the enterprise was losing money faster than Arnold and Helen could provide it.

Sitting in a rocking chair and watching the sun set behind Big Chief Mountain was not Arnold's idea of retirement. He took on consulting

contracts, preparing a brief for the Canada Grains Council's annual meeting in Winnipeg, working with Unifarm on revising its constitution, and
starting the background research for his report on group conflict. He
continued to work closely with the Rural Education and Development
Association, and to be involved with the Department of Agricultural
Economics and Rural Sociology at the University of Alberta, where he
was called in as an external examiner on a thesis. Early in 1977, Premier
Lougheed and several cabinet ministers, including Hugh Horner and Ken
Kowalski, called him to Edmonton for consultation on various issues. He
subsequently took a short-term contract on grain transportation. More
significantly, Arnold also became involved in the issue that led to his last
official role for the provincial government, the issue of how to manage
the water resources in southern Alberta.

The Oldman River Basin was the focus for discussion of water in the
region. Demand for water was increasing. The provincial government,
as part of its commitment to expanding the range of agricultural opportunities, had indicated that it wanted to increase the acreage that was
irrigated. Lethbridge and other urban centres in the region depended on
the Oldman River for their water supply and, as the Oldman River Study
Committee stated in its report,

> The natural flow in the Oldman and its tributaries is highly variable,
> both seasonally and annually, and during low flow years is insufficient
> to satisfy existing demands for water. Water storage developed over the
> years to rectify this situation no longer provides a secure water supply
> during a protracted period of low flow.[38]

Construction of a new dam on the Oldman had been under serious consideration since 1974. The preliminary report, released in June 1976, considered the issue to be significant enough to warrant major study, and the
Minister of the Environment, David Russell, appointed a study management committee in May 1977. Arnold was not part of this management
committee, and he did not assume any public role in relation to its work.
Nevertheless, representatives from the irrigation districts and planning
agencies called on him for advice, and he provided it as it pertained to

the economics of farming under irrigation. To the best of my knowledge, he did not take a stance for or against the construction of a new dam on the Oldman River.

The final, controversial report of the management committee was published in August 1978. It recommended that a new dam be constructed on the Oldman at one of two sites, the Brocket site or the Three Rivers site. The site was to be selected through public hearings to be held that fall. The depth of the controversy was indicated by the dissenting statement of a committee member, Hilton Pharis, which was published as part of the report: Pharis, a rancher from Cowley who lived near the Three Rivers site, opposed the construction of any dam on the Oldman.

When he released the Committee's final report, Minister of the Environment Dave Russell announced that Arnold Platt would chair the public hearings. Minister Russell knew what Arnold could do with controversial issues. Arnold had deflected the controversy over Hutterites when, as Minister of Municipal Affairs, Russell had been responsible for suspending the operation of the Communal Property Board. In addition to appointing Arnold as chair, the government appointed three other members to the Environment Council of Alberta's review panel: Tom Sissons, a businessman from Medicine Hat; Dixon Thompson, associate professor of environmental design at the University of Calgary, whose family was based in the Pincher Creek area; and Alistair Crerar, the chief executive officer of the Environment Council.

The construction of a new dam was at the heart of the controversy. Arnold provided the government with a way out of that controversy, but it was not the way that the government had anticipated. Arnold and the committee interpreted their terms of reference as providing them with enough scope to consider alternatives. Those terms of reference said that

Whereas past water shortages in the Oldman River Basin have indicated a need for improved management of the resource, the Environment Council is therefore requested to:

1.   *Enquire into the conservation, management and utilization of water resources within the Oldman River Basin as outlined in*

> *the Report of the Oldman River Study Management Committee*
> *giving particular attention to:*
> a)   *present water supply*
> b)   *present and future water requirements*
> c)   *the merits of alternative means of providing for future*
>   *water requirements.*
>
> 2.   *Hold Public Hearings at suitable locations throughout southern*
>   *Alberta on the Report of the Oldman River Study Management*
>   *Committee and report to the Minister of Environment as soon*
>   *as possible.*[39]

As directed, the panel held ten public hearings in eight centres in southern Alberta. They also "met with a variety of agencies and consultants who had contributed to the preparation of the report of the Management Committee or who had a particular knowledge or involvement in critical aspects of water management in the area."[40] Although the terms of reference could be interpreted to mean that the panel was to limit its attention to studies already conducted by the Oldman River Study Management Committee, the panel did not follow that interpretation. The panel asked the staff of the Environment Council for new information and commissioned two reports from consultants "on aspects that it felt required additional information."[41] These were

> Price-Quantity Relationships for Irrigation Water in Southern Alberta *by Marv Anderson & Associates (1979) and* The Economic Viability of Increased Beef Feeding in Alberta *by Meat Industry Research Services (1979). The Anderson report is an examination of the impact of price on the consumption of water in irrigation agriculture. The Meat Industry Research report is an examination of Alberta's market prospects for red meat and of the comparative advantage of Alberta in the production of red meats in competition with Ontario and the American midwest.*[42]

These reports signalled the emphasis on the markets for agricultural commodities as a major factor in determining the extent to which irrigation should be expanded. They filled a major gap in the report of the Management Committee, one which had been recognized in Terry McDonald's analysis in The *Lethbridge Herald* on August 28, 1978.

Public controversy focused on the prospect of constructing a dam at the Three Rivers site west of Pincher Creek. If that dam were built, ranchers would be flooded out, sport fishing in some of the best cold-water trout areas in southern Alberta would be ruined, and the ecosystem of the river valley upstream from Pincher Creek would be destroyed. By shifting the focus from environmental issues associated with constructing a dam to economic issues associated with markets for agricultural products, Arnold and the panel shifted from issues having broad appeal to both urban and rural people throughout the province to a technical subject in which a much narrower audience was interested, thus effectively containing the controversy.

The panel determined that expanding irrigation to the fullest extent that a new dam would allow was not economically justifiable. So it began to examine what might be done if the water available without constructing a new dam were used more efficiently.

The efficiency consultant (Stanley/SLN 1978) found the overall irrigation efficiency in the Oldman River Basin between 1968 and 1974 to be about 31 per cent. In order to assess 1978 efficiencies, the Environmental Council reviewed this with irrigation district managers, who suggested that efficiencies had increased to 35 per cent (Table 10).

Stanley/SLN felt it conceivable, eventually to attain an overall basin efficiency of 65 per cent. The Management Committee could not accept this figure and judged 60 per cent to be more realistic. The Environment Council agrees with that judgement.[43]

Increasing efficiency to 60% would require major rehabilitation of the existing irrigation water delivery system, but it would seem that was worth doing regardless of whether or not a new dam was constructed.

Water storage did not just occur "on stream" behind dams on rivers. Various reservoirs providing "off stream" storage had been constructed as irrigation was developed in southern Alberta. The panel determined that the capacity of several reservoirs could be expanded, and at least one new reservoir constructed in an area much less environmentally sensitive that the Three Rivers dam site. It also determined that, because of soil conditions and available heat units, expansion of irrigated acreage should occur only south of the Oldman River. However, that did not significantly limit the acreage that could be added to the already-irrigated land in the region. If the panel's recommended measures to increase efficiency were implemented and if the capacity of the existing reservoirs were increased and another reservoir built, then an additional 200,000 acres could be irrigated. This was only 50,000 acres less than the 250,000 additional acres that the Management Committee had indicated as being possible with the construction of a new dam. Because the economic benefit of expanding irrigation by more than 200,000 acres was extremely doubtful, no new dam was necessary.

As Arnold told a reporter from The *Calgary Herald*, the panel's recommendation was a compromise:

> *"No way you can come up with something that can please everyone,"*
> *Arnold Platt, chairman of the ECA panel, told The Herald today. "We*
> *think we have a reasonable thing that everyone can live with. But what*
> *the hell they (the provincial government) do with it is their business."*[44]

That last remark suggested that Arnold had doubts about the likelihood of the government's accepting the panel's recommendations. He did not believe that a report should contain any surprises for the minister of the environment or the government, and had met with cabinet, including the new minister of the environment, Jack Cookson, on August 15 to present his work.

Arnold left Edmonton knowing that the government was committed to building the dam at the Three Rivers site. He was disappointed in the government's decision to ignore his major recommendation, but he was not disillusioned. He understood the role he had played in this controversy and in the others involving communal property and land use. From 1973 to late 1979, he had been able to use his reputation in rural Alberta to help the government deal with these issues.

As Allan Warrack, Minister of Lands and Forests when Arnold worked with the Land Use Forum, said, "We used Arnold," and Arnold knew this. He understood the workings of government well enough to know that it needed people to deflect the heat of controversy from elected leaders and to test public response to new or alternative ideas.

Arnold used to say, "If you can afford to farm, you don't have to," and he had reached that time in his life when he could afford to farm. He was seventy years old, and deserved to do what he wanted to. Sheep farming allowed him to stay connected with the agricultural industry and, just as importantly for Arnold, it connected him with the farming community in which he and Helen lived. Peggy Prince and her family lived in the other house on the farm, and took over the farm responsibilities when Arnold and Helen wanted to travel. This arrangement gave Helen and Arnold freedom to spend time with their families and with their vast network of friends.

Not having to farm did not mean that Arnold wouldn't take sheep farming seriously. He and Helen studied genetic lines and lambing characteristics, working to develop year-round production of fast-growing lambs at lambing rates approaching 200%. He built a lambing barn with a bedroom, and slept there during peak lambing times. As he had learned in his earliest experiences with farming, producing commodities without attending to markets was bad business, so Helen and Arnold studied the market for lamb. After trying several ways of selling their lambs, including hauling them to the new processing plant at Innisfail and leaving the selling to wholesalers, the couple decided that selling directly to consumers was the best approach. Their red Toyota pickup with the freezer-like box became a common sight in the towns and cities of southern Alberta, as Arnold and Helen delivered some of the best-tasting, leanest, and tenderest lamb available. This method of marketing gave them the opportunity of keeping up old friendships and connections and making new ones, a significant part of the social aspect of their farming operation.

Grain farming continued to interest Arnold as well. He especially loved the rush of the harvest and, until he was eighty-two, he drove combines for his neighbours. While he enjoyed the neighbourliness and the physical work, he was not content with farming that did not involve some

Arnold with the author, mid-1980s.
[Platt Family Collection]

test of his ability to manage. In the early 1980s, he became a director of Farman Agrisystems Ltd., a farm management company involved in managing grain farms primarily in the Peace River country of northern Alberta. Managing the 4,000-hectare farm near Rycroft along with two other agriculturalists gave Arnold one more opportunity to test his idea that ownership of the land did not really matter for certain kinds of farming. As John Schmidt wrote in his column in the *Calgary Herald*, the land was owned by a company headed by an engineer, Ed Davis of Calgary. It was managed by a group that included Arnold, Ralph Erdman, and Ian McKenzie, and was actually farmed by someone who lived on the farm and was part of the community.[45]

Arnold also had time to pursue his hobbies and take up new ones. A passionate and omnivorous reader, he was once again able to indulge his

Arnold with half-brother Jim and half-sister Hazel at Arnold's 75th birthday, 1984.
[Platt Family Collection]

love of literature. He kept informed through subscriptions to everything, from the newsletter of the sheep producers association to academic journals in agricultural economics and plant and soil science, and local and international newspapers. He read because he loved good writing, he loved people, and he loved knowledge. John Schmidt aptly described him in retirement as "a scientist, a thinker, a savant."[46] Arnold liked nothing better than good, informed conversation, and he welcomed his neighbours and friends, who looking forward to stopping by to visit with such an informed and stimulating thinker. Sharing a meal and a drink was often part of a visit, and Arnold would contribute some of the wine he was now making, (Stew Wells having introduced Arnold to this hobby). He discovered that his black currant bushes produced a wine that he could declare to be "not bad."

He loved growing things, and transformed the farmyard to a garden. The growing season on the Ridge was short and the Chinook winds desiccated plants in the winter, but those were welcome challenges. Arnold

Arnold and Helen in the garden at the farm on Milk River Ridge.
[Gerald Schuler Private Collection]

built a greenhouse at the south end of the church addition, using windows he had salvaged. Not since he left his work at the research station had he had time to play around with growing things in a greenhouse. He would take his morning coffee directly from his bedroom to the greenhouse, there to be surrounded by flowers and greenery. Ever the scientist, he explored hydroponic production, succeeding with cucumbers and tomatoes. From the greenhouse, he could also appreciate the attractions of the outdoor garden, sheltered from the Chinook winds by a tall hedge. Arnold delighted in identifying the great variety of birds and other creatures that were attracted to the profusion of flowers and shrubs.

Arnold and Helen involved themselves in their community. They loved to host get-togethers with the neighbours, and they joined in the dances and card parties at the Jefferson Community Hall nearby. Arnold liked to tell of how he continued to have some influence in government: he helped arrange for the Hall to have a license fairly regularly to serve alcoholic drinks—this in the Municipal District of Cardston, where there

Helen, Margaret, Wayne, Arnold (back row); Billy Deneka, Jody and Cathy Oikawa, Barbara Deneka, 1979. [Platt Family Collection]

was no official liquor vendor. They went to ball games and theatre in Lethbridge, rodeos in Fort MacLeod, and on walks to see the springtime wildflowers in Police Outpost Provincial Park. This was home.

But Arnold and Helen were no stay-at-homes. Travelling allowed them to stay connected with their widely distributed family and their friends in Canada and the United States. The importance of family hit close to the heart for Arnold and Helen when their daughter Shirley's husband, Larry Deneka, and son, Billy, were killed in a small-airplane crash in August of 1982. Twelve-year-old Billy had spent part of that summer with Arnold and Helen at the farm, and he and Arnold had grown very close. After the accident, the family often got together for winter vacations in Mexico, Arizona, or, on one occasion, Hawaii.

On that holiday in Hawaii, Arnold, ever the agriculturalist, was nearly charged with trespassing when he stopped to investigate a field of pineapple. Having become intrigued by the possibility of developing strains of nitrogen-fixing wheat, he visited the International Maize and Wheat Improvement Centre (CIMMYT) in Mexico to explore ideas with the researchers there. Arnold revisited the Imperial Valley site in California, where he had multiplied the seed that became Rescue wheat, and called on his old friend Keith Mets, who had made the plots available; Mets and his wife later returned the visit. Arnold and Helen visited their son Wayne and Ann and their sons, who were then living in England, and several times traveled to continental Europe as well.

One of their trips became memorable for the wrong reasons. In early 1986, Arnold and Helen went to Albany, New York, to attend a friend's premiere performance: British composer George Lloyd's Symphony No. 11, which George Lloyd himself was conducting. They drove east, as Arnold never seemed to tire of long trips by car. Their plan included a family gathering in Albany before returning west for a stay in Arizona.

Somewhere in Nebraska, Arnold noticed numbness in his left arm. A visit to the nearest hospital emergency room confirmed that Arnold was having a heart attack. Bypass surgery was needed immediately, and he was taken by air ambulance to Lincoln, Nebraska. Fortunately, the couple had proper medical insurance and Arnold received the best care available. He was soon well enough to allow them to return to Calgary— but it was impossible for them to live on the farm that winter. Arnold would have to work through an extensive program of monitoring and rehabilitation.

Their friend and doctor, Hans Berkhout, arranged for Arnold to join a new program that had been introduced at the General Hospital in Calgary. At seventy-six, Arnold was the oldest person to be selected for that program. Arnold worked through the rehabilitation program with his usual diligence. Although the doctors told him that his pipe-smoking had not had any apparent ill effects, he decided that it was not doing him any good. He quit, and a habit that had been part of his identity for about sixty years was no longer part of him. Their friends the McVeans made a house available to them, and Calgary was home once more. Arnold's recovery was rapid enough that, by late March, Arnold and Helen were once more able to host a houseful of friends. By May, they were back at

Margaret, Shirley, Arnold, and Wayne, Goldeye, 1991. [Platt Family Collection]

the farm to continue the good life. Arnold was stoic about the limitations associated with aging; not for him would a litany of ailments pass for conversation.

But, in the late 1980s, he told those who knew him well that doctors had found a cancerous growth in his outer ear. He figured that what they had found might kill him eventually, but in the meantime he told the medical staff that they might as well "just cut the goddamned thing off." Friends noticed that occasionally his left ear looked as if it had been cut; sometimes it was bandaged, and it seemed to be getting smaller. That ear became his constant intimation of mortality. Whether the cancer in his ear was connected to the development of the tumour in his head, which was diagnosed in 1994, was not established. But there was no doubt about the outcome. His age made the tumour inoperable; its growth could be slowed with radiation, but its eradication was very unlikely.

There were a few more trips to be taken and visits to be made. He was drawn to those places he had known when he was young, the Innisfree district and south western Saskatchewan. In the fall of 1995, together with Pat and Don McVean, Helen and Arnold toured the back roads of the Swift Current area, where Arnold had started his professional career. That was his last trip. Brian Brennan recounts a moment from that visit:

> *He found the area thriving with prosperous farms. As he looked out over a flourishing tract of prairie wheatland, and got down on his hands and knees to feel and smell the earth, he realized his dream had not been impossible.*[47]

Another place was equally important to him: the site of the Grasslands National Park, which was then being established. Prosperous farms in the area showed what human beings applying good science and good management could do to improve nature; and the grasslands reminded Arnold that some things couldn't be improved. Knowing the difference was a mark of his genius; it was also what kept him ordinary.

In 1995, Arnold and Helen returned to live in Calgary. As the level of care that Arnold needed became greater, he had to be close to the offices and clinics of specialists. A friend's house in Crescent Heights was available, and it became a centre for family and friends. Their daughter Margaret still lived in Calgary; Shirley came from Waterloo, and Wayne from Australia, for long visits. Carol Ann Lughtiheid, Helen's daughter, also came from Ottawa.

As his pain intensified and his vision deteriorated, Arnold knew that death was imminent. He neither feared nor welcomed it. Until almost the last, he was able to say that he woke up every morning welcoming the day and curious to find out what it would bring. He died at home on April 7, 1996.

Family and friends came together at the Ranchmen's Club on April 13 to celebrate Arnold's life. He had not wanted a public ceremony to mark the occasion of his death. There were no tributes from politicians or officials of the many organizations with whom Arnold had been associated over his long career. Instead, the people who came together remembered the extraordinary friend that he had been. His granddaughter Barbara, recalling her happiest times, spoke for all who were there when she recalled those times with Arnold:

Recently someone asked me about my childhood—what were the happiest times? Going to my grandparents' farm was my reply. Almost every summer that I can remember, I was at the farm for a visit. I was always greeted with enthusiastic hugs and kisses, and in later years, with some good Scotch. Granddad enjoyed hiking and the two of us set out on many occasions. I was also fortunate to travel with Granddad and the rest of my family to Hawaii, Arizona, and his favourite spot in Mexico. I am very happy that I was able to spend so much time with Granddad because he was wise, kind, and lots of fun. I appreciated how he listened to my left-wing views with an open mind. He always had confidence in me and I know that he loved me very much. As many of you know, my father died when I was a teenager, and Granddad filled a bit of that void.

Those who could call Arnold a friend were blessed.

Conclusion

Arnold accomplished much. Driven by an obligation to do whatever good he was capable of, he showed a remarkable lack of ego as he focussed on accomplishing the task at hand but not on being recognized for it. He was analytical and reflective, but no one recalls that he ever explained his willingness to be the person in the background, the one who shaped the events being given a public face by others in the foreground. He had the intelligence, charm, wit, presence, and oratorical ability to be in the limelight but he consciously chose the other course.

As rational and logical as Arnold was, no such choice is ever entirely rational. It is tempting to suggest that this self-effacing quality derived from environmental influences, that his association with agriculture on the prairies during his era predisposed him to regard all hubristic expression with suspicion. The feeling of human insignificance in the face of nature's force and vastness has become trite; Arnold's character was much too nuanced to allow of such a reductive and deterministic explanation. One of Arnold's favourite books, Wallace Stegner's *Wolf Willow*, suggests that the environment of the prairie does not induce humility in its inhabitants.

Somewhat more plausible might be an explanation drawn from the history of agrarian movements and the nature of leadership to which those movements gave rise. Arnold was brought up during a time when farm movements generally eschewed power, preferring instead to have influence. Even when members of the United Farmers of Alberta stood for election in 1921, they did so with no intention of forming a government. Henry Wise Wood, president of the UFA from 1916 to 1931 and a leader whom Arnold greatly admired, exemplified the pattern. When the farmers' government was formed in 1921, Wood refused to become premier, preferring to exercise influence through farm organizations. Another role model and mentor for Arnold, George Church, adopted a similar position. Undoubtedly the non-partisan, egalitarian ideals of these people and the agrarian movements with which they were associated shaped Arnold's thinking about the effectiveness of leading from behind the scenes.

However, the kind of rural community that gave rise to those ideals was being transformed through the application of science and technology to agriculture. Arnold's training and experience as a scientist reinforced those qualities that inclined him to seek influence rather than power. It is a basic paradox of scientific education that the more one learns, the more one becomes aware of how little one knows. Arnold internalized that understanding of the limitations of knowledge and it made him humble. He could not claim the certainty that would allow for single-minded pursuit. That lack of absolute certainty, developed through his scientific training and complemented by his deep understanding of people, need not have stopped him from being the acknowledged leader if that is what he had wanted to be. But it was not something he wanted.

Why he did not want to put himself forward might have something to do with the way he was raised, with forces of which he was hardly aware. He grew up without a mother and without a home, but the need for what they represented had to be filled. Without that fulfillment, perhaps he lacked the nurturing, the security, and the encouragement necessary for him to take a place in the foreground.

It has been suggested that, inside every behind-the-scenes influencer or advisor, is a disappointed and disillusioned person. Arnold's life gives the lie to this saying. Just as he did not inveigh against the changes that were taking agriculture away from the communitarian past in which his model of influencing had been idealized, he did not resent the societal changes that associated significance with prominence.

The idea of leaving a legacy, of being remembered after his death for his achievements, was as unimportant to Arnold as had been renown and recognition while he was alive. Nonetheless, he was always interested in the future and would no doubt wonder if any of the ideas he had held, the policies he had shaped and promoted, the actions he had taken had an effect beyond the immediate occasion or event. An assessment of this falls outside the scope of an account of his life, although this account provides the necessary basis for one. It has revealed the nature of his involvement and achievement, but it would require the work of a historian of Canadian agriculture to determine the lasting significance of his work.

However, it is my belief that Arnold made at least three lasting contributions. At a time when farmers were near despair, his scientific work gave them reason to have faith in a better future. His research demonstrated the potential of using plant breeding to control insect damage long before methods of genetic manipulation became available. He also introduced the use of plots in southern California to grow two crops a year; Canadian plant breeders continue to follow his lead. At a time when changes to agriculture, brought on by the science and technology of which he was a part, had many people thinking that their way of life was doomed, his own agricultural practice and his leadership in policy-making showed that there was reason to hope.

The new kind of agriculture required education, and maybe that was a good thing, for that education could open up new possibilities for the next generation. It was through his love for young people, for bringing along the next generation, that Arnold left a legacy as valuable as anything else that he did. It starts with his immediate family. His son Wayne completed a Ph.D. in chemistry and had a distinguished career as a research chemist. Shirley was the only woman in her class in medical school and went on to become one of the few female pathologists in Canada. Margaret graduated from the University of Alberta and took on a long career of public service with the Calgary Board of Education. Arnold's grandchildren too have distinguished themselves as students; all have embarked on careers through which they are making significant contributions. Barbara Deneka spoke for them all when she credited Arnold's engagement with their lives for much of their success.

This story of Arnold's life has mentioned only a few of the people beyond his immediate family whose lives and careers he affected profoundly. Gerald Schuler's remark—that one could have no better mentor or more loyal friend than Arnold—captures the feeling of those individuals. There are also many whom Arnold quietly helped when their circumstances had become difficult. And leaders continue to be developed at Goldeye.

Helen Platt recalls a remark Peter Lougheed made to her not long before Arnold died. "The world needs more Arnold Platts."

Notes

One. Farmhouses, Schoolhouses, and the Quest for Home

1. All quotes in this first chapter, unless otherwise noted, are transcribed from the tape recordings Arnold made for his family in 1989.
2. The Loree School, built and opened in 1912, was somewhat unusual in that it was constructed of brick. The first chairman of the school district, J.M. Loree, insisted on brick construction. He believed strongly in education and wanted the school to have the air of permanence associated with brick. He put his own money into the school's construction because the grant from the government covered only a small percentage of the cost.
3. The Platt family papers contain Arnold's written account of the move to Westlock. He also tape recorded his recollections.
4. The transcript does not show mid-term results and Arnold could not remember whether it was two or three exams that he had passed.

Two. Research, Rescue Wheat, and Recognition

1. *Report of Activities Under the Prairie Farm Rehabilitation Act, November 15, 1935*, Library, Lethbridge Research Centre (LLRC).
2. Mark Kilcher notes that five houses were built in 1926 in *Swift Current Research Station 1920–1985* (Ottawa: Agriculture Canada Historical Series, 1986). http://collections.ic.gc.ca/agrican/pubweb/hs250005.asp#hs25_44. Shirley (Platt) Deneka remembers that the family lived on what was known as the South Farm.
3. PFRA report for the year ended March 31, 1936, 7. LLRC.
4. PFRA report for the year ending March 31, 1937, 13. LLRC.
5. Stu McBean, interview October 4, 2004; Baden Campbell, *The Swift Current Research Station 1920–70* (Ottawa: Canada Department of Agriculture, 1971), 31.
6. H.J. Kemp, "Studies on Solid Stem Wheat in Relation to Wheat Stem Sawfly Control," *Scientific Agriculture* 15 (1934): 30–38.
7. Transcript of Chris Farstad's tribute to Arnold Platt on Arnold's resignation from the Lethbridge Research Station. Archival file "A.W. Platt," Library, Lethbridge Research Centre, Lethbridge, Alberta.
8. The story of the development of Rescue wheat that follows is a synthesis of the accounts that Arnold provided in the scientific and popular papers that he published. Those papers are listed in the References.
9. A.W. Platt, "The Influence of Some Environmental Factors on the Expression of the Solid Stem Character in Certain Wheat Varieties," *Scientific Agriculture* 21, no. 3 (1941): 139–51.
10. A.W. Platt, "Breeding Wheats for Sawfly Resistance," *Canadian Geographical Journal* xxxiii, no. 3 (1946): 138–41.

11. Platt, "Influence of Some Environmental Factors."
12. George E. Britnell and Vernon C. Fowke, *Canadian Agriculture in War and Peace, 1935–50* (Stanford, Calif., Stanford University Press, 1962), 108.
13. Interview with Stu McBean, October 4, 2004.
14. Alice Wall's article for the newsletter is included in the archival file "A.W. Platt" held in the LLRC.
15. This memo and other reports are in the collection of Arnold Platt's files on the development of Rescue wheat held in the office of Dr. Ron DePauw, Semiarid Prairie Agricultural Research Centre (SPARC), Swift Current, Saskatchewan.
16. Library and Archives Canada (LAC), RG 17 Vol 2851. Another copy is in the collection of Arnold's files at SPARC.
17. Minutes of the meeting, LAC, RG 17 Vol 3673.
18. The memos that provide the basis for the account that follows are in the LAC, RG 17 Vol 2851.
19. Memo from E.S. Archibald to Deputy Minister, November 28, 1944, LAC RG 17 Vol 2851, File I-44–5.
20. This report is in the LAC, RG 17 Vol 2851. Another copy is in the collection of Arnold's files at SPARC.
21. This report is in the collection of Arnold's files at SPARC.
22. Farstad, tribute to Arnold Platt.
23. Quoted in P.C. 9/9555, A Minute of a Meeting of the Treasury Board, December 28, 1944. In LAC, RG 17 Vol 2851, File I-44–5.
24. Farstad, tribute.

THREE. Never a Bureaucrat

1. LAC, RG 17 Vol 2851.
2. This title is used in Archibald's memo. The document was not published and there is no copy extant.
3. Campbell, *Swift Current Research Station*, 36.
4. The documents that are quoted in and inform the following account are in the Arnold Platt files held at SPARC.
5. "Proposed Plan for Cereal Plant Breeding in Western Canada," Arnold Platt files, SPARC.
6. L.H. Newman, "The Organization of Cereal Work Under Dominion Experimental Farms System," Arnold Platt files, SPARC.
7. Memo, LAC RG 17 Vol 2851.
8. Arnold Platt files, SPARC.
9. Arnold Platt files, SPARC.
10. Arnold Platt files, SPARC.
11. T.H. Anstey, *One Hundred Harvests: Research Branch Agriculture Canada 1886–1986* (Ottawa, Agriculture Canada, 1986).

12. Anstey, *One Hundred Harvests*, Chapter 7, available at http://collections.ic.gc.ca/agrican/pubweb/hs270129.asp.
13. Anstey, *One Hundred Harvests*, Chapter 9.
14. Anstey, *One Hundred Harvests*, Chapter 9.
15. *Lethbridge Herald*, special section, September 17, 1949, 4.
16. *Lethbridge Herald*, September 17, 1949, 4.
17. *Lethbridge Herald*, September 17, 1949, 6.
18. Discussion with author, September 2004.
19. Arnold Platt files, SPARC.
20. Arnold Platt files, SPARC.
21. Alice Wall's profile of Arnold, "Arnold William Platt" was published in the untitled Lethbridge Research Station newsletter, vol 2, no 3, March, 1951. A copy exists in the archival file on Anold Platt at the LLRC.
22. Discussion with author, October 2004.
23. Discussion with author, August 2004.
24. Hoffman J. Powley, *Swift Current and District Memories* (Swift Current, SK: H.J. Powley, 1986), Chapter D, 4.
25. Personal communication, c1976 or 1977. Other than what Arnold told me, no record of this involvement exists and none of his colleagues from that time remembers this activity. However, circumstantial evidence supports his account.
26. *Swift Current Sun*, February 13, 1940.
27. Campbell, *Swift Current Research Station*, 41.
28. LAC, RG 17 Vol 3673, N 10–45A.
29. LAC, RG 17 Vol 3673, N 10–45.
30. LAC, RG 17 Vol 3673, N 10–45.
31. Personal communication, c1976 or 1977.
32. Britnell and Fowke, *Canadian Agriculture*, 142.
33. The Agricultural Institute of Canada does not have an archive as such, but it has compiled several scrapbooks of historical materials, which are stored in its Ottawa office. The past presidents of the organization are included in an archival scrapbook.
34. The archival scrapbook of the Agricultural Institute of Canada contains an undated draft of "A History of the Agricultural Institute of Canada: The First Ten Years" by Dr. M.B. Davis. Pages 13–18 discuss the Institute's views on marketing education.
35. This letter, the only one from this time that Arnold kept, is in the Platt Family Papers, private collection.
36. Jessie Oxford (Spencer) made this point in the interview on September 22, 2004. Helen Platt corroborated the story as one that Arnold had told her.
37. Discussion with Stew Wells, September 2004.
38. This memo and the following ones in this passage are in the archival file "A.W. Platt" at the LLRC.

39. Anstey, *One Hundred Harvests.*
40. "Wheat Stem Sawfly Widespread," Statpub.com, http://www.statpub.com/open/78102.html.
41. Discussions with the author, 2004.

FOUR. The Scientific Farmer and *The Organized Farmer*

1. Hugh Dempsey, *The Gentle Persuader: A Biography of James Gladstone, Indian Senator* (Saskatoon: Western Producer Prairie Books, 1986), 110.
2. Dempsey, *The Gentle Persuader,* 111.
3. Department of Indian and Northern Affairs, File 772/32–2–148–36, vol 1.
4. Department of Indian and Northern Affairs, File 772/32–2–148–36, vol 1.
5. *Organized Farmer,* October 1958, 14.
6. Canada Department of Indian Affairs and Northern Development, File 772/32–2–148–36, vol 1.
7. Carrol L. Jaques, *Unifarm: A Story of Conflict and Change* (Calgary: University of Calgary Press, 2001), 12–13.
8. Norman F. Priestley and Edward B. Swindlehurst, *Furrows, Faith and Fellowship* (Edmonton: Co-op Press, 1967), 246.
9. Priestley and Swindlehurst, *Furrows, Faith and Fellowship,* 249.
10. Interview with Stu McBean October 4, 2004.
11. Priestley and Swindlehurst, *Furrows, Faith and Fellowship,* 269.
12. Harry Patching related the story of how Arnold became involved in the Farmers' Union of Alberta during the interview on November 18, 2004.
13. Arnold Platt's tape recordings, 1989.
14. Personal communication, 1973.
15. *The Organized Farmer* 14, no. 6 (June 1955): 3.
16. This account is based on Gerald Schuler's anecdote, recorded in an interview October 23, 2004.
17. Interview, November 18, 2004.
18. Priestley and Swindlehurst, *Furrows, Faith and Fellowship,* 284.
19. *Organized Farmer,* January 1955.
20. *Organized Farmer,* September 1956, 12–13.
21. *Organized Farmer,* January 1956, 14–15.
22. *A Historical Series of Agricultural Statistics for Alberta—Selected Statistics from the Census of Agriculture,* Agdex 852–4.
23. Discussion with the author, October 2004.
24. *Organized Farmer,* February 1957.
25. *Organized Farmer,* May 1957, 19.
26. *Organized Farmer,* March 1956.
27. *Organized Farmer,* March 1956.
28. *Organized Farmer,* March 1957, 5.
29. *Organized Farmer,* May 1957, 10–11.

30. *Organized Farmer,* July 1957.
31. *Organized Farmer,* September 1957, 10.
32. Denis Smith, *Rogue Tory: The Life and Legend of John G. Diefenbaker* (Toronto: Macfarlane Walter & Ross, 1995), 261–62.
33. *Organized Farmer,* January 1957, 11.
34. *Organized Farmer,* August 1958, 22.
35. *Organized Farmer,* November 1957, 4.
36. *Organized Farmer,* September 1958, 16.
37. *Organized Farmer,* September 1958, 16–17.
38. *Organized Farmer,* September 1958, 3.
39. *Organized Farmer,* October 1958, 4.
40. *Organized Farmer,* February 1958, 4–5.
41. See for example L.H. Newman, "New Wheat Creations and their Significance to Canada," *Canadian Geographical Journal* xvii; no. 4 (April 1939): 208–16, esp. p. 192.
42. Smith, *Rogue Tory,* 224.
43. Discussion with the author, November 2004.
44. *Organized Farmer,* January 1957, 11.
45. *Organized Farmer,* June 1957, 9.
46. *Organized Farmer,* August 1958, 4.
47. *Organized Farmer,* August 1958, 15.
48. *Organized Farmer,* November 1956, 12.
49. Discussion with author, October 2004.
50. *Organized Farmer,* December 1958, 6.
51. Discussion with the author, August 2004.
52. *Organized Farmer,* May 1957, 3–4.
53. Interview with Shirley (Platt) Deneka.
54. Personal communication, 1976.
55. R.H. MacDonald, *Grant MacEwan: No Ordinary Man* (Saskatoon: Western Producer Prairie Books, 1979), 200.
56. *Organized Farmer,* December 1958, 6.

FIVE. Shaping the Future

1. Arnold Platt, quoted in John Schmidt, "Agricultural Alberta," *Calgary Herald,* July 2, 1963.
2. *Organized Farmer,* February 1957, 10.
3. *Organized Farmer,* September 1957, 9.
4. *Organized Farmer,* June 1957, 11.
5. *Organized Farmer,* February 1956.
6. *Organized Farmer,* September 1957, 19.
7. Interview with Alex McCalla, Edmonton, August 2004.
8. Interview with Alex McCalla.

9. Interview with Alex McCalla.
10. Interview with Alex McCalla.
11. Platt family Papers. Arnold kept copies of the documents referred to that are related to the development of the Goldeye Camp, an indication of its importance to him. The change in the statement of "Aim" from "youth" to "people" signals the expansion of Arnold's thinking about the intended participants and beneficiaries. The Camp was to be a place for leadership development of adults as well as youth.
12. Platt Family Papers, Dedication of Blunden Manor.
13. "Address at Dedication of Blunden Manor," Platt Family Papers.
14. "Address at Dedication of Blunden Manor," Platt Family Papers.
15. Jaques, *Unifarm*, 110.
16. Platt Family Papers.
17. Jaques, *Unifarm*, 111.
18. Jaques, *Unifarm*, 117.
19. Platt Family Papers.
20. The Platt Family papers contain Arnold's personal calendars for these years.
21. Desmond E. Berghofer and Alan Vladicka, *Access to Opportunity 1905–80: The Development of Post-Secondary Education in Alberta* ([Edmonton]: Alberta Advanced Education and Manpower, 1980), 28–29.
22. The evidence provided in the minutes of Board meetings corroborates statements Arnold made about the issues that he was involved in.
23. "Notes for the Goldeye Meeting August 5, 1977," Platt Family Papers.
24. Donald Cameron, *The Impossible Dream* (Alcraft Printing and Bulletin Commercial Printers, 1977), 189.
25. *UFA Cooperator* 5, no. 2 (February 1967).
26. Board of Governors, October 9, 1959.
27. Talk at Newest Forum for the Arts, Goldeye Centre, July, 1988. The manuscript is in the Platt Family Papers.
28. Travis Manning, The Department of Agricultural Economics," in *The First Fifty Years: A History of the Faculty of Agriculture 1915–1965*, ed. W. Earl Bowser [Edmonton, AB]: University of Alberta, Faculty of Agriculture, [1965].
29. Discussion with the author, May 2005.
30. Interview, May 26, 2005.
31. UAA, Faculty of Agriculture, Accession 76–25, Box 5.
32. Interview on May 26, 2005. Dr. Warrack graduated with a B.Sc. in Agriculture at the University of Alberta in 1961, then Dr. Ball supervised Allan Warrack's doctoral work at Iowa, and in 1967 Dr. Warrack joined the Department of Agricultural Economics at Alberta.
33. UAA, Faculty of Agriculture, Accession 76–25, Vol 73.
34. UAA, Faculty of Agriculture, 76–25, Vol 75.
35. UAA, Faculty of Agriculture, 76–25, Box 5.
36. Discussion with the author, May 2005.
37. Discussion with the author, October 2004.

38. Personal communication, 1980s.
39. Agricultural Economics Advisory Committee Constitution. UAA, Faculty of Agriculture, Accession 76–25, Vol 75.
40. Agricultural Economics Advisory Committee Constitution. UAA 76–25, Vol 75.
41. Platt Family Papers.
42. Convocation Address.
43. Minutes, Executive Committee 3AU Fund, February 14, 1969, UCA Files 24.01, Accession No. 83.007.
44. Minutes, Executive Committee 3AU Fund, August 13, 1969, UCA File 24.01, Accession No. 83.007.

Six. Not Made in Alberta

1. Charles F. Wilson Fonds, LAC, MG 30 E301, Vol 1, file 10. The file contains memos and reports that inform the account that follows.
2. A.S. Ivanov, *International Wheat Agreements, 1949–1964* (London: International Sugar Council, 1964). This booklet is in the Charles F. Wilson Fonds cited above.
3. Ivanov, *International Wheat Agreements*, 2.
4. Letter from Charles Wilson to J. H. English, Deputy Minister of Trade and Commerce, dated January 7, 1959, Charles F. Wilson Fonds, LAC, MG 30 E301 Vol. 1, file 10.
5. Honourable Gordon Churchill Papers, LAC, MG 32 B9 Vol. 64, file International Wheat Conference 1959, briefing document, 21 October, 1958, Grain Division, Department of Trade and Commerce, Ottawa, p. 1.
6. Alfred P. Gleave, *United We Stand: Prairie Farmers 1901–1975* (Toronto: Lugus Press, 1991), 151.
7. Ivanov, *International Wheat Agreements*, 13.
8. Gleave, *United We Stand*, 152.
9. Gleave, *United We Stand*, 152.
10. Charles F. Wilson Fonds, LAC, MG 30 E301, Vol 1, file 10.
11. Ivanov, *International Wheat Agreements*, 10.
12. Howard Darling,*The Politics of Freight Rates: The Railway Freight Issue in Canada* (Toronto: McClelland and Stewart, 1980), 133.
13. Darling, *The Politics of Freight Rates*, 191.
14. Darling, *The Politics of Freight Rates*, 151.
15. Darling, *The Politics of Freight Rates*, 204.
16. Darling, *The Politics of Freight Rates*, 206.
17. Darling, *The Politics of Freight Rates*, 208.
18. Diefenbaker Papers, MG01/V1/732/T773.51; VI 7494.1 and VI 7494.2, vol 487.
19. Darling, *The Politics of Freight Rates*, 214.
20. Don Thomson, *Lethbridge Herald*, May 21, 1959.
21. Order-in-Council P.C. 1959–577.

22. Darling, *The Politics of Freight Rates*, 213.
23. Darling, *The Politics of Freight Rates*, 198.
24. Darling, *The Politics of Freight Rates*, 214.
25. Discussion with the author, May 2005.
26. Press Release, Volume I, April 10, 1961.
27. Diefenbaker papers, MGO/VI/4462, 323.
28. Arnold and Donna had been unhappy for several years by this point, and were divorced in 1966. Arnold and Helen married in 1967.
29. Flannery O'Connor, *Wise Blood* (New York: Farrar, Straus and Giroux, 1962), 113.
30. Darling, *The Politics of Freight Rates*, 218.
31. Darling, *The Politics of Freight Rates*, 218.
32. *Lethbridge Herald*, February 6, 1960, 2.
33. Darling, *The Politics of Freight Rates*, 218.
34. Darling, *The Politics of Freight Rates*, 218.
35. *Organized Farmer*, September 1958, 16.
36. LAC, RG 33–49 Vol. 68, File 2–7–1, vol. 3.
37. Darling, *The Politics of Freight Rates*, 219.
38. Confidential memorandum from Robert Bryce, Clerk of the Privy Council, to Diefenbaker on January 17, 1961. Diefenbaker Papers, MG01/XII/C/388, 75.
39. Darling, *The Politics of Freight Rates*, 151.
40. *Report of the Royal Commission on Transportation (1959–62)* Volume 1, p. 2.
41. Darling, *The Politics of Freight Rates*, 214.
42. Discussions with the author.
43. Darling, *The Politics of Freight Rates*, 219.
44. Jerry Fast, *Economic Efficiency and National Transportation Policy: A Study of the Turgeon and MacPherson Royal Commissions*, M.A. thesis, University of Manitoba, 1971, 177.
45. *Report*, Volume 2, 2.
46. *Report*, Volume 1, 40.
47. *Report*, Volume 1, 31.
48. *Report*, Volume 1, 49–50.
49. Darling, *The Politics of Freight Rates*, 226.

Seven. The Freedom to Serve Agriculture

1. Platt Family Papers.
2. Sales for 1961 were reported in the "United Farmers of Alberta Board of Directors Report" [to the annual meeting], November 1961. Sales for 1967 were reported in "Excerpts from Mr. McCartney's Report to the Annual Meeting," *The United Farmer*, November 1967, 3. Both documents are contained in the historical materials held at the Lethbridge office of the United Farmers of Alberta Cooperative.
3. Shirley (Platt) Deneka.

4. Report of the Committee on Farm Organization to the Board of Directors of the Alberta Federation of Agriculture, 1963, Appendix 1.
5. *Report*, 1963, 7.
6. *Report*, 1963, 8.
7. Tape recording, PAA, 1970.
8. This is a summary of the case, as presented on pages 15–16 in Platt, A.W., D. Cameron, and L. Nesbitt. *Report of the Committee on Farm Organization to the Board of Directors of the Alberta Federation of Agriculture*, 1963.
9. Tape recording, PAA, 1970.
10. Jaques, *Unifarm*, 73.
11. *Report of the Committee on Farm Organization to the Board of Directors of the Alberta Federation of Agriculture*, 1963, 14.
12. *Report*, 1963, 24.
13. Jaques, *Unifarm*, 57.
14. "Submission to the Royal Commission on Farm Machinery," March 16, 1967, 3.
15. Platt, Brief presented to the Royal Commission on Farm Machinery, the Barber Commission, in March 1967, 3.
16. Platt, Brief to the Barber Commission, 4.
17. Platt, Brief to the Barber Commission, 5.
18. Platt, Brief to the Barber Commission, 11–12.
19. Minutes, UFA Board of Directors, April 26–27, 1966.
20. UFA Board Minutes, February 17–18, 1965.
21. Platt Family Papers.
22. Executive Meeting Minutes, April 25, 1966.
23. Minutes of UFA Board of Directors, January 4 and 5, 1971.
24. L.B. Doscher, *Survey on Farmers Attitudes* (Edmonton: Farmers' Union and Co-operative Development Association, 1965), 36.
25. A.W. Platt, *Agriculture and Rural Development* (Ottawa: Liberal Federation of Canada, 1966), 5.
26. Platt, *Agriculture and Rural Development*, 3.
27. Platt, *Agriculture and Rural Development*, 4.
28. Platt, *Agriculture and Rural Development*, 4.
29. Platt, *Agriculture and Rural Development*, 4.
30. Platt, *Agriculture and Rural Development*, 6.
31. Platt, *Agriculture and Rural Development*, 6.
32. Platt, *Agriculture and Rural Development*, 6.
33. Platt, *Agriculture and Rural Development*, 7.
34. Platt, *Agriculture and Rural Development*, 7.
35. Platt, *Agriculture and Rural Development*, 9.
36. Platt, *Agriculture and Rural Development*, 9.
37. Platt, *Agriculture and Rural Development*, 9.
38. Platt, *Agriculture and Rural Development*, 9.
39. Platt, *Agriculture and Rural Development*, 9–10.

40. Platt, *Agriculture and Rural Development*, 11.

41. Platt, *Agriculture and Rural Development*, 11.

42. Platt, *Agriculture and Rural Development*, 11.

43. Platt, *Agriculture and Rural Development*, 15–16.

EIGHT. The Servant of the People Finds His Home

1.   A.W. Platt, *The Role of Government in Group Conflicts: A Case Study*, 1980, unpublished report, 42–43.

2.   The committee of cabinet included David Russell, Minister of Municipal Affairs; Dr. Hugh Horner, Deputy Premier and Minister of Agriculture; and Bob Dowling, Minister without Portfolio. Dowling had chaired the Select Committee of the Assembly Communal Property that produced the *Report on Communal Property 1972* and recommended the repeal of the Communal Property Act.

3.   *Calgary Herald*, February 24, 1973.

4.   Platt, *The Role of Government*, 89.

5.   Platt, *The Role of Government*, 122

6.   Platt, *The Role of Government*, 123.

7.   Platt, *The Role of Government*, 76.

8.   Platt, *The Role of Government*, 78.

9.   *Calgary Herald*, March 17, 1973.

10. *Calgary Herald*, March 23, 1973.

11. Platt, *The Role of Government*, 79.

12. Platt, *The Role of Government*, 79.

13. *Calgary Herald*, May 10, 1973.

14. Platt, *The Role of Government*, 79.

15. Platt, *The Role of Government*, 76.

16. Platt, *The Role of Government*, 77.

17. Platt, *The Role of Government*, 81.

18. Platt, *The Role of Government*, 81.

19. *Calgary Herald*, November 27, 1975.

20. Speaking notes, Platt Family Papers.

21. Platt, *The Role of Government*, 106.

22. *Alberta Land Use Forum: Report and Recommendations* (Edmonton: Alberta Land Use Forum, 1976), 1.

23. *Alberta Land Use Forum*, i.

24. *Western Producer*, March 1, 1973.

25. *Alberta Land Use Forum*, 174.

26. *Alberta Land Use Forum*, 186.

27. *Alberta Land Use Forum*, 205.

28. Platt Family Papers.

29. *Alberta Land Use Forum*, 1.

30. *Alberta Land Use Forum*, 2.

31. *Alberta Land Use Forum*, 3.

32. *Alberta Land Use Forum*, 129.

33. *Edmonton Journal*, February 1, 1976.

34. *Alberta Land Use Forum*, xxxi.

35. *Alberta Land Use Forum*, xviii.

36. *Alberta Land Use Forum*, xxx.

37. *Alberta Land Use Forum*, xli.

38. *Oldman River Basin—Phase II Studies: Report and Recommendations*, August, 1978, 1.

39. *Management of Water Resources within the Oldman River Basin: Report and Recommendations*, August 1979, 4.

40. *Resources within the Oldman River*, 5.

41. *Resources within the Oldman River*, 5.

42. *Resources within the Oldman River*, 5.

43. *Resources within the Oldman River*, 97.

44. *Calgary Herald*, August 29, 1979.

45. *Calgary Herald*, December 27, 1983.

46. *Alberta Farm & Ranch*, September, 1989, 20.

47. Brian Brennan, *Building a Province: 60 Alberta Lives* (Calgary: Fifth House, 2000), 114.

References

Aamodt, O.S., and A.W. Platt. "Resistance of Wild Oats and Some Common Cereal Varieties to Freezing Temperatures." *Scientific Agriculture* 14 (1934): 645–50.

Alberta Agriculture: A History in Graphs. Edmonton: Alberta Department of Agriculture, c1975.

Alberta Land Use Forum: Report and Recommendations. Edmonton: Alberta Land Use Forum, 1976.

Anstey, T.H. *One Hundred Harvests: Research Branch Agriculture Canada 1886–1986.* Ottawa, Agriculture Canada, 1986. Available at http://collections.ic.gc.ca/agrican/pubweb/hs270129.asp.

Archibald, E.S. *The Story of Canadian Wheat: Hilgendorf Memorial Address 1949.* Ottawa: Department of Agriculture, 1949.

Berghofer, Desmond E., and Alan Vladicka. *Access to Opportunity 1905–80: the Development of Post-Secondary Education in Alberta.* [Edmonton]: Alberta Advanced Education and Manpower, 1980.

Boothe, Paul. *Eric J. Hanson's Financial History of Alberta 1905–1950.* Calgary: University of Calgary Press, 2003.

Brennan, Brian. *Building a Province: 60 Alberta Lives.* Calgary: Fifth House, 2000.

Britnell, George E., and Vernon C. Fowke. *Canadian Agriculture in War and Peace, 1935–50.* Stanford, Calif.: Stanford University Press, 1962.

Cameron, Donald. *The Impossible Dream.* Printed by Alcraft Printing and Bulletin Commercial Printers, 1977.

Campbell, J. Baden. *The Swift Current Research Station 1920–70.* Ottawa: Canada Dept. of Agriculture, 1971.

Canada. *Canada Year Book 1950.* Ottawa: King's Printer, 1950.

Canada. *Canada Year Book 1957–58.* Ottawa: Queen's Printer, 1958.

Canada. *Royal Commission on Transportation (1959–1962).* 3 vols. Ottawa: Queen's Printer, 1961–1962 (vol. 1, March 1961; vol. 2, December 1961; vol. 3, July 1962).

Canada. "Farm and Non-Farm Populations, 1921–2001." http://www.statcan.ca/english/freepub/95F0303XIE/tables/html/agpop14.htm.

Darling, Howard. *The Politics of Freight Rates: The Railway Freight Issue in Canada.* Toronto: McClelland and Stewart, 1980.

Dempsey, Hugh. *The Gentle Persuader: A Biography of James Gladstone, Indian Senator.* Saskatoon: Western Producer Prairie Books, 1986.

Doscher, L.B. *Survey on Farmers Attitudes.* Edmonton: Farmers' Union and Co-operative Development Association, 1965.

Emery, J.C.H., and R.D. Kneebone. "100 Years of Economic Development in Alberta and Saskatchewan and the Prospects for Increased Economic Integration," *C.D. Howe Institute Commentary* no. 190 (November, 2003). Available at www.cdhowe.org/pdf/commentary_190.pdf.

Fast, Jerry. *Economic Efficiency and National Transportation Policy: A Study of the Turgeon and MacPherson Royal Commissions*. M.A. thesis, University of Manitoba, 1971.

Friesen, Gerald. *The Canadian Prairies: A History*. Toronto: University of Toronto Press, 1984.

Gleave, Alfred P. *United We Stand: Prairie Farmers 1901–1975*. Toronto: Lugus Press, 1991.

Glenn, Jack. *Once upon an Oldman: Special Interest Politics and the Oldman River Dam*. Vancouver: UBC Press, 1999.

Historical Series of Agricultural Statistics for Alberta. Edmonton: Alberta Department of Agriculture. Statistics Branch. Agdex no. 852–4, 1995.

Ivanov, A.S. *International Wheat Agreements 1949–1964*. London: International Sugar Council, 1964.

Jaques, Carrol L. *Unifarm: A Story of Conflict and Change*. Calgary: University of Calgary Press, 2001.

Jenkins, R.C., A.W. Platt, and L.B. Thomson. "The Field Increase of Cereals During the Winter Months." *Scientific Agriculture* 27, no. 4 (1947): 157–61.

Johns, Walter H. *A History of the University of Alberta*. Edmonton: University of Alberta Press, 1981.

Johnson, Alex. *To Serve Agriculture—The Lethbridge Research Station 1906–1976*. Ottawa: Agriculture Canada Historical Series, 1977.

Keller, Evelyn Fox. *A Feeling for the Organism: The Life and Work of Barbara McClintock*. San Francisco: W.H. Freeman, 1983.

Kemp, H.J. "Studies on Solid Stem Wheat in Relation to Wheat Stem Sawfly Control." *Scientific Agriculture* 15 (1934): 30–38.

Kilcher, M.G. *Swift Current Research Station 1920–1985*. Ottawa: Agriculture Canada Historical Series, 1986.

MacDonald, R.H. *Grant MacEwan: No Ordinary Man*. Saskatoon: Western Producer Prairie Books, 1979.

Manning, Travis. "The Department of Agricultural Economics." In *The First Fifty Years: A History of the Faculty of Agriculture 1915–1965*, edited by W. Earl Bowser. Edmonton: University of Alberta, Faculty of Agriculture, 1965.

Mason, Gregg. "The Grain Handling and Transportation Commission." *Canadian Public Policy* 4, no. 2 (1978): 235–45.

McBean, D.S., and A.W. Platt. "Differential Damage to Barley Varieties by Grasshoppers." *Scientific Agriculture* 31 (1951): 162–75.

Menzies, Merril W. "Grain Marketing Methods in Canada—The Theory, Assumptions and Approach," *American Journal of Agricultural Economics* 55, no. 4 (1973): 791–99.

National Film Board of Canada. *The Drylanders*. [film], 1963.

Nesbitt, Leonard D. *The Story of Wheat*. Calgary: Alberta Wheat Pool, 1953.

Newman, L.H. "New Wheat Creations and their Significance to Canada." *Canadian Geographical Journal* xvii, no. 4 (April 1939): 208–16.

Newman, Peter C. *Renegade in Power: The Diefenbaker Years*. Toronto: McClelland and Stewart, 1963.

O'Byrne, M.B., Dudley Batchelor, and Arnold Platt. *Report of the Committee Which Considered Allowances and Salaries Paid to: Members of the Legislative Assembly, the Deputy Speaker, The Speaker, The Leader of the Opposition, Members of the Executive Council, the Premier*. Edmonton: Government of Alberta, 1972.

O'Connor, Flannery. 1952. *Wise Blood*. New York: Farrar, Straus and Giroux, 1962.

Olds College. *Golden Echoes: Olds School of Agriculture 50th Anniversary Yearbook*. Olds, Alberta: Olds College, 1963.

Platt, A.W. *Agriculture and Rural Development*. Ottawa: Liberal Federation of Canada, 1966.

——. "Breeding Wheats for Sawfly Resistance." *Canadian Geographical Journal* xxxiii, no. 3 (1946): 138–41.

——."The Effect of Freezing Temperatures and of Defoliation on the Subsequent Growth of Wheat Plants." *Scientific Agriculture* 17, no. 7 (1937): 420–30.

——. "The Effect of Soil Moisture, Hardening, Endosperm Condition and Variety on the Frost Reaction of Wheat, Oat and Barley Seedlings." *Scientific Agriculture* 17, no. 10 (1937): 616–26.

——. "The Influence of Some Environmental Factors on the Expression of the Solid Stem Character in Certain Wheat Varieties." *Scientific Agriculture* 21, no. 3 (1941): 139–51.

——. "Laboratory Magic." *Swift Current: Cooper's Store News*, 1943.

——. *The Reaction of Certain Cereals to Freezing Temperatures*. M.Sc. Thesis. University of Alberta, 1936.

——. *The Role of Government in Group Conflicts: A Case Study*, 1980. Unpublished ms.

Platt, A.W., A.D. Crerar, T.A. Sissons, and D. Thompson. *Management of Water Resources Within the Oldman River Basin: Report and Recommendations*. Edmonton: Environment Council of Alberta, August 1979.

Platt, A.W., D. Cameron, and L. Nesbitt. *Report of the Committee on Farm Organization to the Board of Directors of the Alberta Federation of Agriculture*. Edmonton: Alberta Federation of Agriculture, 1963.

Platt, A.W., and J.G. Darroch. "The Seedling Resistance of Wheat Varieties to Artificial Drought in Relation to Grain Yield." *Scientific Agriculture* 22, no. 9 (1947): 521–27.

Platt, A.W., J.G. Darroch, and H.J. Kemp. "The Inheritance of Solid Stem and Certain Other Characteristics in Crosses Between Varieties of Triticum Vulgare." *Scientific Agriculture* 22, no. 4 (1941): 216–23.

Platt, A.W., and C.W. Farstad. "The Reaction of Wheat Varieties to Wheat Stem Sawfly Attack." *Scientific Agriculture* 26, no. 6 (1946): 231–47.

——"The Resistance of Crop Plants to Insect Attack." Swift Current: Dominion Experimental Station, 1941.

Platt, A.W., C.W. Farstad, and J.A. Callenbach. "The Reaction of Rescue Wheat to Sawfly Damage." *Scientific Agriculture* 28, no. 4 (1948): 154–61.

Platt, A.W., and H.J. Kemp. "Solid Stemmed Wheat Varieties in Relation to Sawfly Control: A Summary of Investigations 1929–1936." Ottawa: Cereal Division,

Central Experimental Farm, 1937.

Platt, A.W., and Ruby Larson. "An Attempt to Transfer Solid Stem from *Triticum Durum* to *T. Vulgare* by Hybridization." *Scientific Agriculture* 24, no. 5 (1943): 214–20.

Platt, A.W., and S.A. Wells. "Shattering, Breaking and Threshability in Barley Varieties." *Scientific Agriculture* 29 (1949): 453–64.

Powley, Hoffman J. *Swift Current and District Memories.* Swift Current, Sask.: H.J. Powley, 1986.

Priestley, Norman F., and Edward B. Swindlehurst. *Furrows, Faith and Fellowship.* Edmonton: Co-op Press, 1967.

Proceedings of the World's Grain Exhibition and Conference, Regina Canada, July 24–August 5, 1933, vol II. Ottawa: Canadian Society of Technical Agriculturalists, 1933.

Public Hearings on Management of Water Resources Within the Oldman River Basin: Report and Recommendations. Edmonton: Environment Council of Alberta, 1979.

Report of Activities Under the Prairie Farm Rehabilitation Act, November 15, 1935. Ottawa: Department of Agriculture, 1935.

Report of Proceedings Under the Prairie Farm Rehabilitation Act for the Fiscal Year Ending March 31, 1937. Ottawa: Department of Agriculture, 1937.

Report on Communal Property 1972. Alberta. Legislative Assembly. Select Committee on Communal Property, 1972.

Report to the Minister of Municipal Affairs—Alberta Special Advisory Committee on Communal Property and Land Use. Calgary: Alberta Special Advisory Committee on Communal Property and Land Use, 1973.

Rolph, William Kirby. *Henry Wise Wood of Alberta.* Toronto: University of Toronto Press, 1950.

Smith, Denis. *Rogue Tory: The Life and Legend of John G. Diefenbaker.* Toronto: Macfarlane Walter & Ross, 1995.

Statpub.com. "Wheat Stem Sawfly Widespread," February 2, 2004. Available at http://www.statpub.com /open/78102.html.

Stegner, Wallace. *Wolf Willow: A History, A Story and a Memory of the Last Plains Frontier.* New York: Viking Press, 1955.

Through the Years: A History of Innisfree and District. Innisfree, AB: Innisfree History Book, 1986.

UFA Co-op. "Submission to the Royal Commission on Farm Machinery," March 16, 1967.

Vermilion School of Agriculture Yearbook. Vermillion, AB: Vermillion School of Agriculture, 1926/1927, 1927/1928, 1929/1930.

Wells, S.A., and A.W. Platt. "The Effect of Loose Smut on the Viability of Artificially Inoculated Barley Seeds." *Scientific Agriculture* 29, no. 1 (1949): 45–52.

Wilson, Charles F. *Canadian Grain Marketing.* Winnipeg: Canadian International Grains Institute, 1979.

Yackulic, George. "Alberta's Bloods," *Western Business and Industry* 27, no. 10 (October 1953): 28–30, 56.

ARCHIVES

Alvin Hamilton Fonds

National Archives, MG 32 B40 Vol 2, file 12.

Canada Department of Agriculture
    Library and Archives Canada (LAC), RG 17 Vol 2851, [Experimental Farms—Swift
    Current Saskatchewan Experimental Station]
    RG 17 Vol 3673 [Dominion Reconstruction Committee].

Canada Department of Indian Affairs and Northern Development
    File 772/32–2–148–36, vols 1&2.

Charles F. Wilson Fonds
    Library and Archives Canada (LAC), MG 30 E301, vol 1, file 10.

Diefenbaker Canada Centre Archives, University of Saskatchewan, MG01/VI/354
    MacPherson Federal Government Administration—Royal Commissions—
    MacPherson 1959–1963. Volume 323;
    MG01/VI/354 McTague Federal Government Administration—Royal Commission—
    McTague. 1959. Volume 323;
    MG01/VI/511 Agriculture—Policy and Price Support 1957—June 1958 Volume 385;
    MG01/VI/732/T773.5R Transportation and Communication—Railway Transportation—
    Department of Transport—Freight Rates—Rape Seed. 1957–1961 Volume 487;
    MG 01/VI/732/T773.51 Transportation and Communication—Railway Transportation—
    Department of Transport—Freight Rates—Increases. 1957—Oct. 1958 Volume 487;
    MG 01/VI/732/T773.51 Transportation and Communication—Railway Transportation—
    Department of Transport—Freight Rates—Increases. Nov. 1958–1963 Volume 487.
    MG01/XII/C/388 Royal Commissions—Transportation n.d., 1960–1961 Volume 75.

Honourable Gordon Churchill papers
    Library and Archives Canada (LAC), MG 32 B9 volume 64, file International Wheat
    Conference 1959, briefing document, 21 October, 1958, Grain Division, Department
    of Trade and Commerce, Ottawa.

Library, Lethbridge Research Centre, (LLRC) File on A.W. Platt
    Farstad, Chris. Tribute to Arnold Platt on Arnold's resignation from the Lethbridge
    Research Station.

Provincial Archives of Alberta (PAA)
    Accession #71.207 a&b, 1970; tape recording of A.W. Platt
    GR1990.11; Special Advisory Committee on Communal Property and Land Use
    GR1990.623 and GR1991.270: Alberta Land Use Forum.

Royal Commission on Transportation
    Library and Archives Canada (LAC), RG 33–49 Vol 13, Vol 68.

United Farmers of Alberta Co-operative
    Minutes of the Board of Directors, 1961–1973.

University of Alberta Archives (UAA)
    Minutes of the Board of Governors, Accession No. 71–164, Vols 16–20
    Faculty of Agriculture, Accession No. 76–25, Vol 35 [Western Canadian Veterinary
    Study Committee]; Vol 40 [President's Committees re Faculty of Agriculture
    Departments 1956–59]; Vol 73 [Department of Agricultural Economics and Farm
    Management 1960–61 Establishment of Department]; Vol 75 [Department of
    Ag Economics Advisory Committee, 1963–71; Vol 78 [Provincial Conference on
    Rural Sociology and Economics 1967]; Vol 232 [Royal Commission on Education

(Cameron Commission)].

Travis Manning Papers, Accession 83–123, Box 11 File 201 [Development of the Department of Agricultural Economics]; Box 14 [Agricultural Economics Advisory Committee; Box 15 File 285 [Departmental Review 1981].

University of Calgary Archives (UCA)

Capital Fund Committee, The Three Alberta Universities (3 AU): Capital Fund Committee, The Three Alberta Universities—1968–1975. File 24.01, Accession No. 83.007.

NEWSPAPERS AND PERIODICALS

Calgary Herald
Edmonton Journal
Free Press Weekly
Lethbridge Herald
Organized Farmer
Swift Current Sun
UFA Cooperator
Western Producer

INTERVIEWS

Bentley, C.F. (Former Dean of Agriculture, University of Alberta, Edmonton, Alberta), in telephone discussion with the author, May 2005.

Deneka, Shirley. (Daughter of Arnold and Donna Platt), in discussion with the author, Calgary, Alberta. August 2004.

DePauw, Ron. (Researcher, Semiarid Prairie Agricultural Research Centre, Swift Current, Saskatchewan), in discussion with the author, Swift Current Saskatchewan. October and November 2004.

Larson, Ruby. (Former Researcher, Swift Current Experimental Farm and Lethbridge Research Centre), in discussion with the author, Lethbridge, Alberta. September 2004.

Lien, Dean. (Former President, Junior Farmers' Union of Alberta, and Head of Public Affairs, UFA Co-op; former Ombudsman for Agriculture Alberta), in discussion with the author, Lethbridge, Alberta. June 2004.

Lore, Jim. (Farmer and Agriculture Consultant, Carstairs, Alberta), in discussion with the author, Calgary, Alberta. May 2005.

Madill, Wally. (Former Chief Executive Officer, Alberta Wheat Pool, Calgary, Alberta), in discussion with the author, Calgary, Alberta. November 2004.

McBean, Lilian. (Daughter of L.B. Thomson, Superintendent of Swift Current Experimental Farm), in discussion with the author, Swift Current, Saskatchewan. October 2004.

McBean, Stu. (Former Researcher, Swift Current Experimental Farm), in discussion with the author, Swift Current, Saskatchewan. October 2004.

McCalla, Alex. (Former President, Junior Farmers' Union of Alberta, Professor Emeritus Agricultural Economics, Davis, California), in discussion with the author,

Edmonton, Alberta. October 2004.

Oikawa, Margaret. (Daughter of Arnold and Donna Platt), in discussion with the author, Calgary, Alberta. August 2004.

Olsen, Arne. (Formerly Head of Human Resources, UFA Co-op, Calgary, Alberta), in discussion with the author, Calgary, Alberta. January 2005.

Oxford (Spencer), Jessie. (Widow of Frank Oxford, sister-in-law to Arnold Platt and Donna [Oxford] Platt), in discussion with the author, Calgary, Alberta. September 2004.

Patching, Harry. (Formerly with Alberta Wheat Pool, Calgary, Alberta), in discussion with the author, Calgary, Alberta. November 18, 2004.

Platt, Helen. (Wife of Arnold Platt, Calgary, Alberta), in discussion with the author, August, September, October, 2004 and January, March, April, 2005.

Platt, Wayne. (Son of Arnold Platt and Donna [Oxford] Platt; now living in Australia), in discussion with the author by email. September 2004.

Richter, Joseph (Professor Emeritus, Department of Agricultural Economics, University of Alberta, Edmonton, Alberta), in discussion with the author, Edmonton, Alberta. May 2005.

Schuler, Gerald. (Former President, Junior Farmers' Union of Alberta; Former Head of Farmers' Union and Cooperative Development Association and the Rural Education and Development Association), in discussion with the author, Kelowna, B.C. October 2004.

Warrack, Allan. (Former Minister of Lands and Forests, Government of Alberta; and Professor of Agricultural Economics, University of Alberta, Edmonton, Alberta), in discussion with the author, Edmonton, Alberta. May 2005.

Wells, Stewart. (Former Researcher, Swift Current Experimental Farm and Lethbridge Research Centre), in discussion with the author, Lethbridge, Alberta. September 2004.

PRIVATE COLLECTIONS

Platt Family Papers

The endnotes cite the materials in this collection as they inform the narrative. They are not inventoried. These materials, at the time of this writing housed in my office, include papers that Arnold left at the farm on the Milk River Ridge after he had destroyed most of his other files. They include about twelve hours of tape recordings that Arnold made in 1989 and early 1990, in which he recalls his earliest experiences and tells the story of his life until the birth of his first child, Wayne, in 1931.

Index

Page numbers in italics refer to photographs.